Marketing Public Relations

Post from the author
2010

1 Comment(s)

During the course of your lifetime you have seen technology change the way that we communicate, shop, and conduct business. Your generation -- raised with ever-more sophisticated media techniques and products, at ease in this environment, and savvy about its potential -- has driven change. This book provides a basis for you to turn your understanding of today's consumer environment into a skill that is in demand by a growing number of companies around the globe. The same changes in communication embraced by your generation have transformed the practice of marketing. We are witnessing a convergence of new and traditional media that will undoubtedly reshape the media landscape of the future. We call the place where new and traditional media meet to publicize businesses, brands, people, and ideas Marketing Public Relations (MPR). MPR is now the most powerful method of promoting products, services, and ideas. It is key to establishing, managing – and sometimes restoring - a company's reputation.

The demand for people skilled in both traditional and new marketing methods is increasing rapidly. Yet, despite the growing importance of public relations and new media to businesses, very few colleges and universities have been addressing this convergence from a business perspective. This text breaks from the norm by presenting public relations using a marketing rather than a communications studies or journalism approach. What's more, it recognizes the similarities between PR, word-of-mouth, and social networking media and creates a framework for constructing marketing strategies that incorporate these highly credible and cost-effective tools. You will learn the theory, and you will also learn how to apply it to "do Marketing Public Relations" in the real world.

Author

Gaetan Giannini is a Professor of Marketing at Cedar Crest College and the author of the forthcoming book, *Marketing Public Relations: A Marketer's Approach to Public Relations and Social Media* from Pearson-Prentice Hall.

Comment:

"...one of the first textbooks, if not the very first, that teaches marketing and public relations in the context of social media. The world has been waiting for this book for years." -Ben McConnell, co-author of *Citizen Marketer* and *Creating Customer Evangelists*

MARKETING PUBLIC RELATIONS

A Marketer's Approach to Public Relations and Social Media

Gaetan T. Giannini, Jr.
Cedar Crest College

Prentice Hall

Boston Columbus Indianapolis New York San Francisco Upper Saddle River
Amsterdam Cape Town Dubai London Madrid Milan Munich Paris Montreal Toronto
Delhi Mexico City Sao Paulo Sydney Hong Kong Seoul Singapore Taipei Tokyo

Editorial Director: Sally Yagan
Editor in Chief: Eric Svendsen
Acquisitions Editor: Melissa Sabella
Manager, Product Development: Ashley Santora
Editorial Project Manager: Kierra Kashickey
Editorial Assistant: Karin Williams
Director of Marketing: Patrice Lumumba Jones
Senior Marketing Manager: Anne Fahlgren
Senior Managing Editor: Judy Leale
Project Manager: Ana Jankowski
Senior Operations Supervisor: Arnold Vila
Operations Specialist: Diane Peirano
Senior Art Director: Steve Frim
Text and Cover Designer: Dina Curro
Manager, Visual Research: Beth Brenzel

Manager, Rights and Permissions: Zina Arabia
Image Permission Coordinator: Jan Marc
    Quisumbing
Manager, Cover Visual Research & Permissions:
    Karen Sanatar
Cover Art: Argosy
Media Project Manager, Editorial: Denise Vaughn
Media Project Manager, Production: Lisa Rinaldi
Full-Service Project Management: Elm Street
    Publishing Services
Composition: Integra Software Services, Ltd.
Printer/Binder: Courier/Kendallville
Cover Printer: Lehigh-Phoenix
    Color/Hagerstown
Text Font: 10/12 Times

Credits and acknowledgments borrowed from other sources and reproduced, with permission, in this textbook appear on appropriate page within text.

Library of Congress Cataloging-in-Publication Data

Giannini, Gaetan T.
  Marketing public relations / Gaetan T. Giannini.
      p. cm
  ISBN 978-0-13-608299-6
  1. Public relations.   2. Marketing—Management.   I. Title.
  HD59.G486 2009
  659.2--dc22

                                                                2009015020

10 9 8 7 6 5 4 3 2 1

Prentice Hall
is an imprint of

PEARSON

www.pearsonhighered.com

ISBN 10:   0-13-608299-8
ISBN 13: 978-0-13-608299-6

Dedication

This book is dedicated to my family. To my father, Gaetan Sr., for teaching me it is all right to dream; to my mother, Arlene, for insisting I never give up; to my wife, Crystal, for sharing this crazy journey with me; and to my sons, Jacob and Jason, for filling me with optimism about the future.

BRIEF CONTENTS

CONTENTS

CHAPTER 3: **MPR and the Organizations it Serves**

ACKNOWLEDGEMENTS

Marketing Public Relations is a text based on both tested and emerging ideas in marketing. As with the birth of any new paradigm, this work was the result of the effort of a team of talented and passionate people at Pearson Prentice Hall, Cedar Crest College, and companies and universities around the world.

At Pearson I have many people to thank. First off, thanks to Melissa Sabella for recognizing the potential for a text that takes marketing in the direction of MPR and for being the driving force in turning a concept into reality. My deepest gratitude goes to Karin Williams for keeping me on track and for her unwavering moral support. I was ever fortunate to work with Karen Misler, whose patience and skill transformed a business and academic writer into a textbook author. Thank you to Charles Morris for his time and patience in working through the permission process, to Ana Jankowski for guiding me through final edits and production, and to Steve Frim for creating a great looking, very functional design. Anne Fahlgren has embraced the concepts in this book and created an innovative marketing campaign.

Every day, I am grateful to be a member of the faculty at Cedar Crest College for its traditions, visions, and amazing students, faculty, and staff. Among those, I thank Rebecca Getz for her assistance and support in writing the text and keeping the Department of Business, Management and Economics running as I worked on this book. A million thanks to Professor Henry Marchand for lending his mastery of the English language to me as I composed my proposal and the early chapters. Thank you to Mary Ellen Hickes of Cedar Crest College for helping me wind my way through final proofs. And to my brilliant department colleagues Ibi Balog, Chris Duelfer, Michael Donovan, Arlene Peltola, and Alice Wilson for their support and for making my job easy and fun.

It's probably no surprise to find out that business people and academics contributed to the creation of a textbook. Despite this fact, I was humbled by the enthusiastic contribution of the marketing community. There are too many people to thank everyone, but I extend a special thank you to:

- Peter Shankman and his "Help A Report Out" service for putting me in touch with countless marketing professionals. (www.helpareporter.com)
- Drs. Donald Stacks and David Michaelson for lending the collateral from their "Zip Chips" study.
- Dr. Douglas Holt at Oxford University for his support for adapting his Brand Author and Brand Value taxonomy to MPR.
- Press Benbow of Benbow International Public Relations for bringing her expertise and client experience to the pages of this text. (http://www.benbowpr.com)
- Kathy Kniss of Clean Agency for her insight and examples of great MPR. (http://www.cleanagency.com)
- Richard Laermer of RLM PR for his *full frontal* contribution to the content of this text. (http://www.rlmpr.com/index.php)
- Ben McConnell, co-author of *Citizen Marketer* and *Creating Customer Evangelists*, for lending his unique perspective and expertise. (http://www.churchofthecustomer.com)

- Gary Vaynerchuk and Matt Sitomer for living on the cutting edge of MPR, giving everything I could ask, and being great people. (http://tv.winelibrary.com)
- Geno Church and Spike Jones of Brains on Fire because, well, they just rock. (http://www.brainsonfire.com)
- David Puner of Dunkin Donuts' for arranging access to one of the world's great brands.
- Grand Pooh-bah of PR, Sean Greenwood of Ben & Jerry's for sharing his philosophy.
- Carla Eberle at BzzAgent for sharing a great case.
- Ruth Farland at Cision for a wealth of information.
- My dear friends and confidants Tom Garrity, Tina Hamilton, Drew Marron, and Tom Roberts for their inspiration.

I'd be remiss if I didn't thank John Moore, editor of the *Eastern Pennsylvania Business Journal* for giving me my start as a writer, and the late Dr. Vince Fitzgerald for introducing me to the world of marketing and public relations.

Last, I'd like to express my sincerest appreciation to the team of academic reviewers who worked so diligently on this manuscript with me.

Reviewers

Chike Anyaegbunam, *University of Kentucky*
Claire Badaracco, *Marquette University*
Duane Franceschi, *Canyon College*
Michael Goldberg, *Berkeley College, Rutgers, University of Phoenix*
Jennifer Gushue, *Rowan University*
Carol Ann Hackley, *University of the Pacific, Stockton*
Joseph P. Helgert, *Grand Valley State University*
Steve Iseman, *Ohio Northern University*
Andrew Lingwall, *Clarion University of Pennsylvania*
Janet Rice McCoy, *Morehead State University*
Sherri Massey, *University of Central Oklahoma, Edmond*
Teresa Mastin, *Michigan State University*
Karen Mishra, *Michigan State University*
Karen S. Olson, *SUNY College at Brockport*
Marilyn Olson, *Chicago State University*
Michelle Rai, *Pacific Union College*
Christine A. Saplala, *De La Salle – College of St. Benilde*
Jonathan Slater, *SUNY Plattsburgh*
Jian (Jay) Wang, *Purdue University*

ABOUT THE AUTHOR

Gaetan Giannini is an assistant professor and chairman of the Department of Business, Management and Economics at Cedar Crest College as well as a sales and marketing consultant and writer.

After earning a bachelor's degree in mechanical engineering technology from Temple University and an MBA from Seton Hall University, Gaetan worked in sales and marketing management for a small, process instrumentation company before moving to a multinational firm in the same industry. After a productive corporate career, he started his own business and marketing consulting firm, Giannini O'Connor LLC, which he ran until entering academia.

CHAPTER 1

An Introduction to Marketing Public Relations

CHAPTER OBJECTIVES

After studying this chapter, you should be able to:

1. Define Marketing Public Relations (MPR).

2. Explain how MPR differs from other elements of the marketing mix.

3. Discuss the different ways MPR contributes to a firm's overall marketing effort.

4. Describe the basic types of MPR opportunities and some fundamental rules for marketers who pursue them.

5. Discuss the values and ethical standards for MPR professionals.

CLASSIC AND CUTTING EDGE *Harry Potter*

If you were anywhere in the civilized world toward the end of June 2006, you probably witnessed public relations working its magic. Although the final installment in the series of Harry Potter novels would not be released until July 21, 2007, the anticipation for the new book began to rise. On a British talk show, author J. K. Rowling mentioned that two familiar characters would meet their doom in book number seven and that one of them might be young Mr. Potter himself. This short dialogue set into motion an avalanche of press coverage. All of the major television networks and their Web and cable counterparts covered the story. *The New York Times* gave the story a prominent spot in its pages and on its Web site. Even the venerable *Wall Street Journal* mentioned it. The story also graced the pages of newspapers across the globe, thanks to news wire services such as the Associated Press and Reuters. Finally, the trade journal *Advertising Age* covered the story and the story behind the story—*the reason this announcement was such a big deal*.[1]

When you look beneath the surface, you see that not only did Ms. Rowling have an interest in keeping her work in the public eye, but so did the book's publisher, the producer and distributor of the popular Harry Potter movies, and the countless companies that make and sell Potter paraphernalia. Since the Harry Potter brand became fanatically popular with children and adults everywhere, television producers, newspaper editors, and magazine publishers also had an interest in covering this announcement. Why? A mere mention of the boy wizard's name got the instant attention of viewers and readers, providing benefits to both the organization covering the story and those who advertised with them. As Michael Drabenstott, a partner in SPARK, a public relations and marketing firm in suburban Philadelphia, says:

> The Harry Potter phenomenon started with a unique product: an engaging, imaginative novel that bridged generations by captivating children and adults alike. Favorable media coverage stemming from the first book made Harry into a "star" who became as newsworthy as anyone on the Hollywood A-list.... The public wanted to know about Harry and journalists willingly obliged. Each successive book stimulated additional excitement and buzz. When people you trust and admire talk about a product, you are more likely to buy it so you, too, can become part of the conversation.

The Harry Potter case illustrates the unique form of marketing in which the firms who initiate the message win because they get the word out about their work; those who deliver the message win because it draws the public to their information outlet; and the consumers win because they gain access to the information that they crave. This is the magic of **Marketing Public Relations**.

What Is Marketing Public Relations (MPR)?

Marketers are living in an exciting time. Over the last decade or so, the way that people communicate has changed drastically. Today, nearly a billion people have Internet access and, as a result, can communicate instantly with others around the world. At no time in the history of the human race have we been able to access people or information so quickly or completely. With this newfound ability has come the desire on the part of consumers to leave behind the model of one-way communication in which companies push unsolicited information about brands and products (in the form of advertisements and other promotional messages) into the marketplace. The preferred alternative is for consumers to seek this information when they are ready and to participate in a dialogue and become a part of a mutually beneficial community that includes the marketers and consumers. This text takes a practical approach to understanding and using this new paradigm; it takes a marketer's perspective on public relations that emphasizes the importance of a two-way brand relationship utilizing both traditional and new media channels in a way that can adapt to the ever-changing marketing landscape.

In their landmark publication *The Fall of Advertising and the Rise of PR*, renowned marketing authors Al and Laura Ries raise concerns about the future of advertising and mark the ascendancy of its cousin, public relations (PR). While the Rieses do not actually predict the annihilation of advertising, their work does signal a shift in how organizations promote products, services, and ideas. Enabled by Internet-driven new media, organizations are looking for more credible and durable ways to create a dialogue with customers and prospects than traditional mass-market advertising. These new avenues have led to marketing strategies that use the fundamentals of classic public relations in innovative ways, fostering interactions among organizations, products, consumers, and the **media** at a pace that is unprecedented in the history of modern marketing.

Traditionally, PR is defined as a firm's efforts to build good relations with its various **publics** by obtaining favorable publicity, building up a good "corporate image," and handling or heading off unfavorable rumors, stories, or events.[2] A firm typically accomplished these goals by working with the media to send a persuasive message to consumers. As far back as 1923, Edward Bernays, now considered the father of modern public relations, obtained media attention for Ivory® soap by staging soap yacht races in Central Park and soap-carving contests for children across the country.[3] Over time, other marketing tools have evolved that share striking similarities to PR. We generally classify these tools as **consumer-generated marketing (CGM)**, in which consumers create marketing messages and other brand exchanges themselves.[4] An example of CGM is 3M's® 2008 Internet campaign called "One Million Uses & Counting," which promoted the company's Post-it® Notes. The firm used YouTube® to invite people to submit videos illustrating their favorite uses for the pervasive sticky paper squares and offered prizes of up to $10,000 for the videos rated best by viewers.[5] This campaign differed from traditional PR in that it went straight to the consumer to create the content and spread the word. We commonly refer to these messages and exchanges by a host of names, including, but not limited to, *word-of-mouth* and *buzz*. The fact that both PR and CGM require the marketer to hand over his or her promotional message to an intermediary in order to reach the ultimate customer is the essence of Marketing Public Relations. As a result, we define MPR as any program or effort designed to improve, maintain, or protect the sales or image of a **product** by encouraging **intermediaries**,

Exhibit 1.1 Marketers rely on an enormous number of media outlets, both traditional and new, to get their message across to consumers.

such as traditional mass media, the electronic media, or individuals, to voluntarily pass a message about the firm or product to their audience of businesses or consumers.

MPR and the Marketing Mix

CHAPTER OBJECTIVE 2

Most businesses consider the Marketing Public Relations function to be part of marketing, in that it does not supersede other types of public relations. Rather, it is public relations used for marketing purposes. Essentially, marketing includes all efforts to change or

---

Key Terms

Media In public relations, media are considered to be any communication methods widely distributed to the consumer or business community. *Media* is the plural form of *medium*. Types of media include television, radio, newspapers, magazines, Web sites, and blogs.

Publics Any group that has an interest in or effect upon the activities of

a firm and that may also be affected by those activities

Consumer-generated marketing (CGM) Marketing efforts designed to encourage consumers to create marketing messages and other brand exchanges themselves

Product Any good, service, idea, or personality to which PR can be applied

Intermediaries Organizations or individuals that pass a message about a product from a firm to consumers; this should not be confused with the term "marketing intermediary," which refers to product distribution channels.

maintain the behavior of consumers or businesses relative to a product. Typically, the behavior in question is the purchase of a good or service or the belief in a certain idea, such as that exercising is good for one's health. The **marketing mix** is the variety of tools available to marketers in their quest to manage this process. They often classify these tools as the four Ps: product, price, place, and promotion. In this context, *product* refers to the design, packaging, features, benefits, and quality of the item; *price* is the cost of acquisition of the product (including purchase price and all other factors, tangible or intangible, associated with the product's perceived value); and *place* refers to the distribution of the product. The final category, *promotion*, which we often refer to as integrated marketing communications, includes MPR. The promotion category also includes several non-MPR activities, such as advertising, personal selling efforts, and trade promotions. These activities do not qualify as MPR because a firm pays for them and/or they do not use intermediaries in spreading the message. While these elements contribute to achieving a firm's marketing goals, the tactics and strategies differ from those of MPR. Because Marketing Public Relations messages are spread voluntarily, consumers perceive them differently than other types of promotion. An organization's marketing professionals need to balance the mix of MPR and non-MPR activities properly to maximize the effectiveness of the marketing program.

Successful organizations realize that public relations is not limited to the marketing people. Whenever *any* representative of an organization interacts with the outside world, a communication is taking place that can affect the sales or image of that organization. The marketing people must manage this process regardless of who the players are, and the organization's executives must give the marketing people the authority and resources to do so.

CHAPTER
OBJECTIVE
3

What Can MPR Do?

MPR's task is ultimately one of communication between an organization and its **stakeholders**. This communication is accomplished through channels—typically interpersonal or media. Savvy organizations and marketing professionals will use their skills to communicate with stakeholders in a way that will assist them in achieving one or more of these related goals:

- Building the identity of the organization or product
- Increasing the visibility of an established organization or product
- Establishing an organization or individual as an expert in a given field
- Educating stakeholders on issues critical to the organization
- Shaping public opinion about an organization, idea, or individual
- Maintaining the image of an organization or product—over time or during a crisis
- Stimulating the trial or repeat usage of a product

The Clorox Company accomplished several of these goals when it partnered with the environmentalist group Sierra Club to launch its line of natural cleaning products, Green Works. Effectively, the attention that the Clorox Company received helped to establish the awareness of this new product line and helped create a public impression of the company as eco-friendly. The partnership with the Sierra Club lent the product line the credibility of a well-known authority on environmental issues and provided additional exposure to consumers for both Clorox and the Sierra Club.

Exhibit 1.2 MPR is an effective tool for informing the public about a new product, especially when that new product can be tied to a current trend.

Shutterstock.

Since MPR manifests itself as the coverage of a story by the media or the recommendation of a friend, prospective buyers often perceive MPR as news or opinion rather than a paid solicitation. As a result, it has higher credibility than other promotional tools like advertising and direct selling. The downside of this implied credibility is that the ownership of the message is transferred from the marketer to the channel. This transfer means that the message can be altered or distorted in a fashion unintended by the marketer.

An example of MPR gone astray is the 2007 efforts of the Cartoon Network to promote its new show, "Aqua Teen Hunger Force." The network's marketing firm placed blinking electronic signs in ten major U.S. cities. Unfortunately, some folks in Boston found the devices suspicious and reported them to authorities. The police subsequently shut down roads in several sections of the city, causing a traffic nightmare, giving the network a black eye, and sticking Boston with at least $500,000 in police costs.[6]

Another challenge faced by MPR practitioners is the need to show how effective their efforts are with respect to the investment the firm makes in them. Calculating return on investment (ROI) has always been challenging for marketers, since marketing goals can be based on changing attitudes and opinions, which are hard to measure. Even when the goal is to increase a product's sales, it is difficult to say which element or combination of elements in the firm's portfolio of marketing activities contributed to

Key Terms

Marketing mix The variety of tools available to marketers in their quest to manage the marketing process

Stakeholders Customers, prospective customers, employees, stockholders, or, in some cases, even the general public

any given change in sales. To further complicate matters for MPR, the firm relies on intermediaries to spread the word about its products and brands, making a direct correlation with MPR activities more difficult.

<table>
<tr><td>CHAPTER
OBJECTIVE
4</td></tr>
</table>

MPR Opportunities

Opportunities for MPR are everywhere. They can include items as diverse as an appearance in the local newspaper or network news, a mention on the Web site of an independent blogger or a globally distributed magazine, a comment from one friend to another, or a recommendation from one of the thousands of trade associations across the world. MPR is the art and science of turning the happenings of an organization into the news of those who should be buying the product, voting for a particular candidate, or aligning their views with the marketer's. The tools of the MPR professional can range from relationships with journalists and bloggers, to using social media like YouTube and Facebook®, to creating events that will interest influential individuals. The tools serve in the interest of creating media mentions and spreading word-of-mouth that influences the behavior of groups of consumers whose actions can have a positive impact on the firm. As you wind your way through the alchemy of MPR, you need to be aware of a few basic rules that apply, regardless of the tools and tactics that you employ to make a campaign a success.

Exhibit 1.3 Social networking sites like Facebook® offer a new way for firms to build connections with their customers.

Chris Jackson/Getty Images, Inc.

Basic Rules of MPR

- *Use MPR.* Although this rule appears obvious, most companies in the United States do not have a formal MPR process. This fact is puzzling, since MPR efforts have the lowest costs of deployment and a high degree of credibility when compared to other marketing tools. For example, for a firm's message to reach an audience by advertising in mass media, the firm would likely pay thousands of dollars. In contrast, mention of one of the firm's products in a news article in the same media outlet would not cost the firm anything. According to Sally Hodge of Hodge Communications, "PR takes on a whole new relevance in tough economic times....Obviously, it costs a fraction of the [total] cost to launch a PR campaign than it does to launch a major ad campaign."[7]

- *Be aware of what's newsworthy.* Once an organization adopts MPR as a marketing method, it may be tempted to notify the media or try to create buzz every time anything happens in the organization. While you should always be on the lookout for MPR opportunities, you need to consider whether a significant portion of a given medium's audience will be interested in what you have to say. If a definable group of consumers or businesses won't care, then it's not news, and you are likely wasting the time of your intended audience and the media. Additionally, reaching out to the media and the public repeatedly with non-newsworthy stories can give you the appearance of "crying wolf" and dampen your chances of getting attention when you do have something worth hearing. Remember that newsworthiness is subjective and dependent on the audience, so while your business moving across town may not be news for the industry's trade magazine, it might be highly significant for the local newspaper—especially if the move can be tied into creating more jobs or revitalizing a section of town.

- *Share the news.* The image of the old-time reporter with the press pass tucked in his hat and on the hunt for the next "scoop" and the hard-hitting, investigative reporter taking on corruption with microphone in hand and camera crew in tow is just that, an image. In reality, the media does not work without the help of the MPR people of companies, trade groups, celebrities, and politicians. Newspapers are printed every day; magazines appear every week or month; blogs are updated frequently; TV news is broadcast at 6 a.m., 5 p.m., 6 p.m., and 11 p.m.; and cable TV and Internet news are 24/7. So, if media companies and bloggers want to stay in business, they must rely on reputable MPR people to help "feed the beast" and make their productions a success.

- *Package it properly.* Despite the small percentage of organizations that use MPR as a part of their marketing strategy, editors, producers, reporters, and popular bloggers are engulfed by people trying to get their attention. In order to pique their interest, be sure to package your solicitation in an easily digestible way that allows the media folks to see the value of covering your story. You need to do this while appearing exciting and professional at the same time. For example, your communications need to be personal so that you show you understand what is important to the person you are trying to entice to cover your story. Impersonal mass e-mails and letters and anything that looks too complicated or too much like a sales pitch is not packaged properly.

- *Get it to the right people.* A media organization consists of a group of individuals working toward the goal of producing a magazine, newspaper, news show, and so on. Even if you have the most newsworthy story, packaged in the most professional and compelling way, that story will not see a drop of ink or a second of TV time if it does not reach the right person within the organization. Know *who cares about what* in the media organizations with which you hope to work. The same rule also applies to CGM. Many individuals and groups disseminate information about many things. You need to know which of the groups will spread the word for you and will do so in a positive fashion. In either case, you need to know which channel will reach which audience.

  For example, you may want to use bloggers to help spread the word about your product, but after checking out Technotati's™ directory of blogs you might discover that there are thousands of blogs out there. The research that you put into finding the right bloggers can be the difference between spreading positive news about your product to the right audience, being heard by the wrong audience while being ignored by the right one, or, in the worst case, having bloggers say bad things about your product to those who should be buying it. The best-produced story about your organization will mean nothing if the consumers it reaches do not care about what they are reading, seeing, or hearing.

- *Be available.* The first indication of a successful campaign is having journalists call for more information. If you get a call, you get the opportunity to discover what they are looking for in a story and to work together to create a piece that meets both your needs and theirs. Since journalists have deadlines and often work crazy hours, you have to make sure that you are available to give them the information they need when they need it. If a story is big enough, plan to keep your cell phone and your laptop next to your bed. Being available increases the chances of having your story covered and strengthens a relationship.

- *Stay engaged.* A constant flow of information occurs between firms, consumers, and the people and organizations that connect them. Make sure that your presence is felt. As you stay in touch with the needs of your customers, you will also discover how they prefer to be reached and how to best involve the media and people that influence them.

- *Realize that MPR has global reach.* The technology that has magnified the importance of MPR as a part of the marketer's toolkit also brings the marketer's message to the entire world regardless of whether that message is delivered by new or traditional media. You, the marketer, must be sensitive to this fact when formulating your message and must be ready to respond to reaction to these messages from around the globe.

- *Ethics are not optional.* From the dawn of commercial society, those in the business of selling and marketing goods and services have developed a reputation of questionable ethics. By the same token, people often consider the media to be self-serving. While these reputations may be deserved in some instances, marketing and media people in general are upstanding professionals who put as much pride into their work and value honesty as much as anyone else. So, although you may be tempted to

Exhibit 1.4 Consumers often discover what is "under the hood" of a story, so MPR professionals can never assume that they can behave unethically because no one will find out.

Selena/Shutterstock.

bend the truth to make a story sound more exciting, don't do it. Remember, small lies will not only haunt you but can burn your organization, your media contacts, and the consumers of media. MPR people who break this rule wind up burning all of their bridges at once and usually destroy their careers in the process. For example, a company called PowerTV and its clients, such as General Motors® and Holly®, have felt the sting of less than transparent attempts at MPR. PowerTV is a marketing company that produces promotional videos for automotive parts companies and that works to have these videos shared on blogs and online forums. However, the folks at PowerTV did not announce themselves as marketers when interacting with Web communities, and they were subsequently outed by the Center for Media and Democracy's Web site PRwatch.org and an activist group at http://www.spankmymarketer.com. Such an occurrence only serves to discredit the firm conducting the campaign and weakens future MPR efforts.

Ethics and Values of a PR Professional

CHAPTER
OBJECTIVE
5

People engaged in MPR for a company work with customers, the media, and outside stakeholders to promote the mission of the organization. They also work with internal constituents to ensure that they understand this mission and are prepared to communicate it properly in all of their external interactions.

Ethics

Routinely, MPR professionals serve many masters as they work their magic. Those who are employed by a PR agency have ethical responsibilities to the firm for which they work, the clients they serve, the media, and the ultimate consumers of the media. This scope of influence is larger than most professionals have in their careers. Not only is this chain of influence broad, but it is highly visible as well. While most business is conducted in the privacy of boardrooms and company offices, MPR is conducted in the most public of public places—the hearts and minds of consumers and in the media.

For this reason, the Public Relations Society of America (PRSA) has published a code of ethics for its members that will give you a constructive way to frame ethical issues in your career.

PRSA Member Statement of Professional Values[8]

This statement presents the core values of PRSA members and, more broadly, of the public relations profession. These values provide the foundation for the Member Code of Ethics and set the industry standard for the professional practice of public relations. These values are the fundamental beliefs that guide our behaviors and decision-making process. We believe our professional values are vital to the integrity of the profession as a whole.

Advocacy We serve the public interest by acting as responsible advocates for those we represent. We provide a voice in the marketplace of ideas, facts, and viewpoints to aid informed public debate.

Honesty We adhere to the highest standards of accuracy and truth in advancing the interests of those we represent and in communicating with the public.

Expertise We acquire and responsibly use specialized knowledge and experience. We advance the profession through continued professional development, research, and education. We build mutual understanding, credibility, and relationships among a wide array of institutions and audiences.

Independence We provide objective counsel to those we represent. We are accountable for our actions.

Loyalty We are faithful to those we represent, while honoring our obligation to serve the public interest.

Fairness We deal fairly with clients, employers, competitors, peers, vendors, the media, and the general public. We respect all opinions and support the right of free expression.

As you might expect, these professional values have had a significant impact on the practice of MPR.

Concept Case 1.1: **An Introduction to The Falcon's Lair**

This text features Concept Cases, which take you through the entire MPR process for a fictitious company, The Falcon's Lair. As you move through the text, you will think about and apply each chapter's MPR topics to The Falcon's Lair.

The Falcon's Lair is a high-end hiking and climbing equipment and accessory retailer located in Allentown, Pennsylvania, that serves clientele within a seventy-five-mile radius from its store. Although it has been successful since its establishment in 1998, the company wants to increase business by strengthening its relationship with its existing customer base (regional, "hardcore" hikers and climbers), establish itself as a resource for families and recreational hikers and climbers, and increase its nationwide Web sales.

Questions:

1. Using the Internet, find three other stores across the country that are similar to The Falcon's Lair and briefly describe each.
2. Go to the U.S. Census Department's Web site (http://www.census.gov) and describe the people who live within a seventy-five-mile radius of Allentown, Pennsylvania.
3. Search the Internet to find the radio, television, newspaper, and magazine media outlets that serve The Falcon's Lair's geographic region.

 Reflection Questions

1. Explain the basic concept of Marketing Public Relations. (Chapter Objectives 1 & 2)

2. Compare and contrast MPR with traditional public relations and advertising. (Chapter Objective 2)

3. Discuss some of the stories that you have read about on the Web, on TV, and in magazines and newspapers? (Chapter Objective 3)

4. Do some topics appear in multiple places? (Chapter Objective 4)

5. Is the coverage of any of these issues affecting those who have a stake in its promotion in a positive or negative way? Explain. (Chapter Objective 5)

Chapter Key Terms

Consumer-generated marketing (CGM) Marketing efforts designed to encourage consumers to create marketing messages and other brand exchanges themselves (p. 4)

Intermediaries Organizations or individuals that pass a message about a product from a firm to consumers; this should not be confused with the term "marketing intermediary," which refers to product distribution channels (p. 5)

Marketing mix The variety of tools available to marketers in their quest to manage this process (p. 6)

Marketing Public Relations (MPR) Any program or effort designed to improve, maintain, or protect the sales or image of a product by encouraging intermediaries, such as traditional mass media, the electronic media, or individuals, to voluntarily

pass a message about the firm or product to their audience of businesses or consumers (p. 3)

Media In public relations, media are considered to be any communication methods widely distributed to the consumer or business community. *Media* is the plural form of *medium*. Types of media include television, radio, newspapers, magazines, Web sites, and blogs. (p. 4)

Product In this text, the term ***product*** will refer to any good, service, idea, or personality to which PR can be applied. (p. 4)

Public Any group that has an interest in or effect upon the activities of a firm and that may also be affected by those activities (p. 4)

Stakeholders Customers, prospective customers, employees, stockholders, or, in some cases, even the general public (p. 7)

Application Assignments

1. Find an issue or a story that is currently getting a lot of media attention. Identify as many media sources as you can, ranging from a short clip in a local newspaper to feature segments on TV news shows to blog entries on the Internet, that refer to this topic.

2. Discuss how the messages differ between media sources and identify any common threads that you may see.

3. As an extra challenge, try to document the originator of this media buzz by finding a press release or some other type of press announcement issued by a PR agency or some other stakeholder in this issue.

4. Find advertisements about the subject of this issue, if they exist, and compare them to the media coverage in both content and the media in which they appear.

5. Explore http://www.prwatch.org to find a current public relations issue you believe to be ethically questionable. Discuss how you think the issue should have been handled by the firm.

Practice Portfolio

Each chapter offers a Practice Portfolio, an activity that relates to the material covered in the chapter. In addition, the activity will allow you to contribute to an MPR portfolio that you will be able to use as evidence of your abilities as a marketing professional. The portfolio can be based on a fictitious company or on a real company that your instructor assigns to you. At this point you should choose your company. Remember to choose carefully, as you will be working with this company all semester long.

CHAPTER **2**

Marketing Public Relations and the Marketing Communications Mix

CHAPTER OBJECTIVES

After studying this chapter, you should be able to:

1. Explain the different variations of exchange and their relationship to Marketing Public Relations (MPR).

2. List and explain the key elements in the marketing communications mix and explain how these elements work together with MPR.

3. Explain the concept of positioning and MPR's role in shaping it.

4. Describe and differentiate between the standard and MPR communications processes.

5. Explain what a connector is and how connectors function in the MPR process.

6. Explain the two types of MPR audiences and the importance of a firm's relationships with them.

Disney® has long been known for its marketing prowess. From its theme parks to its cruise line to its motion pictures, the House of Mouse has been the gold standard for getting people talking about a product. One could argue that this mastery stems from a consistent stream of high-quality products coupled with a relentless yet tactful approach to cross promoting. If you pay attention, you will notice that you hear about Disney theme parks while you are watching the Disney Channel, you are immersed in images from Disney movies and TV shows while at Disney theme parks, and you live a total Disney experience while aboard one of the company's cruise ships. You will even notice references to other Disney movies and characters within movies and TV shows.

The best modern example of an organization embracing public relations and consumer-generated marketing is Disney's promotion of Hannah Montana. What started out as a series on the Disney Channel has become a product line that includes the sale of music, live events, movies, and even a clothing line. The monumental success of the Hannah Montana brand may have gotten its start in a strong product, but it achieved blockbuster status through the skillful implementation of marketing public relations.

By the time Disney launched Hannah Montana, it had perfected a means of promotion that put the consumer (six- to fourteen-year-olds[1]) in touch with the product. Although Hannah Montana was not the first TV show to do so, the merger of the Web with the show allowed fans to enter the world of Hannah for real. The show currently promotes the site through screen snipes (video promotions appearing temporarily on the screen) and through promotional mentions during breaks in the show. The Web site then offers clips, photos, downloads, and information about the characters and the stars who play them. In addition, fans can e-mail the characters, and they have a chance to see their e-mail scrolling along the bottom of the screen during the show itself. The Web site even has a quasi-disclaimer that says, "Anything you send us or do here could end up on TV—on the Disney Channel!"

In addition to the Web-based buzz created by Disney's own efforts in cyberspace, the continuous flow of information about Hannah Montana in the media, coupled with intense fan interest in the brand, has spawned numerous non-Disney fan sites and blogs. These unofficial sites can be a bit dangerous for Disney, as they allow the image surrounding its products to be manipulated by others. The benefits, however, seem to outweigh the risks in that these sites and blogs advance the brand and often link to sites where fans can purchase Hannah Montana products. As a result, this phenomenon not only benefits the fans and Disney, but also the numerous Disney retail partners.

Another stroke of marketing genius resulted from Disney's realization that the market for Hannah included not only the six- to fourteen-year-olds who watched the

iStockphoto.com

show, but also their parents. Preteens do spend money, but they invariably get their funding from their parents. Armed with the knowledge that gaining the favorable opinion of parents would lead to product sales through preteens, Disney began connecting Hannah with moms and dads on Main Street USA. In early 2007, profiles of Miley Cyrus and her success as Hannah Montana graced the pages of publications like *Parade*, *Life*, and *Fortune* magazines, just to name a few. The articles discuss the business success of the Hannah Empire and also subtly remind readers that this is a brand with which parents can feel safe and one that they might even enjoy themselves.

Exchanges and Their Relationship to Marketing Public Relations

CHAPTER OBJECTIVE 1

As discussed in Chapter 1, marketing encompasses all efforts to change or maintain the behavior of consumers or businesses relative to a product. The behavior in question is typically the purchase of a product in exchange for money, but it can take other forms as well. Marketers who employ Marketing Public Relations (MPR) need to understand the variety of forms this behavior may take, because often MPR activities do not directly result in the sale of a good. As Professor David Robinson of the University of California-Berkeley's Haas School of Business writes, "Typically, MPR techniques and campaigns are used to foster communication between a firm and its public constituencies to promote **word-of-mouth** and increase **media mentions** of the firm which, ideally, lead to a positive perception of the firm, its brands, and its product."[2] Positive perception, in turn, leads the consumer to exchange something of value that he or she possesses for something that an organization or individual is offering that he or she wishes to possess. Nineteenth-century English economist William Stanley Jevon explained that in every act of **exchange** a definite quantity of one substance is exchanged for a definite quantity of another: "The quantities to be measured may be expressed in terms of space, time, mass, force, energy, heat, or any other physical units. Yet each exchange will consist in giving so many units of one thing for so many units of another, each measured in its appropriate way."[3] As Table 2.1 illustrates, the notion of exchange includes the adoption or modification of ideas, changes in behaviors, the casting of votes, and the spreading of information, as well as more traditional transactions involving goods, services, and money.

The Marketing Communications Mix

CHAPTER OBJECTIVE 2

MPR is one of the elements in the marketing communications, or promotional, mix. The purpose of the marketing communications mix is to inform, persuade, and remind consumers about products. It traditionally includes the marketing activities of advertising, sales promotion, personal selling, direct marketing, and public relations. Members of an organization use all of these tools in combination to achieve marketing goals in a process that is sometimes referred to as **integrated marketing communications** or IMC. As Armstrong and Kotler explain in *Marketing: An Introduction,* five elements of IMC are as follows:[4]

> **Advertising:** Any paid form of nonpersonal presentation and promotion of ideas, goods, or services by an identified sponsor

Table 2.1 Chart of Modern Exchanges

Commercial Exchanges (Partial List)

Goods	Money
Services	Money
Real Estate	Money
Goods	Goods
Services	Goods
Services	Services
Real Estate	Real Estate
Goods	Real Estate
Services	Real Estate
Votes	Promise of some future action
Adoption of idea	Status/Notoriety
Adoption of idea	Acceptance into a group
Brand preference	Status/Notoriety

Sales promotion: Short-term incentives to encourage the purchase or sale of a product or service

Personal selling: Personal presentation by a firm's sales force for the purpose of making sales and building customer relationships

Direct marketing: The use of direct mail, telephone, direct-response television, e-mail, the Internet, and other tools to communicate directly with carefully targeted individual consumers in an attempt to obtain an immediate response and to cultivate lasting customer relationships

Public relations: Building good relations with the company's various publics by obtaining favorable publicity, building up a good corporate image, and handling or heading off unfavorable rumors, stories, and events

Like IMC, MPR includes components of the advertising, sales promotion, personal selling, and direct marketing elements, but it places greater emphasis on the role of public relations tactics. Let's see how MPR fits together with and differs from the other ingredients in the mix.

Key Terms

Word-of-mouth Information spread from person to person through the spoken or written word where the communication is personal, intentional, and concerns a product

Media mentions The spoken, written, or visual reference to a product presented through mass media or other incidence where one source has the attention of many people or organizations

Exchange A transaction in which a person or organization trades a definite quantity of one substance for a definite quantity of another

Advertising and MPR

Traditionally, advertising and public relations were both delivered through mass media. They were differentiated by the fact that a person or organization paid for advertising but not for public relations. The introduction of word-of-mouth and other types of consumer-generated marketing has blurred the line between the two marketing disciplines, while simultaneously providing opportunities for greater visibility. We can find the most popular example of the synergies between advertising and MPR in the frenzy of publicity that focuses on the television commercials that air during the broadcast of the Super Bowl®.

Starting a few weeks before the game and lasting for weeks afterward, the media and consumers "buzz" about the Super Bowl commercials. Prior to the game, conversations and media commentary abound, concerning everything from the cost of a thirty-second spot ($2.7 million for the New England Patriots–New York Giants showdown in Super Bowl XLII[5]), to who the advertisers are going to be, to rumors about specific commercials. After the game, there is as much analysis of the commercials as there is of the game. The *Wall Street Journal*, *USA Today*, *Advertising Age*, and countless local newspapers, Web sites, and blogs expound on the advertising triumphs and tragedies of the day. There is even a Web site called http://www.superbowl-ads.com where you can view most of the Super Bowl ads from 1998 to the present, as well as a few classics from previous years. Finally, you can leave your own comments on the Web site's message board and stay current on Super Bowl ad news.

When you look at this event from a commercial perspective, you can see why the advertisers were willing to pay large sums of money for thirty seconds of air time. Not only did they get to put their message in front of 97.5 million pairs of eyes[6] during the game, but, after the game, millions of people viewed the commercials on the Web, others wrote and read hundreds of articles, and prospective consumers participated in innumerable conversations about the spots. Without the MPR component, the value of the advertisements themselves would be greatly diminished and their impact would last only for about thirty seconds. With the MPR component, the value is tremendous and you can see effects of the ads for weeks after the final whistle blows. While the Super Bowl advertising represents an extreme example of MPR and advertising working together, this same type of partnership between marketers, the media, and consumers can benefit almost any organization.

Sales Promotion and MPR

Sales promotion's point of intersection with MPR is similar to that of advertising. Sales promotion includes coupons, point-of-purchase displays, special deals within distribution channels, and a host of other items for which the distributor is compensated for carrying a firm's message to the consumer. The overlap between sales promotion and MPR comes in the form of certain types of event marketing, the offering of an extraordinary degree of service or price level, and even what we might call "publicity stunts." Consider, for example, Wal-Mart's® introduction of the $4 price point on prescription medication. Effectively, this is a sales promotion that offers a class of products at a price that consumers perceive as remarkably low. Wal-Mart tested the promotion in Florida in September 2006 and expanded it to eleven more states in November of the same year. By September 2007, the company had put the promotion in effect nationwide. This initiative was an effective sales promotion, because it raised the daily average of Wal-Mart pharmacies' volume by about 22 percent.[7] However, it also served as an MPR effort because it put Wal-Mart pharmacies in the news and on the lips of the American consumer. *A quick search of most any news medium's archives from 2006 to the present will demonstrate the impact this campaign has had for Wal-Mart.* Clearly, the sales promotion created the MPR opportunity, which led to an impressive number of media mentions and considerable word-of-mouth—further enhancing the sales promotion. The combination of the sales promotion and supporting MPR was far more valuable to the firm than the sales promotion alone.

Personal Selling and MPR

Has someone ever attempted to sell you something that you had never heard of before? What was your reaction? If you are like most people, you probably rebuffed the salesperson's advances and did not give it a second thought.

Now suppose that the pitch was for a product that you had just read an article about or had heard about from a trusted friend. Assuming the product was something you need or want and can afford, would you be more open to listening to the sales pitch? Chances are, you would.

Why? Conventional sales management wisdom suggests that salespeople need to establish some trust with a prospect, identify the prospect's needs, offer possible solutions, and help him or her make a decision.[8] Unfortunately, salespeople tend to focus on the third and fourth steps of this process, while consumers tend to offer more resistance during the first and second steps. MPR, however, can help bridge the gap between the seller and the prospective buyer.

Media mentions and word-of-mouth are nonthreatening means for consumers to gain awareness of products and their potential need for them. Therefore, a logical synergy exists between personal selling and MPR, where the MPR campaign creates awareness of the product among prospects and illustrates why the prospect might need or want this particular good or service. Once the campaign has met these goals, the salesperson can approach targeted consumers to help them evaluate purchasing alternatives and make the final decision. The MPR efforts support the salesperson by informing the prospects about the product, thereby turning the initial contact into an effort to continue a relationship rather than a "cold call." After securing the leads, the personal selling activities can then take over and do what MPR cannot, which is to interact with a prospect in real time by answering questions as they arise and even judging a consumer's level of comfort or understanding by watching his or her body language.

We can see evidence of the power of the relationship between personal selling and MPR in a campaign executed by Sistina Software® in conjunction with Schwartz Communications. The campaign reached out to industry media, worked with influential software analysts, and took advantage of speaking opportunities within the software industry to position itself as a major player in its core business of "enterprise infrastructure." Sistina's owners also desired to improve the company's sales and image so they could sell the company profitably. As a result of the word-of-mouth and media mentions created by the campaign, Sistina nearly doubled in size in just twelve months. Shortly thereafter, industry leader Red Hat purchased Sistina for $30 million.[9]

Direct Marketing and MPR

Direct marketing and MPR interface in much the same way as personal selling and MPR do. MPR generates awareness and plants the seeds of need in the minds of consumers, while direct marketing completes the process by attempting to make the sale. Direct marketing can come in many forms, including direct mail, direct response TV and radio commercials, infomercials, and catalogs. These two marketing elements reach their true convergence point on the electronic side of marketing.

Similar to the way consumers are reluctant to engage in a sales conversation about an unknown product, they are also resistant to opening, reading, and remembering e-mail sent to them by organizations. MPR campaigns increase consumer awareness of a product or a company through media mentions and word-of-mouth, resulting in consumers who are more receptive to the direct marketing message. During the early days of the Internet, direct e-mail was an effective marketing tool on its own. However, over time anti-spam legislation and consumer fatigue have inspired marketers to look elsewhere for ways to leverage the benefits of e-mail, leading to the use of **viral marketing**.

We call this type of marketing "viral" because the way people are exposed to the message mimics the process of passing a virus or contagious disease from one person to another.[10] Most often a firm starts a direct marketing campaign with the intent of getting the recipient to buy a particular product and, more important, to pass the information on to others who will be interested in this product as well. Sometimes, however, viral marketers create something that is not directly related to the organization or its products but rather is of great interest or entertainment value to its prospective customers. OfficeMax's® "Elf Yourself"® campaign over the winter holidays in 2006, 2007, and 2008 is a great example of this technique. Accessed at ElfYourself.com, this campaign allowed people to visit a Web site to transpose pictures of their own faces onto a group of dancing elves and then to e-mail this animation to their family and friends. More than 193 million people visited the site in 2007 and they created more than 123 million elves. Users of this site spent the equivalent of 2,600 years either creating or watching short clips of their loved ones as dancing fairy-tale creatures while simultaneously being exposed to the OfficeMax logo. Elf Yourself was also featured on *CNN American Morning*, *ABC World News*, *Good Morning America*, *Fox News*, and the *TODAY Show*.[11] This successful campaign demonstrated how direct marketing and MPR can work in concert to generate an immediate response, foster long-term relationships, spread word-of-mouth, and elicit media mentions.

Public Relations and MPR

As you can see, none of the elements of the marketing communications mix work in a vacuum; they need to be used in harmony to achieve the marketing goals of the organization. MPR is often the element of the mix that starts off a marketing campaign. In addition, it stays around in support of the other elements for the duration of that campaign.

While public relations bridges into other functional areas within an organization as well, MPR represents the deliberate and calculated influence of public relations upon the rest of the marketing mix.

Exhibit 2.1 MPR works together with other forms of marketing to increase the effectiveness of a promotional campaign.

According to Mitchell Friedman, APR (Accredited in Public Relations), an adjunct instructor in communications at the University of San Francisco and a long-time public relations consultant:

> There's a wealth of evidence on the need to integrate all elements of the marketing mix, including public relations, advertising, sales promotion, and others. What I've seen over the years as far as "critical success factors" in this integration include cultivating a cooperative as opposed to a competitive environment (i.e., individual functions work together and don't compete for dollars and resources) and having the individual functions report to one person. In general, it helps a lot if the "integration" message comes from senior management—specifically the CEO. On the public relations side of things, I've seen entire companies assume a specific persona based on the CEO's adoption of the perspective that "public relations matters...it is central to what we do."

Key Terms

Viral marketing The marketing phenomenon that facilitates and encourages people to pass along a marketing message

---

Concept Case 2.1: **Marketing Communications Mix**

As discussed in the chapter, organizations rarely use MPR alone. Rather, they incorporate MPR practices with other elements of the marketing communications mix. Let's examine some of the possibilities for integrating MPR with advertising, sales promotion, personal selling, and direct marketing by listing areas where multitiered promotional opportunities exist for The Falcon's Lair.

- Advertising
  - Solicit media to report on a new advertising technique (blogs, podcasts, launch of new e-commerce site, etc.)
  - Solicit media to report on an innovative or controversial advertisement
- Sales promotion
  - Publicize the visit of a famous climber that occurs in conjunction with a sale
- Personal selling
  - Publicize the knowledge and experience of the sales staff
- Direct marketing
  - Announce the launch of a new catalogue

Questions:

1. Cite some other ways The Falcon's Lair might use MPR together with advertising and personal selling to help improve business.
2. Find an example of a real company using MPR in conjunction with one of the other elements of the marketing mix and explain what you think the company is trying to accomplish.

CHAPTER
OBJECTIVE
3

Positioning

A primary goal in any marketing communications effort is to differentiate a product or product line by ensuring that it occupies a clear, distinctive, and desirable place relative to competing products in the minds of consumers.[12] **Positioning** refers to the place that consumers perceive a product to inhabit on the competitive landscape. MPR shows its strength in positioning a product or overall organization.

A recently established, yet widely held, belief is that information delivered as news or by word-of-mouth has more credibility than similar information delivered via an advertisement or by salespeople. Some research suggests that advertising and MPR techniques are equally effective in establishing consumer awareness of or interest in a product and in getting them to ultimately buy it. Another study suggests that MPR might actually have an edge. This study used a fictional product, "Zip Chips," positioned as a snack food that contained no sodium or fats. The participants were divided into three groups. One was not exposed to any media, another was exposed to a full-color ad created by an award-winning advertising consultant, and a third group was exposed to an editorial commentary created to match those found in *The New York Times* product testing section.

The research found that those who read the editorial (a form of MPR) viewed the product as more closely related to their lifestyles than those who read the advertisement.

Exhibit 2.2 People associate products with their lifestyle better when they receive information about that product through MPR channels as opposed to advertising.

The reason for this distinction appeared to be related to higher levels of overall knowledge about the product from exposure to the editorial.[13]

If advertising and MPR efforts are at least equal in their ability to get consumers to buy products, then organizations have an incentive to shift resources away from advertising and into MPR. The first part of this incentive is financial, as public relations and consumer-generated marketing initiatives simply cost less than advertising campaigns generating similar exposure. In describing the need to shift marketing expenditures away from advertising and into public relations, well-known marketing author Al Ries noted the following in a 2006 interview with *Marketing News*:

> During the boom days of the late 1990s and 2000, there were many Internet Web sites that tried to establish their brands with massive advertising programs, including Pets.com whose Sock Puppet is on the cover of our book. Almost none of the Internet companies that tried to build brands with advertising succeeded. The ones that did succeed usually did so with massive PR, not advertising. Amazon.com and eBay are two classic examples.[14]

The second, and possibly stronger, part of this incentive relates to positioning. Advertising campaigns are limited by budget and can only utilize a relatively small number of media outlets. MPR, on the other hand, is designed to maximize exposure by reaching out to any and all media outlets, consumer groups, or experts that

Key Terms

Positioning The way that consumers perceive a product relative to its competitors connect with the target consumer in one way, shape, or form. Therefore, when we look at positioning as consumers' perceptions of a product relative to the market, we can conclude that greater consumer exposure to information about one organization or its products from sources other than the organization itself strengthens the position of that organization or product relative to its competitors.

Positioning greatly impacts all MPR efforts and the way they interface with the other elements of the marketing communications mix. Most notably, a company's position can affect the choice of media outlets for PR and advertising; the selection of groups and individuals for fostering word-of-mouth; the choice of expert or celebrity endorsers used in advertising and event promotion; the style of writing and presentation used in all promotional material; and the types of events attended or created for promotional purposes.

Positioning Statement

A successful marketing plan for a product or organization includes a **positioning statement**, which describes the way that the marketers intend consumers to perceive the product relative to its competitors. The statement should also identify these consumers and outline the various ways that they are influenced about products. A workable positioning statement is typically four to six sentences long and should serve as a decision-making tool for marketers as they plan a marketing campaign and manage its implementation. For example, marketers should be able to look to the positioning statement when formulating a promotional message or when selecting media or other promotional channels. A good positioning statement should help answer these questions:

- What do consumers think of the product?
- How will consumers learn about the product?

Remember that positioning goes beyond the physical manifestation of the product and includes the product's image and other intangible perceptions of that product. For instance, Volvo® has done an outstanding job positioning itself as a leader in automotive safety, while BMW® has positioned itself as the Ultimate Driving Machine. Although both are luxury cars, they have managed to position themselves differently. As you evaluate successful positioning efforts, you will see that MPR has had a hand in all of them.

Concept Case 2.2: **Positioning Statement**

Following is a possible positioning statement for The Falcon's Lair:

The Falcon's Lair is a premiere hiking and camping store that serves everyone from the master climber to the youth hiker. Our products are a collection of the best hiking and camping equipment available, and our staff is experienced, knowledgeable, and helpful. Our customers rely on their relationship with us to make their time hiking and camping safe and enjoyable, and they know that personal service is part of every product we sell.

Questions:
1. What are the strengths and weaknesses of this positioning statement?
2. How could you improve it?

The Communication Process

As indicated by the term *integrated marketing communications*, the activities that reside in the promotions segment of the marketing mix are types of communication. The communication process that most of these promotional tools employ follows the classical model, which is very similar to the pattern that people engaged in conversation follow. The conversation model begins with a sender who encodes a message into a form that is intelligible to a receiver. This message is then transmitted to the receiver via some channel. Finally, the receiver decodes the message and offers some feedback—either solicited or unsolicited—in a way that reassures the sender that the receiver understood the meaning of the message. In a conversation, the sender and receiver are people, the message is the topic of conversation, and the channel is the human voice. In marketing, however, the sender is usually an organization with a product to sell or an idea to foster and the message is designed to change or reinforce the behavior of the receiver. The channel is the media, or the words and actions of people, and the receivers are the consumers that the sender hopes to persuade. Finally, the desired feedback is the purchase of a product or the acceptance of an idea. Feedback, in this case, is the measurable consumer behavior that results from attending to a promotional message. In business the communication needs to take place in an open environment where there are literally thousands of other competing messages creating lots of **noise**, thereby creating some uncertainty as to whether the sender's messages reached and were understood by the receiver.

Exhibit 2.3 In the Classic Communication Process the message reaches the receiver as intended by the sender.

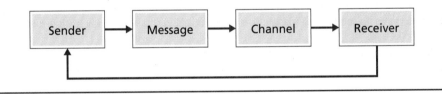

Connectors

In MPR, the sender is an organization that wants to influence or inform some sector of the public or business community relative to a particular product or issue. The message needs to take the channel into account to ensure that the organization reaches the right audience and that the combination of message and channel contributes to attaining the

Key Terms

Positioning statement A statement describing the way that the marketers intend consumers to perceive the product relative to its competitors

Noise Anything tangible or intangible that interferes with the transmission of a message from a sender to a receiver or with the comprehension of the message by the receiver

ultimate goal. Since we know that the objectives of Marketing Public Relations are to obtain media mentions and to create word-of-mouth, we can easily deduce that the media and groups or individuals who influence others are the prime MPR channels. We call these channels **connectors**.

The method of making contact with connectors varies with the types of connectors selected and the goals of a particular campaign. Regardless of these factors, however, once the connectors receive the message, they have the ball. Media outlets can choose either to ignore the message or to cover it. Similarly, influential groups and individuals can choose to disregard the message or to spread the word. If the connectors choose to act on the message, they then decide how much exposure to give the story, how they will present it, and when. This initial exposure comes in the form of media mentions and word-of-mouth and is the first form of feedback that the sender receives. However, this is not the end of the MPR communications process. The connectors have the option to repackage the message and present it in a way that suits their own needs and the interests of their audience—what media theorists call *gatekeeping*. Consumers and businesses, the ultimate audience, then need to absorb the message that the connectors conveyed to them and to behave accordingly. This behavior is the second form of feedback and usually takes the shape of consumers buying a product or displaying new attitudes.

Since the message is filtered through connectors, consumers tend to trust PR and consumer-generated marketing more than other types of promotional efforts, such as advertisements and direct selling. However, members of the media can, and will, alter the message to put it into the context of their specific medium. In addition, they often offer their opinion of the message. You must remember that the medium through which a consumer receives the MPR message gives it its context. As a result, the meaning of the message can change depending upon the channel through which it is delivered. Imagine two people saying the same thing, yet one is smiling and displaying open arms while the other is scowling and brandishing a gun. Clearly, you will hear that message

Exhibit 2.4 In the MPR Communication Process, the sender gives up control of the message.

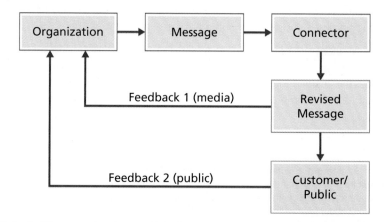

differently from these two different messengers. Marketers need to be aware that the connectors they choose are equally as important as the message with which they entrust them. Legendary communications scholar Marshall McLuhan went as far as to say that the "medium is the message."

Anheuser Busch® scored an MPR victory with its Swear Jar campaign by combining advertising with MPR to reach millions of potential beer drinkers. The company began by posting a Web-only advertisement depicting an office that has taken up swearing in order to raise money to buy some Bud Light®. The ad is very funny, but the language is too rough for TV. The winning combination of new technology, humor, and irreverence hit home with a variety of connectors and started a viral epidemic. Stories on the Associated Press and *Tribune* news wires spurred coverage in newspapers, including the *Chicago Tribune*, *Denver Post*, *Orlando Sentinel*, and even the usually conservative *Forbes Magazine*. Bloggers specializing in entertainment and marketing posted commentary and links to the commercial, and there were more than 200 postings to YouTube, resulting in tens of thousands of views. Using the Internet as a connector allowed Anheuser Busch to create a message that was not appropriate for traditional media but was very popular with consumers. This combination of lewd humor and a tremendous popular response in turn led to considerable coverage in traditional media.

Audience

CHAPTER OBJECTIVE 6

An understanding of the term *audience* is essential to the success of any MPR effort. When speaking of **audience** in marketing, we are typically referring to the intended receivers of a promotional message. This holds true for MPR as well, but you must remember that we really have *two* audiences: the intended receiver and the connectors. The challenge is to manage the relationship with the connectors in order to reach the intended audience and to create and maintain relationships with its members. First, you must understand your intended audience, the media that its members follow, and the groups and individuals that influence them. You must also understand the connectors that reach your intended audience and their respective styles and preferences.

In short, you need to do your homework. The more you know about the media outlet, the more successful you will be in getting coverage by that outlet. If you, as a marketing professional, can help a media organization serve its audience better, or give a connector something he or she feels is important to say, you are likely to be successful in getting positive media mentions and word-of-mouth, and you are likely to be called on in the future for more. The better your knowledge of the audience and the connectors, the better your relationships will become. The better your relationships, the more success you will have in using MPR as a marketing tool.

Key Terms

Connectors Media, groups, or individuals who act as a channel for a marketing message resulting in media mentions or the creation of word-of-mouth

Audience The intended receivers of a promotional message

Reflection Questions

1. People commonly perceive a marketing exchange to be the trade of a good or service for money. List and describe other types of exchanges that do not include a good, a service, or money as part of the exchange. (Chapter Objective 1)

2. Explain the five elements of the marketing communications mix. (Chapter Objective 2)

3. Discuss how MPR is used in conjunction with the other elements of the marketing communications mix. (Chapter Objective 2)

4. What is a positioning statement and how does it serve the marketer? (Chapter Objective 3)

5. Describe and differentiate between the standard communications process and the MPR communication process. (Chapter Objective 4)

6. Explain what a connector is and list several examples. (Chapter Objective 5)

7. For each of the following industries, list as many companies or products as you can, and discuss their positioning in their respective markets: (Chapter Objective 6)

   a. Fast food
   b. Automobiles
   c. Airlines
   d. Soft drinks
   e. Coffee (retail, by the cup)

Chapter Key Terms

Advertising Any paid form of nonpersonal presentation and promotion of ideas, goods, or services by an identified sponsor (p. 16)

Audience The intended receivers of a promotional message (p. 27)

Buzz Synonymous with *word-of-mouth* (p. 15)

Connectors Media, groups, or individuals who act as a channel for a marketing message, resulting in media mentions or the creation of word-of-mouth (p. 26)

Direct marketing The use of direct mail, the telephone, direct-response television, e-mail, the Internet, and other tools to communicate directly with carefully targeted individual consumers in an attempt to obtain an immediate response and to cultivate lasting customer relationships (p. 17)

Exchange A transaction in which a person or organization trades a definite quantity of one substance for a definite quantity of another (p. 17)

Integrated marketing communications The concept under which a company carefully integrates and

coordinates its many communications channels to deliver a clear, consistent, and compelling message about the organization and its products (p. 16)

Media mentions The spoken, written, or visual reference to a product presented through mass media or other incidence where one source has the attention of many people or organizations (p. 16)

Noise Anything tangible or intangible that interferes with the transmission of a message from a sender to a receiver or with the comprehension of the message by the receiver (p. 25)

Personal selling Personal presentation by a firm's sales force for the purpose of making sales and building customer relationships (p. 17)

Positioning The way that consumers perceive a product relative to its competitors (p. 22)

Positioning statement A statement describing the way that the marketers intend consumers to perceive the product relative to its competitors (p. 24)

Public relations The function of building good relations with the company's various publics by obtaining favorable publicity, building up a good corporate image, and handling or heading off unfavorable rumors, stories, and events (p. 17)

Sales promotion Short-term incentives to encourage the purchase or sale of a product or service (p. 17)

Viral marketing The marketing phenomenon that facilitates and encourages people to pass along a marketing message (p. 20)

Word-of-mouth Information spread from person to person through the spoken or written word where the communication is personal, intentional, and concerns a product (p. 16)

Application Assignments

Select one of the following companies in order to answer questions 1 through 4:

    a. Ralph Lauren

    b. Rolex

    c. Hollister

    d. Coach

    e. Mercedes-Benz

1. Explain how the company you selected uses each element of the marketing communications mix to promote its products. (Hint: Explore the company's Web site and conduct a Web search using the company name along with terms like *marketing*, *advertising*, *sales*, and *public relations.* Also investigate popular magazines and TV programs where you think you might find mention of the company.)

2. Identify areas where this company is not using a specific element of the marketing communications mix and suggest ways it can improve.

3. Describe this company's position and contrast it to the position of its major competitors.

4. List the specific media, groups, and individuals that can be considered connectors for this company.

5. Watch a morning or an evening news program on one of the major television networks. List the stories you saw and name the ones you believe to have been influenced by marketers. Explain who did the influencing and why. (Note: This question does not involve the company selected in question 1.)

Practice Portfolio

This Practice Portfolio can be based on a fictitious company or on a real company that your instructor assigns to you. (If you used a company in the previous Practice Portfolio exercise, continue to use that company.) Add your completed assignment to your portfolio to present to prospective employers.

- List some non-MPR elements of the marketing communication mix that your practice company would most likely use. Identify any areas where the company could combine conventional marketing methods with MPR. Describe how the company could achieve that goal and discuss the benefits of doing so.

- Write a positioning statement for your practice company, meeting all of the criteria described in the chapter.

- List the likely connectors for your practice company and divide them into media, groups, and individuals. Name actual media outlets and groups whenever possible. You may need to generalize somewhat for individuals, but provide as much detail as you can.

CHAPTER 3

MPR and the Organization It Serves

CHAPTER OBJECTIVES

After studying this chapter, you should be able to:

1. Explain how MPR serves an organization in marketing, employee relations, and investor relations capacities.

2. Discuss how changes in technology and consumer attitudes have contributed to changes in firms' management philosophies over time.

3. Illustrate how MPR supports an organization's strategic plan and implementation.

4. Describe MPR's role in creating brand authors.

5. Explain the importance of MPR in building and supporting a brand value.

6. List and explain the five elements of S.M.A.R.T. goal setting.

If successfully employing marketing public relations requires a company to engage popular culture, customers, and other influencers as **brand authors** to create a brand culture, then Red Bull® is the epitome of an MPR-focused company. It has infused itself into the areas of popular culture where fun and energy intersect. Specifically, the company is part of the fabric of extreme and conventional sports whose teen and young adult fans feed off of the energy of their sport by day and the energy of partying with Red Bull in hand by night. The company has accomplished this goal through its sponsorship of these sports, by its omnipresence at events and in clubs frequented by its target customers, and by its use of the Web to create social networking sites that keep these customers engaged with each other. Red Bull is the unobtrusive, yet ever-present, backdrop to all of these events and interactions. And the result? Despite stiff competition from well-financed competitors made by Coke® and Pepsi®, Red Bull maintains a share of about 50 percent in the energy drink market.[1]

While Red Bull has done a fair amount of traditional advertising, the company created its multibillion-dollar worldwide stampede for Red Bull through a highly ingenious "buzz-marketing" strategy that herds consumers to exclusive and exciting events with high media coverage.[2] The company created this buzz by engaging consumers not as a soft drink marketer, but as a partner in traditional and extreme sporting events where it acts as sponsor and sometimes owner of teams and events.

In addition, the company has created a multifaceted Web presence with Web sites that act as social networking platforms for enthusiasts of the given sport. The company has associations, and corresponding Red Bull Web sites, for surfing, motocross, Formula One racing, and major league soccer. One immediately striking aspect of these Web sites is that they are information-sharing venues for people interested in the sport. The sites do not overtly sell the Red Bull drink. Yet the company is still the market leader and sells millions of cans a year. Red Bull has branded itself as a lifestyle product and has aligned itself with the lifestyle associated with action or extreme sports and motor sports.[3] In so doing, it has captured the power of interaction. Red Bull has also relied on virtual interaction between the company and its target market. For instance, Red Bull has developed a social-networking site aimed at fostering innovation and providing young consumers support for their ideas. The Flugelbinder site, which carries minimal Red Bull branding, allows users to create a Thought Locker— a profile page where they can securely store ideas, photos, and business proposals.[4]

The company also uses both traditional and new media to influence its consumers. For example, Red Bull took a page from the playbook of Benetton® when it decided to produce controversial advertisements. While the advertisements themselves are not MPR, the buzz created in the media and with consumers surely is. One such ad, which ran on Italian television, depicted

Shutterstock.

four wise men, instead of three, visiting Mary and the baby Jesus in Bethlehem. The fourth wise man bore a can of the soft drink. An outcry from the Catholic Church prompted Red Bull to pull the ad from television.[5] However, the outcry generated its own wave of media coverage and sent thousands of people to view this ad on YouTube.

YouTube itself has been important to Red Bull. The company posts and encourages the posting of video clips from consumers whether they are viewing or participating in a Red Bull–sponsored sport or participating in the "Red Bull lifestyle." In addition, Red Bull has used YouTube to display videos of famed base jumper (and Red-Bull sponsored) Felix Baumgartner, who routinely jumps off tall buildings sporting a Red Bull suit and parachute. Videos of Baumgartner's jumps have garnered hundreds of thousands of views at a minimal cost to Red Bull.

The Red Bull brand clearly has tremendous value. As with its ability to enlist brand authors, the company has been able to build brand value in all categories. The Red Bull company has a reputation for being associated with all that is active and edgy. It continuously interacts with its customer base to create relationships that transcend energy drinks and create an "energy culture." The experience of consuming the drink is consistent with participating in or watching one of its branded events or social networks. Holding the Red Bull can or donning Red Bull–logoed clothing are symbolic of living the fun and fast-paced Generation Y lifestyle.

CHAPTER
OBJECTIVE
1

Marketing Public Relations in an Organizational Setting

Traditional public relations serves three constituencies within an organization: the marketing, human resources,[6] and investor relations departments. While this text focuses on the use of public relations techniques in the marketing capacity, you should understand how organizations can use these principles to serve the other two functions as well.

Human Resources and MPR

Human resources departments typically have three areas of responsibility—namely, recruiting and retaining employees, managing employee benefits, and training and professional development of employees. Other responsibilities of the human resources department may include policy and procedure creation and employee recognition. Although communication with employees is not a true MPR function, organizations can apply elements of MPR to this aspect of human resources (HR) known as **employee relations**. Consider that a typical communication from HR informs employees about organizational issues that relate to them and has the goal of ensuring that employees remain satisfied with their jobs and perform as productively as possible. The communication channels that connect the sender (the organization) and the receiver (the employees) are internal to the organization and are almost entirely controlled by the organization itself. These channels can take the form of company newsletters (both paper and electronic); informative e-mails; message board postings (again, both paper and electronic); and meetings, seminars, or other types of group sessions.

Exhibit 3.1 Employee relations use many of the same tools and techniques used in MPR.

Dmitriy Shironosov/Shutterstock.

The area where communications from human resources directly intersects with communications from marketing is the recruiting function, because the overall public image of the company comes into play when an organization is courting prospective employees. We assume that the best employees want to work for the best companies. Therefore, the company's public image is as important to its recruiting efforts as it is to its marketing efforts.

Marketers are usually put in charge of maintaining the company's relationship with the media and other connectors because they have the task of communicating with stakeholders to build brand image and promote sales. However, a conflict may arise if a prospective employee is turned off by a firm's marketing, or if internally generated word-of-mouth finds its way to customers in a manner that is unfavorable to the firm. Managers need to be aware of these possible negative repercussions when they design organizational structure and plan the marketing and HR functions of the firm. They may find the situation challenging, since these two disciplines have significantly different missions within an organization. However, when the two groups work together

Key Terms

Employee relations A public relations function that deals with managing communication with existing and prospective employees

in using MPR tools, they can enhance the company's brand as an employer, which in turn helps recruit better-qualified employees and improves the morale and engagement of current staff.[7] As Oliver Blanchard of the Brand Builder Blog says:

> Employees are the core element of a company's identity. Beyond professionalism and happiness at one's job, an employee's sense of worth within the context of this identity directly affects the quality of the service they provide in the eyes of their customers. Unhappy employees can turn even the best companies into "has beens." In contrast, happy employees can turn even the most average companies into word-of-mouth worthy lovebrands.[8]

D. Mark Hornung, senior vice president of employer brand practice at the Bernard Hodes Group in New York, calls Google® an example of a company that uses its brand right. Google keeps its prospective employee pipeline full by spreading the word to people whose way of life aligns with the brand.[9] "The most effective employment branding is word-of-mouth—what people say at parties, on weekends—when they get asked, 'How do you like working there?'" says F. Leigh Branham, owner of Keeping People Inc. "That spreads like crazy."[10]

Investor Relations and MPR

In a typical business, marketing tends to be in charge of managing the relationship with customers, prospective customers, and even competitors, while HR takes the lead on the relationship with employees. Companies that trade shares of ownership (**stock**[11]) on the open market have a third group of stakeholders with whom they need to manage relationships and because of whom they need to work with the media and other types of connectors. The people or organizations in question are the company's stockholders. These **publicly traded companies**[12] rely on the positive opinion of shareholders to keep the demand for the company's stock high and, therefore, the stock price strong.

This opinion is driven not only by the company's performance and the words of its executives, but also by the opinion of analysts who monitor corporate performance. These analysts may be employed by the financial media or by large brokerage firms and insurance companies. In every case the news they share about the financial performance of a corporation has material impact on the business and all of its stakeholders. In addition, the presence of intermediaries, such as financial analysts, reporters, and even the company's own executives, illustrates how the function that we commonly call **investor relations** needs to utilize MPR methods to sustain positive opinion about the organization's financial viability. The company needs to use these analysts and the financial media to get information to the investing public in an expedient manner so they can make informed decisions. By demonstrating good **corporate governance**[13] and greater **transparency**,[14] investor relations can help achieve overall business objectives.[15] As is the case with employee relations, marketers must coordinate with investor relations personnel to ensure that they do not duplicate efforts and that they are not working at cross purposes.

Note that only a small percentage of companies are publicly traded and, therefore, need to concern themselves with investor relations. Many of the smaller public firms combine their investor relations function with marketing. However, for those companies that need it, the investor relations function is extremely important, as it can significantly impact the market value of a public company.

Exhibit 3.2 MPR and Investor Relations practitioners work together to ensure a positive image of a firm among all stakeholders.

Just ASC/Shutterstock.

Other Business Functions and MPR

In addition to HR and investor relations, the operations, finance, and service functions of a business can impact marketing, generally in one of two ways, both of which involve word-of-mouth. First, employees in these functional areas often have contact with customers, **vendors**,[16] and the general public as a part of performing their duties. This contact may take the form of the delivery of a product, a phone call to clarify an invoice, or the performance of a service. This interplay will, invariably, influence opinions and instigate word-of-mouth. Secondly, employees adopt their own opinions about companies and their products and share these opinions with those outside of the organization. Marketers rarely have any authority or control over employees in these areas, but the results of the messages sent by these workers to the world at large can have a considerable impact on marketing. Therefore, managers need to structure the organization so that they can recognize how customers and the public perceive all aspects of the company. They need to do so in a way that ensures that all stakeholders send a consistent and positive message to the greater world and that they can take corrective action when perception is inconsistent or negative.

Key Terms

Investor relations A public relations function that manages the communication between a publicly held corporation, its shareholders, and the media and analysts who report on the corporation's financial situation

For an example of how the different facets of public relations can affect a business, look no further than Southwest Airlines®. Southwest uses MPR-rooted tools to facilitate "employee branding" that simultaneously increases employee satisfaction and reduces employee turnover while increasing customer satisfaction and loyalty. The company pays careful attention to ensure that all messages emanating from the organization align with its **mission**[17] and **vision**.[18] This uniformity applies to messages that have sources and channels that are both formal and informal in nature, as well as internally and externally generated communications. For instance, formal messages that reinforce Southwest's commitment to its employees and customer service are communicated internally by its human resources management team. Formal external sources include messages that are disseminated by the company's PR department and target the general public. Informal sources include employee word-of-mouth (internal) and customer feedback (external). In all cases the messages enhance Southwest's overall reputation among all of the company's stakeholders.[19]

<table>
<tr><td>CHAPTER
OBJECTIVE
2</td><td>

Organizational Marketing Philosophies Evolve Toward Embracing MPR

</td></tr>
</table>

Since the late eighteenth century, businesses have regularly reoriented their philosophy of marketing management as the sophistication of consumers and technology has evolved. The Industrial Revolution gave birth to the earliest of these philosophies, the **production concept**. This concept assumes that consumers will favor products that are most widely available and attractively priced. As manufacturing and transportation technologies improved, however, competition heated up and led many organizations to attempt to differentiate their products through product quality, performance, and available features. This approach is known as the **product concept**. This same wave of competition inspired other companies to focus on large-scale promotional and selling efforts in order to gain market share, which is an approach called the **selling concept**. As the twenty-first century neared, firms realized that consumers had become increasingly savvy and that simply offering the right product or selling aggressively was not enough to maintain market share. This realization that they needed something more ushered in the era of the **marketing concept**, the philosophy of centering the organization's goal on satisfying the needs of the customer.[20] While even today's companies continue to embrace all four of these concepts, the marketing concept has been given the most attention for several decades.

New marketing orientations and concepts are beginning to emerge that appear to build on the marketing concept. The first of these, which goes beyond a concentration on the consumer and considers the long-term interests of society at large,[21] is the **societal marketing concept**. This concept includes both green and cause-related marketing and is integrated into what is now known as *corporate social responsibility* (CSR). While the academic and professional media have offered much praise for the societal marketing concept, it is also an area of question. The primary concern is whether firms are espousing social responsibility to truly benefit society or if they are using this rhetoric just to garner the favor of the increasing numbers of socially aware consumers.

As changes in technology and consumer attitudes continue to accelerate, modern firms are pressuring marketing managers to demonstrate the success of their efforts down to the individual customer level. They can demonstrate this success most profoundly in the increased number of two-way multimedia interactions between firms and consumers. This enhanced level of communication has facilitated a shift from marketing orientation to interaction orientation.[22] Amazon.com® is a prime example of a company that embraces customer interaction. The Amazon Web site allows customers to rate and review books and other products with comments that are then available for other customers to read before making a purchase. The site also analyzes individual customers' buying patterns and recommends products to them via e-mail and on the Web. As Amazon CEO Jeff Bezos noted, "The majority of our customers that come to us every day are coming by word of mouth. I think that the best money we spend on acquiring new customers is actually spent on customer experience."[23]

This shift toward interaction orientation can either alter the marketing concept to include the feedback loop that exists between firms and consumers, or we can classify it as a new business philosophy, the **interaction concept**. Regardless of its label, this concept focuses on a firm's need to demonstrate that customers are important partners when they interact with the firm and even when they interact with each other. Marketers are looking to the interaction concept to increase profitability by more efficiently acquiring and retaining profitable customers and by improving customer-based relational performance, which consists of customer satisfaction and positive word-of-mouth.[24]

MPR and a Firm's Strategy Objectives

CHAPTER OBJECTIVE 3

A firm's strategic plan is a forward-looking document that defines the organization's mission and vision, analyzes the company's business environment, sets goals for the company, and explains how the management of the firm intends to take the company from where it is now to where it wants to be in the future. Obviously, the strategic plan encompasses far more than just the marketing function, but marketing is often overlooked or undervalued as a part of the strategic planning process. When marketing activities are tightly aligned with corporate strategy, they drive growth. But in too many companies, marketing and strategy are poorly linked.[25] In order to frame the notion of business strategy and relate it to MPR, we will use the Business

Key Terms

Production concept A business philosophy that assumes that consumers will favor the most widely available and attractively priced products

Product concept A business philosophy that assumes that consumers will favor products with a higher degree of quality, performance, and available features

Selling concept A business philosophy in which companies focus on large-scale promotional and selling efforts in order to gain market share

Marketing concept The business philosophy of centering an organization's goal on satisfying the needs of the customer

Societal marketing concept A business philosophy that goes beyond concentrating on the consumer and considers the long-term interests of society at large

Interaction concept A business philosophy that assumes that a firm's two-way interaction with customers is essential to long-term profitability

Exhibit 3.3 The Business Strategy Diamond identifies five critical elements of strategic planning.

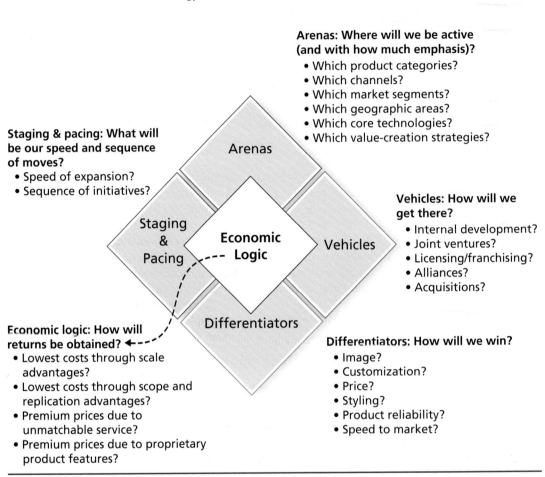

**Arenas: Where will we be active
(and with how much emphasis)?**
- Which product categories?
- Which channels?
- Which market segments?
- Which geographic areas?
- Which core technologies?
- Which value-creation strategies?

**Staging & pacing: What will
be our speed and sequence
of moves?**
- Speed of expansion?
- Sequence of initiatives?

**Vehicles: How will we
get there?**
- Internal development?
- Joint ventures?
- Licensing/franchising?
- Alliances?
- Acquisitions?

**Economic logic: How will
returns be obtained?**
- Lowest costs through scale
  advantages?
- Lowest costs through scope and
  replication advantages?
- Premium prices due to
  unmatchable service?
- Premium prices due to proprietary
  product features?

Differentiators: How will we win?
- Image?
- Customization?
- Price?
- Styling?
- Product reliability?
- Speed to market?

Source: Carpenter, Mason, Sanders, Gerry, Strategic Management: Concepts, 2nd. Electronically reproduced by permission of Pearson Education, Inc., Upper Saddle River, New Jersey.

Strategy Diamond as the foundation of our discussion.[26] As illustrated, the diamond identifies five critical elements of strategic planning, along with a series of questions that managers should consider when formulating a strategic plan. Let's explore MPR's role in each element.

Economic Logic

Economic logic is often seen as the primary motivator for any business venture. The chief strategic question relative to economic logic tends to be, "How will we realize a return on our investment?" The entire marketing function, including MPR, is instrumental in determining the products that need to be delivered to a particular market at a particular price. In essence, management should look to its marketers to locate a substantial customer base who find significant value in its product, thereby creating long-term profits for the organization. MPR professionals, with their customer interaction focus, are also instrumental in acting as a conduit between management and the consumer, so that managers create a strategy that simultaneously serves both the organization and the customer.

Arena

Arena decisions and strategies include determining the products the firm will offer and the distribution channels it will use to get the products to the consumer. These components are clearly analogous to the *product* and *place* elements of the marketing mix. In addition, selecting the target market, or group of consumers to whom the company wishes to sell, is also an arena decision. MPR contributes to the strategic plan by communicating the knowledge gained by interaction with consumers to the firm's management, thereby helping managers to offer the right products to the right customer base through the right channels, with the goal of maximizing customer satisfaction and profitability.

Vehicles

Vehicles are the means to enter or conduct business within a given arena. They are also the main mechanisms for getting the company from its present state to where it wants to be in the future. These vehicles can include decisions about initiating joint ventures with other organizations, entering into product licensing agreements, or acquiring another business. The MPR function, in concert with marketing research and feedback from the firm's sales force, is a vital link between the firm's management and the marketplace that will help ensure that the firm aligns its strategic implementation with the needs of the customer.

Differentiators

Differentiators are the attributes of a company or product that create its competitive advantage in the marketplace. While MPR plays an essential role in providing important customer and market information to a firm's management team for the other elements of the Business Strategy Diamond, this element gives MPR its primary focus. As the principal goals of MPR are to produce media mentions and promote positive word-of-mouth, the organization's strategy must include the use of MPR to ensure that it communicates its key differentiators to its various stakeholders. When a firm communicates these factors successfully, consumers begin to understand why they should change or maintain their thoughts or behaviors relative to a product or company. In addition, when a firm uses MPR correctly, it will also be able to gauge whether consumers perceive the same factors to be differentiators that the company does.

Staging

Staging refers to the speed and sequence of implementing a strategic plan. Successful strategic implementation requires that all stakeholders be aware of the varying phases of the plan at the appropriate times. MPR professionals have an important role in ensuring that the firm executes the plan at a pace that allows for efficient communications and that the firm carries out effective communication practices throughout the duration of the implementation.

As you can see, each element of the Business Strategy Diamond reinforces the need for firms to embrace good communication practices, which, at least in part, falls to the MPR function of the organization. In fact, research has shown that "information flow" is one of the building blocks of organizational effectiveness.[27] A recent study concludes that traits such as information about competitive environments flowing quickly back to headquarters, information flowing swiftly across organizational borders, and few conflicting messages being sent to the market are being vital to the effective implementation of a firm's strategy. While one might consider good communication to be either a strategic advantage or a core competency in its own right, it is critical to creating and maintaining strategic advantages for a firm.[28]

Concept Case 3.1: **Strategy**

Let's look at how the owners of The Falcon's Lair interpret the elements of the Business Strategy Diamond to create a business strategy that will help the company grow.

Let's begin with economic logic by asking, "How are they going to make money?"

Using the positioning statement created in Chapter 2 as our guide, we can see that their *economic logic* is to realize profit from a premium pricing strategy made possible by the sales of the highest-quality products supported by unmatched customer service.

They define their *arena* by two market segments: hardcore hikers and climbers and family-recreational hikers in their defined geographic area who are interested in purchasing premium merchandise and attending high-end events.

The *vehicle* for reaching their customers is their highly engaged staff who works with customers to ensure that they buy the right equipment and know how to use it properly and who offers advice for making the most out of their hobby. In addition, the company hosts hiking and climbing events in the geographic region and maintains a Web site that offers the same level of interaction between The Falcon's Lair staff and customers.

Their key *differentiator* for The Falcon's Lair is a high level of interaction with customers that offers expertise and support beyond that offered by any competitor.

Questions:

1. How would using a low-cost, average-quality strategy as their economic logic impact the other elements of the Business Strategy Diamond?
2. Describe some specific things the owners of The Falcon's Lair can do to increase the interaction with customers that reflects their positioning statement. Be sure to consider initiatives conducted in the store, on the Web, at an event, or any combination of the three.
3. Explain how staging will come into play as the owners of The Falcon's Lair plan their strategy.

CHAPTER OBJECTIVE 4

MPR's Role in Creating Brand Authors[29]

Although we typically think of brands as a collection of names, logos, and design features, the true meaning of a brand is deeper than these overt artifacts. Famous brands have logos and other distinctive design elements as a part of their brand, but they also have a history of customer experience, well-known advertising, a library of media coverage, and a place in our everyday conversations. This history lifts a brand beyond a collection of words and symbols to a brand culture. This culture is the perceptual frame through which customers understand the value and experience of the product. As a result, customers never experience a brand objectively, but rather see it through the lens of the brand culture.

We can also think of brand culture as a set of stories, images, and associations related to the entire product experience. These stories, images, and associations are created by "authors" and accumulate over time. Authors can take one of four forms:

1. Companies
2. Popular culture
3. Customers
4. Influencers

Companies

Companies shape their brands through all of the product-related activities that touch the customer. This interaction happens in many ways, including traditional marketing methods such as advertising, distribution, sales, and the use of the product itself. However, a firm uses MPR to help manage the three other types of authors. That is, the company uses MPR to create stories, images, and associations for its products within popular culture, with customers, and among connectors.

Popular Culture

Products are part of popular culture and frequently show up in films, on television, in print, and on the Internet. While we can argue that paying to place a company's products in films and popular television shows is akin to advertising, most other intersections between products and popular culture are MPR. When companies host events surrounding the use of a product, create contests, or position their products and experts at the center of some larger issue, they are attempting to write their brand into the popular culture.

Let's look at how Gillette® has used YouTube, along with sports celebrities Tiger Woods, Roger Federer, and Thierry Henry, to promote the Phenom version of its Fusion Power razor in a contest format. This contest is an attempt to write the Phenom into popular culture by combining a web-based format and celebrities who are at the epicenter of popular culture for this product's target market. Gillette's apparent tactic is to create consumer interaction and entertainment by offering a prize to guys who submit a video demonstrating their "phenomenal ball skills." The contest and supporting video and Web material make little to no mention of shaving or the features of the razor. Rather, they associate the product with symbols of excellent performance that are immediately recognizable to the people who are most likely to buy that product.

Customers

Customers create stories about how they use or consume products and then share them with their friends. These stories then become the fuel for word-of-mouth. The MPR professional helps customers recognize when they have a **consumption story** and helps them share it as well. Web-based technology such as del.icio.us®, MySpace®, Facebook, Stumbleupon.com®, YouTube, and a host of other sites have given firms a hand in allowing customers to share their product experiences. Before this enabling technology emerged, companies relied on referral programs, promotional products (giveaways with the company's logo on it), publicity stunts, and customer testimonials in their advertising to remind customers to tell their own stories to their friends. Companies still use these "low-tech" tactics today, often in combination with their high-tech cousins.

Fiskars®, the folks who make the scissors with the orange handles, have capitalized on the phenomenon of consumption stories with the creation of a virtual community of "Fiskateers." Fiskars realized that one of its identified market segments—scrapbook enthusiasts—are passionate about their hobby and need good scissors and other Fiskars products to do what they do. Fiskars also noticed that their brand lacked passion. The company decided to actively engage scrapbookers with efforts to associate the passion for the hobby with a passion for the brand.[30] From this notion, the Fiskateers were born. Four real scrapbooking enthusiasts, who happen to be compensated by Fiskars, lead this group. They moderate the conversation and share information about their favorite pastime and Fiskars' products. The community has not only led to increased sales, but also to assistance in product development and customer service. It represents a win-win situation for the firm and for some of its best customers.

Exhibit 3.4 Fiskars® connects with its customers by encouraging them to share their experiences at the "Fiskateers" Web site.

Influencers

Influencers are the people, groups, and organizations that were defined in Chapter 2 as connectors. They can include media outlets, product mavens, experts, and so on. Influencers reside in the classic public relations field of play. In this arena, a firm's MPR staff creates relationships, not with the customers themselves, but with the outside forces that reach the customers. The power of influencers lies in the fact that consumers do not perceive them to be selling anything, but rather providing opinion and analysis. The archetype of the modern influencer is none other than talk show host Oprah Winfrey. Simply getting on Oprah's yearly "Favorite Things List" has been known to transform books, beauty products, and foods into sales blockbusters.[31]

Concept Case 3.2: **Brand Authors**

Let's identify The Falcon's Lair's non-company brand authors. The role of popular culture in the perception of hiking and climbing depends on the set of customers. The hardcore hikers and climbers set define the sport and the people who participate in it as "extreme." They participate in the sport for the thrill of doing something a bit dangerous, and by that means they differentiate themselves from others. On the other hand, the family-recreational hikers see themselves as living active, outdoor lifestyles and often think of themselves as environmentally conscious.

Customers appear to be the company's biggest potential brand authors. Ideally, the customers will tell stories about the reason they started coming to The Falcon's Lair and about how a staff member helped them find just the right piece of equipment, arrange the ultimate hiking or climbing trip, or just shared an incredible experience with them.

Local media can also influence people in their area to try hiking or climbing and can help build awareness of The Falcon's Lair. Getting press in the national media may be of some value as well. Finally, the company's vendors might be good influencers, particularly since some of them pay hiking and climbing pros as spokespeople.

Questions:

1. Describe how popular culture influences your perception of a particular retailer, brand, or product.
2. Discuss one way that The Falcon's Lair can encourage customers to share their consumption stories.
3. What might interest the local and national media covering The Falcon's Lair? How would local and national interests differ?
4. How might The Falcon's Lair partner with its vendors to create brand authors?

Key Terms

Consumption stories Stories created by consumers about how they use or consume products, which they then share with their friends and which become the fuel for word-of-mouth

Influencers Media, groups, or individuals who act as channels for a marketing message resulting in media mentions or the creation of word-of-mouth; synonymous with *connectors*

Exhibit 3.5 The Brand Culture Diagram illustrates the many facets of brand value.

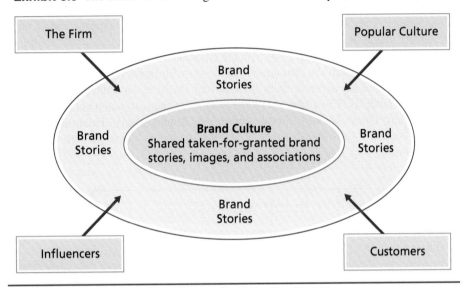

Source: Brands and Branding (Harvard Business School Case No. 503–045).

The Importance of MPR in Building and Supporting a Brand Value

CHAPTER
OBJECTIVE
5

MPR professionals are the stewards of the narrative generated by all of these brand authors. Their particular charge is to create and cultivate brand value. From this perspective, they need to manage four components:

1. Reputation value
2. Relationship value
3. Experiential value
4. Symbolic value

Reputation Value

Reputation value shapes the perceived quality of a product and acts as a signaling mechanism to increase customers' confidence that products will provide a given level of quality, reliability, and functionality. For example, marketers at Volvo® look to work with customers and influencers to generate word-of-mouth and garner media mentions that will foster its reputation for producing safe automobiles.

Relationship Value

Relationship value communicates that the customer can trust the firm to act as a long-term partner who will meet both present and future needs. For example, successful hospitals and health networks use the media, community newsletters, and even blogs to communicate the value of maintaining a relationship with their doctors and facilities, not only as a mechanism for treating illness, but also for living a long and productive life. Many of these organizations focus on highlighting the specific values they share with the community that they serve.

Experiential Value

Experiential value relates a particular benefit delivered by the product that can provide a decision-making shortcut and allow the consumer to make effective product choices. When they examine experience from the MPR perspective, marketers need to look to the customers to understand the value they derive from using the firm's product and to reinforce this experience by promoting word-of-mouth or illustrating it through media coverage. Disney is a master, not only at creating an experience, but in spreading the word about the potential for a great experience when using its products. Stories about its theme parks, cruise line, movies, and television shows are on the lips of many and are constantly in the media. The company even has a Web site, http://www.disneyexperience.com, which promises to be the "online source for adding a touch of Disney magic to your computer and your home."

Symbolic Value

Symbolic value is reflected in the symbols that express the status, lifestyle, politics, and other social aspirations of the customer. What better illustration of symbolic value is there than the diamond? While diamonds are not as rare as many people think (red rubies are actually the rarest gemstone), we instantly associate them with the concepts of romance and affluence.[32] This association could just as easily have been granted to another gemstone or precious metal if it had not been for a successful meeting in New York between Harry Oppenheimer and the president of advertising agency N.W. Ayer & Son, Gerold M. Lauck, in September 1938.

Harry Oppenheimer was the son of the founder of the company that would become the most successful cartel of the twentieth century, De Beers Consolidated Mines, Ltd.® In addition to launching an advertising campaign, Ayer engaged jewelers to give talks, lectures, classes, and informal meetings to thousands of young women. Ayer also arranged for movie stars to appear at social events adorned with diamonds. The agency used its influence to modify film scripts and movie titles to feature diamonds more prominently.[33] They even sent representatives to high school home economics classes to teach girls about the value of diamonds and to feed them romantic dreams. The diamond went from being a status symbol to an emotional one—love measured in carats.[34]

Concept Case 3.3: **Brand Value**

An organization cannot conduct successful MPR if it doesn't understand the value of its own brand. Since the value of any brand can be broken into four components—reputation value, relationship value, experiential value, and symbolic value, let's break down brand value for The Falcon's Lair.

The company's positioning dictates that it create and maintain a reputation for having the best products sold by knowledgeable, enthusiastic people. This reputation fosters relationships with customers, and even people who aren't customers know

(continued)

> ### Concept Case 3.3: (Continued)
>
> that The Falcon's Lair personnel have customers' best interests in mind and are a reliable resource for anything that has to do with hiking and climbing.
>
> The company's goal is to create an experience in which shopping at The Falcon's Lair is like becoming one of the family and becoming part of the culture of the sport.
>
> For hardcore hikers and climbers, having gear from The Falcon's Lair is a symbol that lets other climbers know they're for real, or at the very least, want to be perceived that way.
>
> The family and recreational set feel secure shopping there and like to show off the Lair's logo on their clothes, as it proves that they are part of the hiking and climbing culture. It is also a symbol of affluence, since customers know that quality and service don't come cheaply.
>
> **Questions:**
> 1. Describe another opportunity for creating brand value at The Falcon's Lair.
> 2. Explain which brand authors will be instrumental in communicating brand value to customers and why.

CHAPTER
OBJECTIVE
6

S.M.A.R.T. Goal-setting Brings Together MPR's Strategic and Tactical Functions

As illustrated throughout this chapter, MPR serves the organization from a "big picture" strategic function, where it works with the firm's management to create or support the overall image of the company. It works tactically as a part of the firm's marketing function to create a brand culture and, ultimately, to sustain the sales volume and profitability of the organization. In some organizations a single department has both the strategic and the tactical responsibilities, while in others separate departments handle those responsibilities. In larger organizations MPR duties may also be broken down by individual brands or product lines. Since MPR pervades an organization, MPR professionals may find themselves working on long-term strategic implementations or individual campaigns. Regardless of the level, successful MPR efforts need to have set goals and objectives that contribute to the mission and vision of the organization and/or of a given campaign. Goals and objectives are, by definition, very similar. For the purposes of this text, however, goals are long-term, strategic aspirations that a firm hopes to achieve in a year or longer or over the life of a campaign. Objectives, on the other hand, are short-term, tactical targets that a firm needs to accomplish en route to realizing its goals. A good rule of thumb is a set of criteria known by the acronym S.M.A.R.T., which will help ensure the effectiveness of goals and objectives.

The Anatomy of S.M.A.R.T. Goals® and Objectives[35]

Good goals and objectives need to meet *all* of the following criteria:

1. Specific: To accomplish something, the task must be clearly defined. A clear, specific definition helps in both planning and implementation. Answering questions such as *who*, *what*, *where*, and *why* contributes to specificity.

2. **M**easurable: A goal or objective cannot truly be achieved if it cannot be measured. You must be able to answer the question, "How do I know when the goal is reached?"

3. **A**ttainable: Are the resources needed to reach the goal or objective available? If they are not, then the goal is designed to fail.

4. **R**ealistic: While goals and objectives should stretch organizations and individuals to new levels of accomplishment, goals that are set too high may discourage someone from pursuing them because of the difficulty of achieving success.

5. **T**angible: Let's face it, unless the impact of goals and objectives can be perceived for those pursuing them, they are more likely to be put off and are less likely to be completed. Tangibility also includes bounding the goals and objectives with deadlines or other time constraints.

Concept Case 3.4: **Goals**

Let's start to sketch out some goals for The Falcon's Lair. Although you still need to learn more about MPR opportunities and tactics before setting any specific objectives, let's lay out some preliminary, strategic goals that will result from strengthening the brand through MPR.

Remembering that goals need to be S.M.A.R.T. (specific, measurable, attainable, realistic, and tangible), here is a list of possible goals:

1. Increase product sales, in dollars, by 10 percent a year over the next five years.

2. Increase the number of customers in the hardcore hikers and climbers and family-recreational segments by 5 percent per year over the next five years.

3. Increase the number of times The Falcon's Lair gets mentioned in the media to at least once per month in one year's time and increase it to twice a month in five years.

4. Create a customer community that is both live and virtual that allows customers to communicate with each other and The Falcon's Lair staff. Twenty percent of The Falcon's Lair customers will participate in this community in five years' time.

Questions:
1. What are the strengths and weaknesses of these goals?
2. How could you improve them?
3. Are there any goals you would add?

Understanding how MPR fits into the overall strategic landscape of an organization enables you, as a marketer, to plan and execute an MPR strategy that contributes to achieving the goals of the entire organization.

 Reflection Questions

1. How is MPR different from employee relations and investor relations? (Chapter Objective 1)

2. How do MPR, employee relations, and investor relations affect each other? (Chapter Objective 1)

3. Explain the changes in business orientation over the course of the last century. Start with the production concept and end with the marketing concept. (Chapter Objective 2)

4. What is the interaction concept and why might it replace the marketing concept as the dominant business orientation? (Chapter Objective 2)

5. Define each of the five elements of the Business Strategy Diamond and discuss how MPR contributes to each element. (Chapter Objective 3)

6. Discuss MPR's role in branding. (Chapter Objective 4)

7. What are the various types of brand story, image, and association authors? (Chapter Objective 4)

8. Define the concept of brand value and discuss its different forms. (Chapter Objective 5)

9. Discuss the difference between goals and objectives. (Chapter Objective 6)

10. What are the five elements of S.M.A.R.T. goal setting? (Chapter Objective 6)

 Chapter Key Terms

Arena The combination of products a firm offers and the distribution channels it uses to get the products to the consumer (p. 39)

Brand authors The companies, customers, and influencers, along with popular culture, who create the stories, images, and associations between brands and consumers (p. 31)

Consumption stories Stories created by consumers about how they use or consume products, which they then share with their friends and which become the fuel for word-of-mouth (p. 42)

Corporate governance A generic term that describes the ways in which rights and responsibilities are shared between the various corporate participants, especially the management and the shareholders (p. 34)

Differentiators The attributes of a company or product that create its competitive advantage in the marketplace. (p. 39)

Economic logic The means by which an organization realizes a return on its investment (p. 38)

Employee relations A public relations function that deals with managing communication with existing and prospective employees (p. 32)

Human resources The division of a company that is focused on activities relating to employees. These activities normally include recruiting and hiring of new employees, orientation and training of current employees, employee benefits, and retention. (p. 32)

Influencers Media, groups, or individuals who act as a channel for a marketing message, resulting in media mentions or the creation of word-of-mouth. Synonymous with *connectors*. (p. 43)

Interaction concept A business philosophy that assumes that a firm's two-way interaction with customers is essential to long-term profitability (p. 37)

Investor relations A public relations function that manages the communication between a publicly held corporation, its shareholders, and the media and analysts who report on the corporation's financial situation (p. 34)

Marketing concept The business philosophy of centering an organization's goal on satisfying the needs of the customer (p. 36)

Mission A firm's core purpose and focus (p. 36)

Product concept A business philosophy that assumes that consumers will favor products with a higher degree of quality, performance, and available features (p. 36)

Production concept A business philosophy that assumes that consumers will favor the most widely available and attractively priced products (p. 36)

Publicly traded companies Companies that have issued securities through an offering and that are now traded on the open market (p. 34)

Selling concept A business philosophy in which companies focus on large-scale promotional and selling efforts in order to gain market share (p. 36)

Societal marketing concept A business philosophy that goes beyond concentrating on the consumer and considers the long-term interests of society at large (p. 36)

Staging The speed and sequence of implementing a strategic plan (p. 39)

Stock An instrument that signifies an ownership position (called *equity*) in a corporation, and represents a claim on its proportional share in the corporation's assets and profits (p. 34)

Transparency Essential condition for a free and open exchange whereby the rules and reasons behind regulatory measures are fair and clear to all participants (p. 34)

Vehicles The mechanisms for a firm to enter or conduct business within a given arena and to achieve its goals (p. 39)

Vendors Companies that supply parts or services to another company; also called *supplier* (p. 35)

Vision An organization's aspirations in the mid-term or long-term future. It is intended to serve as a clear guide for choosing current and future courses of action. (p. 36)

Application Assignments

1. Visit the Web sites of the following companies, determine which business concept they are oriented toward, and explain why. Decide which of these companies is most aligned with the interaction concept and explain your reasoning.

   a. 3M (http://www.3m.com)

   b. Amazon (http://www.amazon.com)

   c. Apple® (http://www.apple.com)

   d. Boeing® (http://www.boeing.com)

   e. Dell® (http://www.dell.com)

   f. Nordstrom® (http://www.nordstrom.com)

   g. Southwest Airlines (http://www.southwest.com)

   h. Victoria's Secret® (http://www.victoriassecret.com)

2. For one of the companies listed in Application Assignment 1, describe what you perceive to be its strategic differentiators, and discuss how this company communicates these differentiators to consumers. (Remember *differentiators* are the attributes of a company or product that create its competitive advantage in the marketplace.)

3. From the list of companies in Application Assignment 1, identify and describe one example of each of the following brand author types: popular culture, customer, and influencer.

4. Use the list of companies in Application Assignment 1 to find examples of each of the four types of brand value. Explain why your choices fit the category.

5. Construct a list of goals and objectives for yourself for this class.

Practice Portfolio

This Practice Portfolio can be based on a fictitious company or on a real company that your instructor assigns to you. (If you used a company in previous Practice Portfolio exercises, continue to use that company.) Add your completed assignment to your portfolio to present to prospective employers.

- Explain how the MPR function fits into the overall strategy of your practice company. (Hint: Think about MPR's role in each of the five elements of the Business Strategy Diamond.)

- Develop a list of goals for establishing and maintaining your brand that can be facilitated by MPR. (Remember that goals are long-term and strategy-focused. You will set specific objectives as you progress through the text.)

- Describe how your company will use MPR to engage external authors in developing its brand stories, images, and associations.

- Describe your company's brand value and categorize the different elements of value by the four brand value components discussed in the chapter. (Remember: Not every company has brand value in each of the four components, and a given company may have multiple brands that offer different value sets.)

CHAPTER **4**

The MPR Framework: Objectives, Target, Connectors, Message, and Measure

CHAPTER OBJECTIVES

After studying this chapter, you should be able to:

1. List and explain the five elements of the MPR process and describe how they relate to each other.

2. Explain the purpose of setting objectives for an MPR effort.

3. Map the consumer decision-making process and explain how marketers can influence the various steps in the process.

4. Define *market segment* and *target market* and explain how an organization would go about selecting its target market.

5. Describe the three primary methods for classifying market segments.

6. Understand the different types of connectors and their role in the MPR process.

7. Define *message* in an MPR context and explain its dual purpose.

8. Explain the need for measuring the effectiveness of an MPR effort.

In early 2008 Starbucks® was making headlines in newspapers, on television news, and on the Web. This time the headlines were not about the company's explosive growth or much-loved product. Instead, its stock price had fallen by nearly 50 percent in less than a year and the company had just announced that it was eliminating 600 jobs from its workforce. At the same time, *The Wall Street Journal* reported concerns among market analysts about Starbucks's brand becoming a commodity and increased competition coming from the likes of McDonald's® and Dunkin' Donuts®. Starbucks even brought back Howard Schultz as CEO to help refocus the organization. Shortly after Schultz took the reins, he told employees in a video recording that, "Over the years we kind of lost our way."[1] Not only was the java giant struggling organizationally and on Wall Street, it was also seeing the traditional media, bloggers, and consumers begin to froth with negative news about its future. To complicate matters further, any actions Schultz took had to take into consideration Starbucks's customers, employees, and stockholders. The situation posed no small challenge.

The solution was training—with a marketing twist. On Tuesday, February 26, 2008, Starbucks closed all of its approximately 7,100 stores between 5:30 and 9:00 p.m. According to the company's press release, the purpose of these closures was to "perfect espresso." The company did in fact train its employees for these three and a half hours, but the genius of this strategy was the attention it received. Newspapers from *The New York Times* to *USA Today* to small-town dailies ran stories about it. Business media like *The Wall Street Journal* and American Public Media's *Marketplace* radio show ran pieces. Blogs and Web sites from *The Huffington Post* to *The Onion* chimed in. The major TV networks even ran spots on their news shows. Everyone from college students to C-level executives was buzzing. Brilliant! Why? First, a company that does very little conventional advertising managed to get countless minutes of broadcast air time, loads of ink from the news press, and Web mentions galore. This alone was worth the equivalent of millions of dollars in paid advertising costs and carried the credibility of news. Combined with the fact that the company temporarily cut off the caffeine supply to thousands, if not millions, of the Starbucks faithful, the result was that people were talking about Starbucks coffee everywhere.

This strategy was masterful as well because it addressed all three of the audiences with whom Starbucks needed to make up ground. Customers got to see Starbucks caring about them and their favorite beverage once again. Employees not only got some actual training but were assured from the very top of the organization that what they do matters. Finally, stockholders saw that the ship was being righted and that Starbucks was in the hands of strong leaders and on track to continue its success and position as an industry leader.

Elena Ray/Shutterstock.

Schultz's *objectives* were to energize three *target* audiences (customers, employees, and stockholders), to get the *connectors* (media, bloggers, etc.) back into Starbucks's corner, and to keep sales growing with a *message* that worked for the connectors and was meaningful to all three groups of stakeholders. It seems that he did what he set out to do.

CHAPTER
OBJECTIVE
1

Elements of MPR Process

Now that you have a basic understanding of what MPR is and how it fits into an organization, you need to see how it works. To the casual observer, the publicity that the news media or an enthusiastic consumer generates seems random and sporadic. While, indeed, occasionally a journalist will uncover something unexpected about an organization or a zealous customer will elevate a product to a new status, this rarely happens. Even the best-intentioned connectors have difficulty pulling off a publicity coup without having at least tacit assistance from the organization in question. Companies that sit around hoping for some good PR and word-of-mouth rarely get it. Despite what Ralph Waldo Emerson said, simply building a better mouse trap will probably not cause the world to beat a path to your door. You have to let the world know about your mouse trap and make it want to come to your door with cash in hand. To do so, you need to understand the underlying process that makes Marketing Public Relations work.

Your first step is to set some objectives that focus on the behaviors you desire from a particular group of consumers. These behaviors will typically be tied to your marketing goals (increased sales, brand awareness, support for a cause, etc.). For example, before the 2008 Olympics, swimsuit maker Speedo® set out to use the Games to increase its market share. Ingeniously, the company supplemented its advertising with an MPR campaign that featured endorsements from prominent Olympic swimmers and splashy details about the performance of their new high-tech Speedo suits. The campaign's media success exceeded expectations and elevated Speedo's market share to a commanding 61 percent. According to Craig Brommers, Speedo's VP of marketing, "The suit itself was such a revolution in technology, but the media hype has far exceeded our expectations, and the interest from the general consumer has really exceeded our expectations."[2]

You accomplish these goals by reaching the consumers with a specific message sent through a set of connectors. This message is the information that you direct to potential consumers to effect the desired behavior. The consumers must be accessible in sufficient numbers and generate adequate profit to make your investment of money and time worthwhile. In addition, as with all business goals and objectives, you need to be able to measure the success of this process.

The process for creating a successful campaign or individual effort is as follows:

1. Determine the desired objectives of your efforts. (Objectives)
2. Verify the consumers you wish to influence in order to reach your objectives. (Target market[3] selection)
3. Decide on the media, groups, and individuals that will be able to reach your target market most effectively. (Connectors)

4. Communicate compelling reasons for consumers in your target market to pursue exchanges with your organization, and give connectors a reason to pass on your information to the consumers within their sphere of influence. (Message)

5. Measure the amount of activity generated by selected connectors and the resulting behavior of your target market relative to your goals. (Measure)

Objectives

As a marketer, you will need to set goals that are consistent with the long-term mission, vision, and goals of your organization. In addition, you will need to react to events in the greater marketing environment so that the organization can continue toward its goals during times of crisis or change. In any case, you must still use your skills and resources to change or maintain the behaviors of consumers relative to your product. Typically, these behaviors are *action*, *attitude*, or *information-oriented*. **Action-oriented behavior** can include trying or buying a product for the first time, continuing to buy a product, casting a vote, visiting a Web site, and so on. **Attitude**,[4] on the other hand, refers to a belief about a particular product. For example, a public relations campaign goal may be to ensure that your target market believes that your product is of the highest quality or that your company is environmentally responsible.

When Xerox® decided to transform consumers' attitudes about the company, it used viral marketing. The objective was to get people to forget about the stoic "Document Company" image and to think of Xerox as something more energetic and exciting. Xerox's "Extreme Offices" campaign used a Web video depicting a company adding "something" to the water in order to boost worker productivity. This approach ends in humorous chaos for the company in the video and positions Xerox as the smart way to make your company more productive. As Barbara Basney, Xerox's director of global advertising, said, "It's not only that people are expecting [interactive experiences and entertainment], but it helps make your advertising message break through. It sets Xerox in a different place."[5]

Information-oriented behaviors are designed to make an audience aware of something about a given product, usually with the goal of supporting an action-based outcome at some point in the future. For example, in the summer of 2006, Dell computer had to recall approximately 4 million computer batteries. With the objective of making sure that customers got the message, Dell posted a news release on its Web site and corporate blog and had its media relations team work with TV, print, and radio outlets to announce the recall to its customers. This recall also helped restore a diminished reputation by creating an opportunity to show the company acting to protect its customers as well as the ease and speed of working with Dell customer service.[6]

Key Terms

Action-oriented behaviors Marketing behaviors that include the performance of a specific task, such as trying or buying a product for the first time; continuing to buy a product; casting a vote; visiting a Web site

Attitude A person's overall evaluation of a concept; a response involving general feelings of liking or favorability

Information-oriented behaviors Becoming aware of some aspect of a given product, usually with the goal of supporting an action-based outcome at some point in the future

Consumer Decision-making Process

Most marketing efforts have multiple objectives intended to influence a combination of all three types of behavior. In order to understand these behaviors and the marketer's role in influencing them, let's look at the consumer's decision-making process. The process begins when a consumer realizes that he or she needs or wants something. Conscious of this desire, the consumer searches for information about how to satisfy it. During the quest for information, the consumer identifies different alternatives that he or she evaluates using other data uncovered during the search. A successful evaluation ends with a decision and some critical thought about whether that decision was a good one.[7]

Need Recognition

Many factors can instigate the recognition of a need. Simple things such as being hungry and needing food or having to commute to work and needing transportation can signify physiological or utilitarian needs. Needs based on social or cultural standards or one's need for self-esteem or self-fulfillment are more complex. Twentieth-century psychologist Abraham Maslow explains this pattern in his work on the hierarchy of human needs. Maslow's theory suggests that humans fulfill their most basic needs first before setting out to satisfy more complex ones. As you can see in Exhibit 4.1, the most basic classification of need is physiological—the necessities of life, including food to eat, air to

Exhibit 4.1 In a 1943 Psychological Review article entitled "A Theory of Human Motivation," Abraham Maslow suggested that humans fulfill their most basic needs first before setting out to satisfy more complex ones.

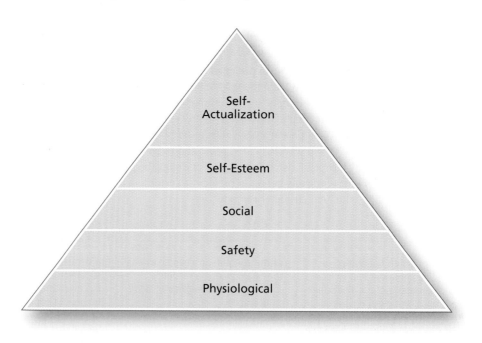

breathe, and the opportunity to sleep. Once those needs are met, people look to safety, such as shelter from the elements and security from threats. When they are physically sustained and reasonably secure, individuals then look to be a part of a social group and long for love and companionship. Once they have a firm standing in a social unit, people subsequently look to differentiate themselves from others and to create a heightened level of personal worth or self-esteem. At the pinnacle of existence, once they have attained a sufficient level of self-esteem, humans look to reach their full potential and gravitate to self-actualizing activities that elevate body, mind, and spirit to new heights.

Marketers can be instrumental in getting consumers to recognize a need or want by identifying a target audience that has a gap between its ideal and current states. This **consumer potential** can take many forms. For example, the South Carolina Department of Parks, Recreation, and Tourism ran a campaign in Chicago in the winter of 2008 called "Time to Thaw." The campaign began with a press announcement about a video of a cold Chicago winter with a song about "getting warmer" performed by the Webb Brothers. The video was interspersed with "warm" images that were part of the advertising portion of the campaign and prominently displayed the Web address. The video, which was originally intended for internal use only, had more than 750 views just days after posting.[8] A marketer could use this same difference between the ideal state of being warm and the actual state of being cold to highlight the need for a host of other products and services, such as warm coats, hot drinks, tanning salon services, and so on.

Information Search

Once a consumer recognizes a need, he or she looks for information that will help satisfy it. This data has two primary sources: externally available information and internal information, commonly called "mental files." External sources can be Web sites, advertisements, the media, friends and family, or the opinions of experts. Mental files are the sum total of the information that an individual has stored in his or her mind. These files not only store objective facts, but facts influenced by the person's values, attitudes, beliefs, and past experiences. In this part of the decision-making process, the marketer's job is to make sure that consumers who possess a need that can be satisfied by his or her product have ample information available. Since this information reaches the consumer through connectors, the marketer also must ensure that the information that the connectors disseminate is not only abundant and available, but accurate and favorable toward the marketer's product.

Evaluation of Alternatives

The evaluation process is similar to the search for information in that an individual consumer takes cues from external sources about how to value or rank different alternatives. Likewise, a person's values, attitudes, beliefs, and past experiences

---

Key Terms

Consumer potential The gap between a consumer's current and ideal state of being

come into play. Therefore, one of the marketer's objectives is usually to have the consumer use a set of evaluation criteria that will lead to the desired outcome. It is not unusual for savvy marketers to use connectors to popularize certain criteria for making a specific choice. For example, you may see articles about the "Ten Things You Need to Ask Before Selecting a Doctor," or you hear people spreading the word about the best way to configure a personal computer for graphic artists. In many cases these evaluation tools originate from the providers of the products or services.

A marketer may also need to contest any negative mental files that exist from previous experience with a product or class of products. Unfortunately, consumers do have negative opinions about or experiences with certain products. Sometimes these stem from the past actions of the marketer's organization. At other times they originate from the marketing efforts of a competitor with a similar product or from the greater marketing environment. In any case, a marketer must be aware of these negative mental files and make an effort to influence them. A classic example of a marketer needing to overcome a negative experience was the incident in 1982 in which someone poisoned several bottles of the pain reliever Tylenol with cyanide, resulting in several deaths. This story was national news and resulted in Johnson & Johnson removing all Tylenol from store shelves. This could have been the end of this brand. However, rather than discontinuing the product altogether, Johnson & Johnson modified the product and its packaging to greatly reduce the possibility of a similar incident and kicked off a campaign that restored consumer confidence in the product. Tylenol is once again an extremely popular pain reliever and this case is a classic example of how MPR contributes to the long-term success of products.

Decision and Post-decision

The decision is a moment in time when the consumer commits to a certain behavior. This commitment is usually action-oriented, as when he or she decides to buy a product for the first time. It can also be attitude or information-oriented, as when a consumer changes or affirms one of his or her beliefs. Regardless of the decision type, the mere act of making a decision triggers the final phase of this process—the post-decision evaluation.

In this phase the consumer appraises the decision made and catalogs the result of this choice into his or her mental files. A consumer typically considers whether, if given the opportunity, he or she would make the same decision again. In addition, the consumer compares the experience of making this decision to those made in the past. This evaluation may determine whether this consumer becomes a connector him- or herself. If the post-decision evaluation is positive, the consumer will likely become a repeat customer and, hopefully, a connector who will spread the word about the product. On the other hand, if the evaluation is negative, the company will likely lose this customer. Worse yet, the customer is apt to speak, write, or blog negatively about the product.

As you can see, the marketer may need to set several sub-objectives (assistance in recognizing need, product information, and/or evaluation criteria) throughout the decision-making process that leads to the prime outcome (buying the product).[9]

Concept Case 4.1: **Objectives and Influencing the Decision-making Process**

Let's explore how the management team of The Falcon's Lair might attempt to influence the consumer decision-making process in order to reach its marketing goal of strengthening its relationship with three target groups.

The management team can use several MPR tools, such as expert articles and word-of-mouth campaigns, to help its target audience recognize a number of needs.

Next, since information needs to be abundant and positive, the team can use connectors to spread the word about its expertise and make its story available to anyone interested in hiking and climbing.

The Falcon's Lair management group should make every effort to use connectors to give consumers some criteria for making decisions when purchasing hiking and climbing equipment and for choosing an equipment retailer. For example, the group could create a chart that compares the products and services it sells with those of its competitors and thereby define the advantage of shopping at The Falcon's Lair.

Finally, as with the evaluation of alternatives, The Falcon's Lair team can work through connectors to give consumers criteria by which to assess the quality of the product they purchased and the overall purchasing experience. This information should reinforce The Falcon's Lair's position in the marketplace, validate the consumer's decisions, and, perhaps, put some doubt in the minds of consumers who bought their hiking or climbing equipment elsewhere. This goal can be accomplished by using the media to showcase its customers performing well or having fun hiking or climbing and to demonstrate how The Falcon's Lair staff, products, or services made this outcome possible.

Questions:

1. List some topics that The Falcon's Lair might incorporate into its expert articles or word-of-mouth campaigns that can help the company achieve its marketing goals.
2. Give some examples of connectors The Falcon's Lair should pursue.
3. What type of information should The Falcon's Lair make available to connectors?
4. Describe some other ways that The Falcon's Lair can use connectors to help consumers choose to shop at The Falcon's Lair rather than its competitors.

Segmentation and Target Markets

CHAPTER
OBJECTIVE
4

In MPR, consumers are defined as the ultimate users of a product regardless of whether the product in question is a good, service, person, place, organization, idea, or a mix of these. These consumers can be individuals or organizations. Since most companies cannot market their product to everyone, they need to learn who their current customers or best prospects are and where they live, and then they need to locate more people like them. Conventionally, we call a group of consumers with identifiable, shared characteristics a **market segment**, and the market segments that a firm pursues are **target markets**.[10]

Selecting a Target Market

Marketers typically look for five characteristics within a given market segment to determine whether that segment is an appropriate target market. Ideally, market segments chosen as target markets should be identifiable, accessible, substantial, durable, and differentiable.[11]

- *Identifiable*: The marketer must be able to define the audience using some tangible criteria such as age, income, lifestyle, and so on.
- *Accessible*: The marketer must be able to convey its message to this audience using one of the tools within the communications marketing mix. For the purposes of MPR, consumers must be exposed to connectors and be open to being influenced by them.
- *Substantial*: The market must be large enough to make economic sense to pursue. The needed market size will vary with the profitability of the product being sold and the cost to reach the specific market. The high level of credibility and relatively low cost of conducting MPR has allowed marketers to pursue segments that are not substantial enough to pursue using other elements of the marketing communications mix, particularly advertising and direct sales.
- *Durable*: The segment needs to remain in existence long enough for the marketer to make a reasonable return on the resources invested to reach the market. The quick and powerful nature of MPR, however, in addition to its affordability, allows more companies to pursue quickly changing or "fad" markets. In effect, MPR has lowered the bar on durability.
- *Differentiable*: A segment should be significantly different from other segments under consideration. If segments contain characteristics that are highly similar, a marketer can often benefit from combining them into a single segment. The proliferation of Web and print media that target increasingly specialized areas of interest, along with an improved understanding of how messages spread among people, allows marketers to identify micro-markets—such as those for obscure books or movies that never made it to the theater—and to reach them with a message tailored specifically to them.[12]

We can illustrate target market selection criteria by the changes in the music industry that began around the year 2000. The pre-2000 model for selling music focused on creating "hits" that sold millions of copies of records, tapes, or CDs. This meant that record companies sought music that would appeal to the large markets (substantial) that could be reached through the mass media (accessible). The mass market (identifiable) approach also proved to work in the long term considering that all of the top twenty-five best-selling albums of all time were released before 2000 (durable). In fact, the number one album, the *Eagles' Greatest Hits, 1971–1975*, sold about 29 million copies and was released in 1976.[13]

Selling music through record stores and promoting it through mass advertising, radio stations, and concerts suited this model but made it difficult for record companies to sell the music of artists who had a strong niche following but who did not appeal to the masses. As a result, the industry was missing out on the profits from selling to a market that was differentiable from the masses because the markets were hard to identify, not accessible, and believed to be insubstantial with limited durability. However, since 2000, record companies have discovered that the Internet is a low-cost yet effective way to reach (identify and access) smaller markets. The sum of smaller markets for differentiated products has proven substantial and durable enough to sustain the industry. We can observe similar changes in sales in the video and book markets as well.[14]

Classifying Market Segments

CHAPTER
OBJECTIVE
5

A marketer can identify these five characteristics by studying market segments demographically, psychographically, and behaviorally.

Demographics

Demographics[15] are characteristics about consumers that are quantifiable and include such factors as age, income, gender, education, and location (for consumer markets), and annual revenue, number of employees, and industrial classification (for business-to-business markets). Demographic data are particularly useful because marketers can obtain them easily and analyze them statistically. Sources for this information include a host of marketing research organizations and the U.S. government, particularly the U.S. Census Bureau. For example, marketers often categorize a group of consumers geographically, by partitioning them by state, county, or ZIP codes. Marketers also use Metropolitan Statistical Area (MSA) designations available from the U.S. Census Bureau because of the depth and breadth of socioeconomic data available about these regions. Designated Market Area (DMA) information created by The Nielsen Company® is considered the segmentation standard for most of the broadcast industry, because DMAs are based on the geographic reach of TV signals from the early television network affiliate stations.

When classifying businesses demographically, marketers commonly use the U.S. Census Bureau's North American Industry Classification System (NAICS) to differentiate businesses by industry and by the products they produce. The NAICS assigns two- to six-digit codes that increase in specificity as digits are added. For example, NAICS code 11 is for Agriculture, Forestry, Fishing and Hunting; 111 represents crop production; 1111 is indicative of oilseed and grain farming; 11111 designates soybean farming; and 111110 remains open for additional subcategories of soybean farming. This classification system allows MPR professionals to compare their target market with the audience of media outlets they are evaluating for use in a campaign.

Key Terms

Market segment A group of consumers who respond in a similar way to a given set of marketing efforts

Target market A set of buyers sharing common needs or characteristics that a company decides to serve

Demographics Criteria for dividing a market into groups based on such variables as age, gender, income, occupation, race, and nationality

Exhibit 4.2 This map shows Metropolitan Statistical Areas (MSAs) as defined by the U.S. Census Bureau.

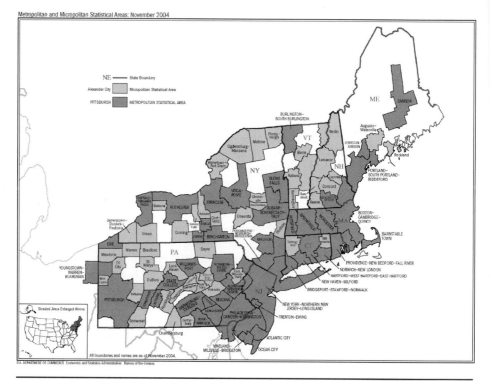

Metropolitan and Micropolitan Statistical Areas: November 2004

Psychographics

Psychographics[16] relate to characteristics of a market segment that are more complex than demographics, not always easy to quantify, and are open to more interpretation. They are focused on attitudes, values, lifestyles, and opinions. Psychographic analysis is particularly important on several fronts. Psychographics can tell us things that demographics simply cannot. For example, consider two families living in the same upper-middle-class housing subdivision in Suburbia, USA. Let's assume that the two families have similar-sized houses, income, and education levels, and the same number of children who are about the same age. In essence, they look the same demographically. A closer look, however, may reveal that one family enjoys the performing arts, spends much of its leisure time indoors, is culturally conservative, watches the History Channel and PBS, and spends its money on attending cultural events and music lessons for the kids. Meanwhile, the other family enjoys watching sports, spends most of its leisure time participating in youth sports or outdoor family activities such as mountain biking and hiking, watches the Discovery Channel and ESPN, is culturally liberal, and spends its money on sporting gear and tickets to sporting events. As you can see, these families are vastly different to a marketer with regard to what they buy, their attitudes about and opinions toward certain products, and how the marketer can reach them with a promotional message.

Exhibit 4.3 The North American Industry Classification System categorizes business from the broad to the specific.

Code	NAICS Sectors
11	Agriculture, Forestry, Fishing and Hunting
21	Mining
22	Utilities
23	Construction
31–33	Manufacturing
42	Wholesale Trade
44–45	Retail Trade
48–49	Transportation and Warehousing
51	Information
52	Finance and Insurance
53	Real Estate and Rental and Leasing
54	Professional, Scientific, and Technical Services
55	Management of Companies and Enterprises
56	Administrative and Support and Waste Management and Remediation Services
61	Education Services
62	Health Care and Social Assistance
71	Arts, Entertainment, and Recreation
72	Accommodation and Food Services
81	Other Services (except Public Administration)
92	Public Administration

Psychographics are typically applied to consumer marketing, but marketers can use them in the segmentation of businesses as well. While there are no generally accepted models for doing so, business-to-business marketers should think about the values and attitudes held by certain businesses and industry groups.

Business Psychographics:

- *Values*: Many companies publish their values on their Web sites and in other company literature such as their annual report to stockholders. Understanding the underlying value structure of an organization is beneficial to marketers because it can help them differentiate a company's buying preference from other companies that look similar demographically. For example, when you read the following statement of core values

Key Terms

Psychographics Criteria for dividing a market into groups based on such variables as social class, lifestyle, or personality characteristics

Exhibit 4.4 Whole Foods® shows its commitment to its values by posting them to its Web site.

Whole Foods.®

of Whole Foods®, you get a much broader picture of the company than you would have if you just looked at it demographically.

- *Attitudes*: While consumer attitude studies are widely available, attitude studies about businesses and industries are not. This information, however, is available internally. Sales and customer service people often have a wealth of knowledge about the attitudes of the people in certain companies and industries and marketers should view them as a resource when designing a marketing campaign.

Behavioral

Behavioral segmentation traditionally identifies consumers according to how they buy or use a product. Typical behavior segments include *Occasion*, *Benefits*, *Usage Rate*, and *Customer Loyalty*:

- *Occasion:*[17] Marketers can segment consumers according to the **occasions** on which they typically make a purchase or some other type of marketing exchange. This could include the cup of coffee someone buys each weekday morning or the flowers the consumer buys for a loved one every Valentine's Day. It could even include the purchase of a new stroller on the occasion of having a child.
- *Benefits:*[18] Some consumers buy products based upon the **benefits** that they receive from acquiring or using that product. Under this scenario different consumers might find different benefits in the purchase of the same product. For instance, one person might buy a particular automobile for its fuel economy, another for its styling, and yet another for its safety. Although the product is one specific car, it has three different benefits-based segments.

- *Usage Rate*: Knowing who buys how much and how often is extremely useful to marketers. The **usage rate** strategy often breaks down consumers by quantity of total purchases and segregates them into light, medium, and heavy users. Frequency of purchase is also a popular segmentation criterion and is divided into units such as purchase per day, per week, and so on.
- *Customer Loyalty*: In essence the **customer loyalty** measure tells us how likely a given consumer is to switch from the brand he or she is currently using to a different brand.

Behavioral segments specific to MPR revolve around a consumer's exposure to media and the likelihood that the consumer will be influenced by a given medium. In addition, marketers are interested in knowing how people rely on and are affected by word-of-mouth and expert opinions in their roles as consumers. Marketers characterize these segments as follows:

- *Media consumption by medium*: This segment relates individual media to those who consume it.
- *Media consumption frequency*: This segment examines how often certain individuals or groups consume or are exposed to a given medium.
- *Reliance on word-of-mouth recommendations:* This segment focuses on how certain social, cultural, and business groups put differing values on information obtained via word-of-mouth sources.
- *Reliance on expert opinion:* This segment separates consumers by their quest for expert opinion and the types of experts that they consult during the consumer decision-making process.

Concept Case 4.2: **Target Market**

We know that The Falcon's Lair serves clientele who are classified as either 1) regional hardcore hikers and climbers or 2) regional families and recreational hikers and climbers. In addition, the company has a third classification that it refers to as nationwide Web sales. In looking at the regional hardcore hikers and climbers segment, the company discovered the following:

- Thirty-five percent of these customers are between the ages of thirty-five and fifty-four years old and are married, with two to three children between the ages of five and eighteen.
- Sixty percent are between the ages of eighteen and thirty-four years old and are unmarried.
- Ninety percent of these customers have or are pursuing an undergraduate college education.
- Approximately seventy percent are male.
- Most consider themselves environmentally conscious.

(continued)

Concept Case 4.2: (Continued)

- Most claim to take advice about products and tips about the practice of hiking and climbing offered by The Falcon's Lair staff seriously.
- Most of these customers routinely climb and hike with the same group of people.
- Most of this segment obtain or share climbing/hiking information on the Web via http://www.climbing.com, http://www.urbanclimbermag.com, Facebook, or MySpace.
- Most of this segment subscribe to or frequently read *Climbing Magazine* or *Urban Climber*.
- Most rely on the recommendation of their friends for information about new equipment and places to climb and hike.
- A majority pursue leisure activities that are outdoors and are physically exhilarating.
- Almost all of them claim to put a high value on fun.
- Many put a high value on spending time with family and friends.
- Many subscribe to climbing and hiking blogs, especially http://www.rock-climbing-for-life.com.
- The average customer in this segment visits the store two to four times per month from April to November.
- They live or work within a fifty-mile radius of the store in Allentown, Pennsylvania, which puts 736 ZIP codes[19] in their sphere of influence and within the Allentown-Bethlehem-Easton MSA and the Philadelphia DMA.

Questions:

1. Sort the findings into demographic, psychographic, and behavior characteristics.
2. Discuss the type of demographic, psychographic, and behavioral data you would want to collect for the family and recreational hikers and climbers target market.

Types of Connectors

The main difference between MPR and all other types of marketing is the connectors that spread the message. Given that the marketer hands over control of the message from the start, a crucial part of his or her job is to find connectors that have a clear influence on the firm's target market. As Paul M. Rand, CEO of Zocalo Group[SM] writes:

> Depending on the organization, key influencers (connectors) besides the media can include authors, academics, analysts, associations, celebrities, civic and governmental leaders, gurus and researchers. One manufacturer of game-toy software discovered that a lone teenage boy, whose personal Web site includes his take on new offerings, holds enormous sway over his peers who value his judgment on video games. Through word-of-mouth, teenagers let others know of his take on some new game—and they base their purchasing decision on his word alone.[20]

The growing relevance of non-media connectors has been changing the landscape of the marketing and public relations world over the last decade. Stan Stalnaker, the founder of *Hub Culture,* an international online and off-line social network writes,

> "Peer-to-peer networks have thrown the media industry into turmoil, changing the flow of information from a one-to-many model (with newspaper publishers, etc., as the sources) to a many-to-many (with blogs, YouTube, etc., as venues). The ability of individuals to both consume and create content greatly threatens traditional players."[21]

Message

MPR is unique in that the communications process has an extra step: There is always another party between the marketer (the sender) and the receiver (the consumer). While they serve as connectors to carry messages to the consumer, these intermediaries can also edit the message as they see fit. As a result, the marketer loses control of the message. Imagine having a conversation with someone who speaks another language through an interpreter. What happens to the meaning of this conversation if the interpreter decides to edit or materially alter what the two conversers are saying? Things could go wrong fast; at the very least, the parties attempting to communicate could have grave misunderstandings. For this reason marketers need to employ all of the strategies of message creation used in other areas, plus a few that are unique to MPR.

You can think of a message in the same way that creative directors think of an advertisement. That is, a message should attract attention, stimulate interest, convey credibility, induce desire and, ultimately, result in an action. This action, ideally, satisfies the marketing objectives. Accomplishing these goals gets you where you need to be with the consumers and part of the way with the connectors. With regard to the connectors, you must recognize that their job is to disseminate information to a certain audience. So, you need to consider a few things:

- Is the information worth spreading?
- Is this information actually news?
- Does this information matter to the intermediary's audience?
- Does spreading this information positively affect the image or standing of the intermediary in the eyes of its audience?
- Does disseminating this information benefit the intermediary?

You will need to create specific types of messages and message vehicles that allow you to achieve your marketing goals while also providing material benefit to the connectors and consumers.

Measurement

Return on investment (ROI) for marketing has been a hot topic in corporate circles for some time. Companies are concerned by the difficulty of quantifying just how dollars invested in marketing efforts turn into sales and other marketing-oriented outcomes. Famous retailer John Wanamaker is claimed to have stated, "Half the money I spend on advertising is wasted; the trouble is, I don't know which half." With increased price pressure from competitors around the globe and pressure from investors to increase profitability, many companies are looking for marketing techniques that are not only effective, but cost-efficient and quantifiable as well. When assessing MPR efforts, marketers need to measure the effectiveness with both the target market and the connectors. Standard marketing metrics such as sales, profitability, and changes in market share, market penetration, and brand awareness apply to MPR efforts much the same way they do to other marketing efforts, such as advertising and sales promotion. These valuable metrics measure changes in the behavior of the target market. Since most organizations have more than one component in their marketing mix, they have difficulty identifying which effort is having what impact on marketing effectiveness. By observing the behavior of connectors, you can measure the effectiveness of a particular component with some certainty, especially when the connector is a member of the media. Through media monitoring and street level market research, you can determine who is passing your message along to whom and how often. You can also get an idea of the tone and context with which they are spreading the message.

Reflection Questions

1. Explain and describe the elements of the MPR process. (Chapter Objective 1)

2. How do MPR objectives differ from marketing goals, and how are they related? (Chapter Objective 2)

3. Identify one current example of how marketers use MPR for each step of the consumer decision-making process. (Chapter Objective 3)

4. Describe the difference between a market segment and a target market, and explain how to determine if a specific market segment should be considered a target market. (Chapter Objective 4)

5. Compare and contrast the three major market segmentation categories. (Chapter Objective 5)

6. Describe the concept of a "connector," and explain how the existence of connectors makes MPR different from other elements of the marketing communications mix. (Chapter Objective 6)

7. What are some types of organizations, groups, or individuals that you might consider to be connectors? (Chapter Objective 6)

8. Explain the dual role of the message in MPR. (Chapter Objective 7)

9. Why is measurement a key element of the MPR process, and how does it differ from the measurement of standard marketing communications efforts? (Chapter Objective 8)

Chapter Key Terms

Action-oriented behaviors Marketing behaviors that include the performance of a specific task, such as trying or buying a product for the first time, continuing to buy a product, casting a vote, or visiting a Web site (p. 53)

Attitude A person's overall evaluation of a concept; a response involving general feelings of liking or favorability (p. 53)

Benefits A behavioral segmentation that groups buyers according to the different benefits they seek from a product (p. 62)

Consumer potential The gap between a consumer's current and ideal state of being (p. 55)

Customer loyalty A behavioral segmentation that groups buyers according to how likely they are to switch from the brand they are currently using to a different brand (p. 63)

Demographics Criteria for dividing a market into groups based on such variables as age, gender, income, occupation, race, and nationality (p. 59)

Information-oriented behaviors Behaviors designed to make an audience aware of some aspect of a given product, usually with the goal of supporting an action-based outcome at some point in the future (p. 53)

Market segment A group of consumers who respond in a similar way to a given set of marketing efforts (p. 58)

Occasion A behavioral segmentation that groups buyers according to when they get the idea to buy, actually make their purchase, or use the purchased item (p. 62)

Psychographics Criteria for dividing a market into groups based on such variables as social class, lifestyle, or personality characteristics (p. 60)

Target market A set of buyers sharing common needs or characteristics that a company decides to serve (p. 58)

Usage rate A behavioral segmentation that groups buyers according to how frequently they buy or use a product (p. 63)

 ## Application Assignments

1. Think of the most expensive purchase that you made over the last three months, and explain how you journeyed through the consumer decision-making process, noting what influenced you along the way. Be sure to explain the impact that your mental files and connectors had on your decision and provide details about your post-purchase evaluation.

2. For the purchase you described in question 1, list all of the connectors that played a part in this purchase and describe how they influenced you. What message did you receive about this product from each connector? Describe how these messages differed from what you think the producer of the product would have liked to portray to you.

3. Explore the Web sites of BP (http://www.bp.com) and Exxon (http://www.exxon.com) and discuss how these companies might differ psychographically and behaviorally.

4. Using the U.S. Census's NAICS list (http://www.census.gov/naics/2007/NAICOD07.HTM) as a guide, identify two companies in each of the following NAICS codes and list the name and number of the six-digit code by which you believe they should be classified.

   a. 212   **c.** 441
   b. 311   **d.** 611

 ## Practice Portfolio

This Practice Portfolio can be based on a fictitious company or on a real company that your instructor assigns to you. (If you used a company in previous Practice Portfolio exercises, continue to use that company.) Add your completed assignment to your portfolio to present to prospective employers.

- List some basic objectives for conducting a public relations consumer-generated marketing campaign for your practice company.

- Outline the buying process for your company's products and discuss what you can do as a marketer to influence this process.

- Using demographic, psychographic, and behavioral criteria, define as many potential market segments for your company as you can identify.

- Considering the five criteria for effective target segmentation selection, narrow the list of market segments you have listed to one to three target markets. Explain why you chose to keep the ones you kept, disqualify those you eliminated, and combine those you consolidated.

- List as many types of media, groups, and individuals as you can think of that would be appropriate connectors for your company. Briefly explain why you chose each one.

- Recall the positioning statement that you created in Chapter 3. What message could you distribute to your connectors that would be of value to them and would also effectively translate to your target audience to meet your objectives?

CHAPTER 5

About the Media

CHAPTER OBJECTIVES

After studying this chapter, you should be able to:

1. Differentiate between news media and advertising media.

2. Classify media types according to demographics, format, geography, size, and topic.

3. Describe the importance of relationships, beats, and ethics in the interaction between marketing and media professionals.

4. Discuss the different kinds of media opportunities available to MPR professionals.

5. Describe the concept of media convergence and how it is affecting the media industry and marketers.

How do you get your news? Chances are that the way you get your news today is very different than the way people got it just a generation or two ago. As recently as the 1970s, people had the choice of the local newspaper, their local TV and radio news broadcasts, the evening news from one of the networks, or one of a handful of news magazines. Things began to change when Ted Turner launched CNN® in 1980, ushering in the era of 24/7 news. Access to cable television allowed anyone with a TV to get news updates whenever he or she wanted them. The Internet and other technology—developed in the mid-1990s and widely available by 2005—has made it easy to obtain news not only when you want it, but where you want it. During this time period, the number and variety of sources offered to news consumers soared.

To illustrate how news media production, distribution, and consumption have changed over time, let's look at ABC® News. RCA® launched the company in 1927 as the Blue Network and in 1943 sold it to Life Savers® candy magnate Edward J. Noble. By 1946 the renamed ABC owned 100 radio stations. By 1953 the company had expanded into television with fourteen affiliates.[1] In the late 1970s, under the guidance of President Roone Arledge, ABC News successfully launched the magazine news format with *20/20* and *Nightline*. In the 1990s Disney purchased ABC and spun off the radio portion of the business, although it maintains the Radio Disney network.

After decades as a thriving news organization, ABC looked to technology, particularly the World Wide Web, to position itself for the future. According to Mike Davidson, one of the key designers of the company's current Web site, "ABC's Web team sought to broaden its online initiatives past the familiar narrowband Web."[2] Today ABC makes news available in more ways and forms than ever.

The ABC News Web site (http://abcnews.go.com) delivers news as it happens in both video and written formats. The news is organized in a fashion that is similar to a newspaper, with categories like world news, U.S. politics, money, health, and so on. You can also explore the site by program title through links to programs such as *Good Morning America*, *20/20*, and *Nightline*. In addition, a "News in Brief" section summarizes the headlines of the top stories.

The rest of the Web site uses multiple media forms. Nearly a quarter of the content is in video form, including a fifteen-minute "World News Webcast," designed with a younger audience in mind. The webcast offers a lineup and format different from those on the traditional evening newscast and is first available to users live at 3 p.m. Eastern Standard Time. The site also uses audio, podcasts, poll data, photos, and more slide shows than any other site studied.[3] Executive producer Jon Banner said of the site: "What it has become is much more of a broadcast aimed at people who use the Web

Shutterstock

and who are much more Web-savvy than people who watch the broadcast. You still get a lot of things that are on the broadcast every evening, but they're done in a much more Web-friendly style."[4]

In addition to having access to news from ABC on TV or the Web site, you can also download it to your portable music device as a podcast, send it to your mobile phone, or have it delivered to you as a feed, thus giving you access anytime and anywhere. Furthermore, you can interact with those who deliver and consume the news by commenting on stories on the Web site. All the network news sites now offer podcasts or "**vodcasts**," but ABC News vodcasts are consistently among those most frequently downloaded on Apple's iTunes. Reuter's has reported that in September 2008, there were 5.2 million downloads of the "World News Webcast."[5]

The enhanced distribution of news and the ability of consumers to interact benefits the MPR professional in several ways. With the need to provide continuous news through an ever-increasing number of channels, the media is constantly looking for story ideas and subject matter experts. When marketers give journalists real news and commentary when they need it, the result is often a positive media mention of the marketer's product or organization. Technology is also on the marketer's side in that it allows people to consume news when they have the time. For example, if you are not able to watch *World News Tonight*'s TV broadcast, you can watch the segments that interest you on the Web whenever you have the time. When you share news stories with your friends, you are actually helping marketers by ensuring that the media mentions in the news segment get passed along to people who may be interested in the product.

News Media versus Advertising Media

CHAPTER
OBJECTIVE
1

Chapter 1 defined media as any communication methods widely distributed to the consumer or business community. As a professional in Marketing Public Relations, however, you must drill down this definition a bit further. Most marketing practitioners are concerned with **advertising media**. These are the various mass media that carry advertising messages to potential consumers of products, services, organizations, or ideas. These media include newspapers, magazines, direct mail advertising, the Yellow Pages®, radio, broadcast television, cable television, outdoor advertising, transit advertising, and specialty advertising.[6] While this classification is important, it defines a type of media in which the firm retains control of the message by way of a *paid* advertisement.

Since the point of Marketing Public Relations is to create media mentions and generate word-of-mouth inexpensively by handing the message over to connectors, the advertising aspect of media is not appropriate for MPR purposes. To find the right point of view, we have to break down the wall that has existed between news and advertising since the dawn of time.[7] That is, in order to effectively use MPR, marketers have to look past advertising media and discover **news media**.[8] The **content** of news media is produced by the media themselves and is not paid for by the persons or organizations that are the subject of the coverage. MPR professionals have to understand that, unlike their other marketing colleagues, they are working on the news side of the business.

Occasionally, the line between controlled media (advertising) and out-of-control media (MPR) does get blurry. For example, marketers will run provocative advertisements hoping to get media coverage and spread word-of-mouth. Marketers will also use "advertorials"—paid advertisements that look like editorial copy—in order to leverage some of MPR's credibility for an ad.

Basic News Media Classifications

CHAPTER
OBJECTIVE
2

We can categorize news media into the following major groups: print (newspapers, magazines, and trade journals), broadcast (television and radio news), organizational publications (newsletters, reports, and Web sites produced by companies and associations), and electronic (news Web sites and blogs). We sometimes refer to electronic media as "**new media**" and categorize it with **social media**.[9] Classic examples of social media are Facebook, MySpace, and LinkedIn®, which represent a shift in how people discover, read, and share news and information and content. While social media is of great importance to marketing public relations, it is really a platform for non-media connectors to communicate, and Chapter 10 of this text will address it separately from other media formats.

As a simple stroll through the magazine section of your local "megabookstore" or a few minutes surfing your cable TV listings will illustrate, there is an almost unfathomable amount of news media opportunities available to marketers. This abundance of media choice makes it imperative for marketers to identify the media that are best suited to reach a target audience. Marketers can further classify news media by demographics and psychographics, format, geography, audience size, and topic.

Demographics and Psychographics

All media serve a range of consumers that vary in age, income, education, ethnicity, gender, and even the language that they speak. You can obtain demographic information on a particular medium from the media outlet or from third-party auditing firms. To get a sense of the psychographics of an audience, marketers rely on the medium itself. Because there is no standardized format for quantifying psychographics, however, this data is subjective and open to interpretation. A good example of a medium that understands its demographic base is *Sports Illustrated*. Having long been the standard in sports magazines, *Sports Illustrated* realized that there are populations that enjoy reading about sports but that could be served better. For example, *SI* observed that the youth market is substantial and has a unique set

---

Key Terms

Vodcast A video podcast

Advertising media Segment of the media business focused on generating revenue through the sales of advertisements

News media Any person or entity that gathers information of potential interest to a segment of the public,

uses its editorial skills to turn the raw materials into a distinct work, and makes its products available to the general public through purchase, subscription, or free distribution

Content All non-advertising elements of media, including but not limited to

articles, columns, feature stories, and editorials

Social media Online technologies and practices that people use to share opinions, insights, experiences, and perspectives, including text, images, audio, and video

of needs. Specifically, kids need a magazine that is easier to read, and they prefer more humor and cartoons than adults. Accordingly, the organization launched *Sports Illustrated Kids* in 1989 for kids from ages six to seventeen.[10]

Format

A medium's format of delivery affects the type of content it distributes, as well as the manner in which it presents that content. Since each medium has its own strengths and weaknesses, MPR professionals seek a balance across media types when planning a campaign. Consider that television may do a wonderful job of generating awareness for a given campaign, but it may fall short in building preference, relationships, or trust. Magazines can do a great job of providing more detail and rationale, but they may not necessarily do a great job of creating broad awareness. The Web also might not be able to generate huge awareness, but it can do a great job of connecting prospects to deeper information and word-of-mouth sources who can build trust or even help facilitate a purchase.[11]

Broadcast Broadcast media have two delivery platforms—television and radio— and each has its own set of news platforms. Television, for example, has shows such as the evening news programs that are aired on the major networks, local news shows aired by network affiliates, 24-hour news networks like CNN, magazine news shows like *20/20* and *Dateline*, and talk shows like *The Oprah Winfrey Show* and *The Ellen DeGeneres Show.* Radio has stations with 24 hour news formats, all-talk formats, individual programs that carry the news, as well as those that broadcast general news at different intervals during the course of the day.

Print We can separate print into two segments—newspaper and magazine. Newspapers come in weekly and daily varieties and typically focus on the happenings of a specific geographic region. Some papers, such as *USA Today* and *The New York Times*, have a national scope. Other papers, both large and small, focus on a specific topic such as business or entertainment. Like newspapers and broadcast media, magazines can have a very broad focus, but they can also be very specific and topic-focused. For example, magazines like *Newsweek* take a sweeping look at all the news, while others, like *Model Railroader Magazine,* cover a single hobby. A trip through the magazine section of your local megabookstore will give you a good understanding of the breadth of topics covered by magazines.

Electronic Electronic media has been radically changing the media business since the 1990s. Media organizations' Web sites and **blogs**[12] have not only changed the physical medium by which the news is distributed, but they have also changed the business itself. As consumers have drifted away from using print and broadcast media as news sources, many media organizations have been offering much of their content online in addition to their traditional format. We can see evidence of this transition in the fact that newspaper circulation has dropped from more than 62 million subscribers in 1980 to around 54 million subscribers in 2004, while evening network news viewership has fallen from over 50 million to less than 30 million viewers over the same period.[13] In addition, the number of consumer magazines in the United States dropped more than 10 percent from 1996 to 2006, while the number of consumer magazines with Web sites increased by 67 percent between 2003 and 2006.[14] While media companies have expressed concern regarding the ability of their online component to replace the revenue lost by declining readership/viewership, Web sites of traditional media companies are consistently among the most highly viewed sites on the Web.[15] Bloggers have also changed the way news is aggregated, distributed, and consumed. Now everyone with a computer can be a journalist. More than 100 million blogs are in existence currently, and the most highly viewed blogs receive millions of views each month.[16] In fact, there are 15.5 million active (updated within the last 90 days), English-language blogs that generate approximately 495,000 new postings per day, and approximately 57 million American adults read blogs.[17] Examples of some popular public relations blogs include:

- Richard Edelman's blog: http://www.edelman.com/speak_up/blog/
- Steve Rubel's Micropersuasion: http://www.micropersuasion.com/
- Ben McConnell and Jackie Huba's Church of the Customer: http://www.churchofthecustomer.com/
- Joan Stewart's Publicity Hound: http://publicityhound.net/
- Cision's Cisionblog: http://blog.us.cision.com

Trade Trade media consist of business-to-business magazines and electronic media. This format class combines media platforms (typically print and electronic) to concentrate on bringing business or professional information to business and trades people. The **trade journal** has been the workhorse of trade media. It is similar to a magazine in its look and feel, but it differs because it caters to the content needs of a particular industry or trade rather than to a segment of consumers. The typical trade journal has a companion Web site to increase its penetration into its audience.

Geography

Media geography is a concern to marketers because it is an indicator of the audience served by a particular medium. For example, a local newspaper provides the people in its area the news that they want. That means that, in addition to national news, it provides the local news that is relevant to the community it serves. Conversely, a global media outlet like CNN is interested in providing news that will bring in the most viewers from around the world.

Key Terms

Blog A hybrid form of Internet communication that combines a column, diary, and directory. The term, short for "Web log," refers to a frequently updated collection of short articles on various subjects with links to further resources.

Trade journal A print publication similar in form to either a magazine or newspaper that focuses its content on a specific industry or profession

Broadcast media are geographically classified by DMA. Other types of media can be classified by MSA, state, county, and, occasionally, ZIP code.

Size

For marketers, measuring the size of a medium is not necessarily related to its sales revenue or number of employees. Instead, measuring size is about gauging how many people consume a particular medium. For television, size equates with viewership; for radio listenership, that is how many people listen to a given broadcast. For print media, marketers measure circulation and look at numbers of subscribers as well as newsstand (nonsubscription) sales. Determining the size of an online media outlet is challenging, as the medium is fairly new and measurement standards are still evolving. Two main companies, Nielsen/NetRatings and ComScore, measure online audiences. Both of these organizations report total audience, time spent (on a site), frequency of use, and page views.[18]

Topic

The topic of a medium drives the content and is an indicator of the types of stories that it will cover. The topic identifies the mission of the medium; it explains how a particular medium intends to serve its chosen audience. Most media outlets will cover subtopics that fall within the scope of the primary topic while still serving the mission of the medium. Rodale is an example of a publishing company that is topic-driven. Its overall mission focuses on health, fitness, and wellness, yet it publishes magazines on several topics within this broader category. Its magazine titles include *Prevention*, *Men's Health*, *Organic Gardening*, and *Runner's World*. This focus on narrower topics allows the editorial staff to provide specific content to a specific group of people with defined interests. These in turn translate into specific demographic and psychographic segments.

<table>
<tr><td>CHAPTER
OBJECTIVE
3</td><td></td></tr>
</table>

Media Organizations and People

Since a codependency exists between business and the media, Marketing Public Relations specialists need to understand what makes media organizations, editors, producers, and journalists tick. The relationships between marketers and the news media enhance marketers' ability to do their jobs effectively while supporting the role of the journalist. As author Richard Laermer says in his book, *Full Frontal PR*, "When they are at a loss for news, reporters rely on creative, connected business people and a gaggle of experts for the news about the topics they are most interested in."[19] Relationships, journalistic interests (beats), and ethics are key elements that play into the interaction between marketing and media professionals.

Relationships

Journalists, editors, producers, and even the most serious bloggers are professionals looking for good ideas, so if you can respect them as professionals and be a consistent source of story ideas, you will have created a lasting and productive relationship. One aspect of respecting them is recognizing that they must work within deadlines. For example, journalists have hard deadlines that range from a month or more for a magazine editor to possibly less than an hour for a CNN producer. Regardless of whether a deadline is measured in months or minutes, the marketer needs to remember that media organizations hold the keys to the vehicle that will bring the message to the customer. The marketer's job, therefore, is to deliver material to the journalist when he or she needs it.

Respecting a journalist's time is as important as respecting his or her deadlines. So, if you are communicating with an editor who is interested in running a story about your firm, you need to get to the point as quickly as possible. Be sure that you have done your homework and are able to convey the value of your story to the editor and his or her audience. If your **pitch** is not newsworthy, then you are wasting the journalist's time.[20]

Marketers also have a responsibility to follow up with journalists. Journalists don't like pests, but they do appreciate follow-up and marketers who can act as expert resources. Once a journalist bites at a story, the marketer needs to be attentive and quick in supplying him or her with statistics, quotes, contact names, or anything else that will reduce the amount of research that the journalist needs to do. Successfully becoming a resource for a journalist is the key to creating a mutually productive, long-term relationship.[21]

Beats

Just as media outlets concentrate on specific topics, some journalists have **beats**. Beats can be very specific; for example, a given medium that covers business may have one journalist covering new businesses, another reporting on retail businesses, and another for finance. Knowing which journalists cover which beats saves time and aggravation for both the marketer and the journalist, as it keeps the marketer from proposing stories in which a particular journalist will not be interested.

Ethics

While the marketer's role is to influence a journalist in order to get the best coverage for his or her story, both marketers and journalists must remember that there is an ethical code they need to follow. A news source must be objective in order to be credible to an audience. If a journalist or media organization is known to be unduly influenced by a company or other outside force, the public will lose trust in that news source.[22] As the preamble to the Code of Ethics for Society of Professional Journalists points out, journalists are bound by a responsibility centered on the belief that public enlightenment is the forerunner of justice and the foundation of democracy, and it is the duty of the journalist to further those

Key Terms

Pitch A marketer's attempt to convince a journalist to report on a topic relevant to his or her product or company

Beat A journalist's area of interest or specialty

ends by seeking truth and providing a fair and comprehensive account of events and issues. Conscientious journalists from all media and specialties strive to serve the public with thoroughness and honesty.[23] The Marketing Public Relations professional must assist journalists in living up to their responsibilities of seeking and reporting the truth while acting independently, minimizing harm to others, and being personally accountable to their audience.[24]

Breaches of ethics can have a negative impact on the reputation of firms and media outlets as well as destroy the career of journalists. For example, Scripps Howard News Service® (SHNS) stated in 2006 that it was severing its business relationship with columnist Michael Fumento, who was also a senior fellow at the conservative Hudson Institute. SHNS's action came after inquiries from *BusinessWeek Online* about payments Fumento received from agribusiness giant Monsanto®—a frequent subject of praise in Fumento's opinion columns as well as in a book he wrote. In a statement released on January 13, 2006, Scripps Howard News Service Editor and General Manager Peter Copeland said that Fumento "did not tell SHNS editors, and therefore we did not tell our readers, that in 1999 Hudson received a $60,000 grant from Monsanto." Copeland added: "Our policy is that he should have disclosed that information. We apologize to our readers."[25]

In an attempt to avoid such lapses, many media publish ethics policies that spell out how those involved with creating editorial content should interact with other stakeholders. The following illustrate typical media guidelines and are excerpted from The New York Times Company Policy on Ethics in Journalism:

- The relationship between the company and advertisers rests on the understanding that news and advertising are separate.

- Journalists should maintain their independence by avoiding discussions of advertising needs, goals, and problems except where those are directly related to the business of the newsroom.

- No one in our news departments (except when authorized by top news executives) may exchange information with the advertising department or with advertisers about the timing or content of advertising, the timing or content of news coverage, or the assignment of staff or freelance news people.[26]

Concept Case 5.1: **Local Media**

The Falcon's Lair has only a single location, and the company has decided that print and broadcast media will help it focus on the geographic area that it serves. Following is a working copy of the company's media list:

- Print
  - Newspapers
    - *The Morning Call* (Allentown); Frequency—Daily; Demographic—Broad
    - *The Express Times* (Easton); Frequency—Daily; Demographic—Broad
    - East Penn Press (seven community papers); Frequency—Weekly; Demographic—Broad

- Magazines
  - *Lehigh Valley Style Magazine;* Topic—Lifestyle; Frequency—Monthly; Demographic—Affluent singles and families
  - *Lehigh Valley Magazine;* Topic—Lifestyle; Frequency—Monthly; Demographic—Affluent singles and families
- Television (Network Affiliate)
  - Allentown
    - WFMZ
    - WLVT (PBS)
  - Philadelphia
    - WKYW (CBS)
    - WCAU (NBC)
    - WHYY (PBS)
    - WPHL
    - WPSG (CW)
    - WPVI (ABC)
    - WTXF (Fox)

Questions:

1. Are news and talk radio stations appropriate for The Falcon's Lair? Explain.

2. What electronic opportunities might be available to the company?

3. Is The Falcon's Lair missing important MPR opportunities by not forming relationships with national media? Explain.

4. Explore one medium in each class listed above and select a journalist who is an appropriate contact for The Falcon's Lair MPR efforts. Explain why you selected that person.

Media Opportunities

CHAPTER
OBJECTIVE
4

Since media are constantly on the lookout for ways to serve and inform their audiences, they rely on a partnership with businesses and public relations professionals to capture the most current news from the marketplace. As a result, items like new product announcements, product reviews, the hiring or promotion of key personnel, change in location, or the acquisition of a lucrative new contract all present opportunities for getting a media mention.

Regional business newspapers, local newspapers, and many trade journals have sections dedicated to announcing new hires, promotions, and new contracts and partnerships for companies that are within their audience's scope of interest. Similarly, media organizations regularly dedicate space to highlighting industry trends, providing "how to" guides to help their audience solve common problems, showcasing accomplished businesses or leaders, and providing question-and-answer sessions with experts.

Media opportunities take many forms, of which the following are the most conspicuous:

- Editorials
- Expert articles
- Cases
- Events
- Interviews

Editorials

Newspapers as well as other media often produce content that is somewhat subjective in nature in the form of editorials, opinions, or **op-eds**. According to a writer in *Directory Journal*, "These opinion pieces are designed to offer an alternate position, generally from an expert in the industry or subject area (or occasionally a more general reader in the case of local news angles). In a general sense, they are offered to educate members of the public about an issue, beyond what the media outlet may have been covering independently."[27] The opinion or editorial offered must analyze an issue and not simply be a covert sales pitch for a company or a product. Blogs may be considered the new media cousins of editorials in that they tend to be subjective in nature. Since many blogs lack the oversight of an editor or producer, self-serving editorials have a higher chance of appearing in them than in a newspaper.

Expert Articles

Media are also willing to consider articles written by an expert within an organization if they are of interest to their audience. For example, *Parenting Magazine* and its associated Web site http://www.parenting.com have a feature called "Ask an Expert" where parenting experts comment on topics that are of significance to the magazine's audience. These specialists build their own credibility by contributing an article or response to a question while also gaining a media mention for the company for whom they work or for the book they have written.

Cases

Case histories or case studies are another opportunity for getting media mentions. These items typically have a problem-solution format or showcase a product or service. Cases are most often written by an organization, but occasionally they are written by a reporter assigned by a media outlet. For example, *Security Management Magazine*, a trade journal for security professionals, has a recurring "Case Study" section that appears every month and spotlights the use of a product or service in a security management setting. In order to get such a piece mentioned by the broadcast media, an organization has to demonstrate the product or solution in such a way that it is of interest to a medium's audience.

Events

Events[28] are an area where there is a symbiotic relationship between media and companies. Events are attractive to media when their audience is participating in the affair, and when they have the opportunity to cover a celebrity or product their audience cares about. This attention increases the number of people engaged with the medium and simultaneously benefits both the media outlet and the sponsors. Organizations use events as MPR both to get media mentions as well as to create word-of-mouth. The 50 Million Pound Challenge sponsored by State Farm Insurance® is an excellent example of the power of an event to garner media mentions. The nationwide event was an "effort in the African-American community to help people get fit, lose excess weight, and stem the toll of weight-related diseases that threaten millions of Americans."[29] *The New York Times* and *The Washington Post,* as well as the Reuters news wire, mentioned the event. To top things off, the company also won the Silver Anvil award from the Public Relations Society of America (PRSA) for multicultural public relations.

Interviews

A quick surf through the cable channels any evening, a brief glance through your favorite newspaper or magazine, or even a few minutes on a media Web site will quickly demonstrate how much the media rely on others for news and that the vehicle they use most frequently is the interview. Although good journalists often find the executives and experts they want to interview, good MPR pros also find the journalists who should be quoting their organization's thought leaders.

Concept Case 5.2: **Events**

People who participate in hiking and climbing consider those sports to be events. To capitalize on this fact, The Falcon's Lair hosts two annual happenings: the Falcon's Frolic (a climbing contest and music festival for hardcore climbers) and the Falcon Fun Weekend (offering guided hikes and instructional sessions for families).

Questions:
1. Discuss media opportunities that the two annual events could generate.
2. What other media opportunities are suited to promoting The Falcon's Lair? Explain why you have chosen each.

Key Terms

Op-ed An opinion piece, often published in newspapers, and more recently in online publications. The term *op-ed* means opposite the editorial. In newspapers, it describes the common placement of an op-ed piece on the page opposite an editorial.

Event A special activity, showing, display, or exhibit designed to demonstrate products or to connect the product to favorable products or activities

Media convergence The trend of media organizations shifting toward a multiple-format approach to producing and distributing content. This trend is driven by innovations in technology and changing consumer preferences.

Exhibit 5.1 Media rely on experts to help tell a story, which, in turn, leads to media exposure for the expert and his or her firm.

Courtesy of *The New York Times.*

Media Convergence

The advent of the Internet and other communications technology has had a tremendous impact on the way that news is produced, distributed, and consumed. Digitization of news production has eroded the borders that have traditionally separated the creation of content for print, the Internet, radio, and television, thus allowing **media convergence**.[30] Technology has changed the way that journalists collect and report information as well as added new ways to deliver the content to those who consume it. This melding of different media types is illustrated by the growing Web presence of traditional media organizations. In fact, a 2008 survey conducted by *PR Week* and PR Newswire found that more than 38 percent of journalists across all media expected to contribute titles to their outlet's online version, and almost 56 percent contribute to other media outside of their official duty.[31]

In the summer of 2008, the *The Washington Post* decided to merge its print and online news operations. The *Post*'s Web site had a separate newsroom and was not under the direct control of the publisher, a situation that led to duplication of efforts and turf wars. As a part of consolidating the two operations, publisher Katharine Weymouth hired former *Wall Street Journal* editor Marcus Brauchli as executive editor. She chose Brauchli both for his journalistic integrity and for his ability to help navigate the new world of media.[32]

While convergence increases journalists' workloads by adding to the number of ways that a given media organization reaches its audience, it also puts an additional burden on marketers by adding complexity to the MPR landscape. Modern marketers must not only identify the right media organization, but they must also find the appropriate journalists within the organization, determine which of the organization's formats will showcase their products best, and craft a message that is suitable for each journalist *and* each format.

Exhibit 5.2 Many media outlets are now delivering their content through a variety of channels.

Radu Razvan/Shutterstock.

Reflection Questions

1. Compared to news media, advertising media provide a marketer with much more control over messaging. What are some ways in which such control can be helpful and how can it hinder a marketer? (Chapter Objective 1)

2. Discuss how a medium's format is related to the demographics of its audience. (Chapter Objective 2)

3. Why is building relationships with journalists beneficial to marketers, and why is ethical behavior important in these relationships? (Chapter Objective 3)

4. Explain how the principle of journalistic ethics affects the Marketing Public Relations professional. (Chapter Objective 3)

5. Why would an article written by a company executive be more effective in achieving the firm's marketing objectives than an advertisement? (Chapter Objective 4)

6. How has media convergence changed how marketers have to think about media? (Chapter Objective 5)

Chapter Key Terms

Advertising media Segment of the media business focused on generating revenue through the sales of advertisements (p. 70)

Beat A journalist's area of interest or specialty (p. 75)

Blog A hybrid form of Internet communication that combines a column, diary, and directory. The term, short for "Web log," refers to a frequently updated collection of short articles on various subjects with links to further resources. (p. 72)

Content All non-advertising elements of media, including but not limited to articles, columns, feature stories, and editorials (p. 70)

Event A special activity, showing, display, or exhibit designed to demonstrate products or to connect the product to favorable products or activities (p. 79)

Media convergence The trend of media organizations shifting toward a multiple-format approach to producing and distributing content. This trend is driven by innovations in technology and changing consumer preferences. (p. 80)

New media Electronically delivered media (p. 71)

News media People or entities that gather information of potential interest to a segment of the public, use their editorial skills to turn the raw materials into a distinct work, and make their products available to the general public through purchase, subscription, or free distribution (p. 70)

Op-ed An opinion piece, often published in newspapers, and more recently in online publications. The term *op-ed*

means "opposite the editorial." In newspapers, it describes the common placement of an op-ed piece on the page opposite an editorial. (p. 78)

Pitch A marketer's attempt to convince a journalist to report on a topic relevant to his or her product or company (p. 75)

Social media Online technologies and practices that people use to share opinions, insights, experiences, and perspectives, including text, images, audio, and video (p. 71)

Trade journal A print publication similar in form to either a magazine or newspaper that focuses its content on a specific industry or profession (p. 73)

Vodcast A video podcast (p. 70)

 Application Assignments

1. Search the Web for a nationally advertised product that is familiar to you. Go to the company's PR page (it could be labeled "public relations," "in the news," "press releases," "media center," or something similar) and review the material on this Web site. Then use the Web, your library, or a newsstand to find mentions of the product being pitched by the company whose Web site you've chosen.

   Some suggestions:

   a. http://sealyinc.com/newsroom/

   b. http://www.apple.com/pr/

   c. http://www.southwest.com/about_swa/press/prindex.html

2. For each of the following media, list the demographics of its audience, format(s) that it uses, size, and topic. (If the medium has multiple formats, be sure to note any differences in demographics, size, and topics between each channel.)

   a. *Maxim*

   b. *Wine Enthusiast*

   c. The *Today* show

   d. *The Onion*

   e. *Financial Times*

3. In 2003 the CEO of Apple, Steve Jobs, gave an interview to *Rolling Stone* magazine and defended the then-fledgling digital music business. This article foreshadowed the forthcoming success of this industry and Apple's role in it. Explain why Jobs and Apple's marketers saw *Rolling Stone* as the appropriate place for an interview of this type and why it was effective. (To read the interview, go to http://www.rollingstone.com and search "Jobs interview.")

4. Search the business and popular media for another example of an executive giving an interview to promote his or her company, and explain what you perceive to be the goals and outcomes of that interview.

5. For each of the following beats, find a journalist who covers it in each media format and cite an example of his or her reporting. Include as many media formats as you can and point out evidence of media convergence.

   a. Business

   b. Environment

   c. Federal government

   d. Health care

   e. Technology

 Practice Portfolio

This Practice Portfolio can be based on a fictitious company or on a real company that your instructor assigns to you. (If you used a company in previous Practice Portfolio exercises, continue to use that company.) Add your completed assignment to your portfolio to present to prospective employers.

- Using your positioning statement from Chapter 2 as a guide, list the media classifications that will best help you to reach your MPR goals. Briefly explain why you chose each classification. (Hint: Creating a table of all media classifications and listing their pros and cons relative to your company is an effective method for completing this task.)

- Using the list you created for the Practice Portfolio in Chapter 4 as a starting point, select the media outlets that best fit the classifications you have chosen above. You may add or delete media from your list based on this analysis.

- Explore four media outlets on your list and identify the journalists who would be most interested in covering your company or products. List their names and their beats. (Hint: A single medium may have more than one journalist who would be interested in your company or products.)

- List the types of media opportunities that will contribute most effectively to achieving your goals and briefly explain your selection. In addition, find an example of each opportunity within one medium on your media list.

CHAPTER 6

Non-media Connectors and Word-of-mouth

CHAPTER OBJECTIVES

After studying this chapter, you should be able to:

1. Explain what non-media connectors are and why they are important to marketers.

2. Explain why word-of-mouth is such a powerful marketing tool.

3. List and discuss the factors needed to create and sustain viral word-of-mouth for a product.

4. Describe reference groups and list some common examples.

5. Describe experts and opinion leaders and list some common examples.

6. Define "Citizen Marketers" and discuss the different types.

7. Discuss how blogs can be tools for media as well as non-media connectors, and how internally generated blogs can benefit a firm.

8. Explain the relative value of online versus offline word-of-mouth.

Feeling the pressure that music downloading was putting on independent record stores, Earshot Music in Greenville, South Carolina, decided to make some radical changes. Earshot transformed the shop into a new urban retail store like no other, centered on Mix & Burn™ technology (an interactive retail system that allows customers to find and download music to a CD or to a portable device). To accomplish this, they partnered with Brains on Fire, a marketing firm with a flair for word-of-mouth promotion. This collaboration led to a campaign that shunned advertising and focused on finding people who influenced others when making music-buying decisions and on giving customers an experience worth talking about.

"Our goals for Earshot were pretty straightforward," explains Brains on Fire partner Geno Church. "We had to re-introduce a music retail shop into downtown Greenville in a way that kept pace with technology, while creating an inspiring yet social retail experience. And, of course, it had to be done in a way that allowed Earshot to be profitable."

Brains on Fire's research and experience told the owners of Earshot that they had to engage the community prior to opening the store. So they set about building relationships with connectors who had the ability to reach out to diverse social groups like musicians, attorneys, young professionals, and downtown visitors. They started by sending out personal invitations to locally influential people, asking them to come and experience Earshot. One of these people, the mayor of Greenville, responded enthusiastically to his invitation. In turn he threw his support behind the project.

"Our first strategy involved making noise in quiet downtown Greenville," says Church. "We sent out calls to Greenville citizens who love music, any kind of music. Then we photographed them listening, dancing, whatever they felt like doing while listening to their music. These photos were turned into window banners that blocked every window of the building during construction. This began to build some buzz within the connectors' circles and started some chatter and anticipation with the public."

The next phase turned into an experience for all of Greenville. All of the connectors identified during the initial phase received a direct mail CD invitation to come create their own music at Earshot. The grand opening party was held over three days. As a result of using an eclectic group of connectors, the attendees were a diverse group of people who mirrored Earshot's variety of musical offerings. "What a success!" exclaims Church. "Though we didn't advertise, we didn't forget the media altogether. They

were invited; they just weren't treated special. They were simply asked to experience Earshot as music lovers."

As a result of this campaign, Earshot became the talk of downtown as well as a destination retailer. The campaign also resulted in media mentions ranging from local to national publications. "We also got a lot of attention in the music business because it broke some norms," concludes Church. "A higher percentage of Baby Boomers were creating music than expected. That fact goes against the national trend and made the story even more newsworthy."

To top it all off, Earshot has become the number one destination for creating downloadable, customized CDs in the southeastern United States. With 25 percent of the company's customers burning entire CDs (five times the industry average), its profitability is sound.[1]

<table><tr><td>CHAPTER
OBJECTIVE
1</td><td></td></tr></table>

Non-media Connectors

Media are not the only vehicles for getting a promotional message from a firm to a potential customer. While they have existed for as long as marketing itself, techniques for using **non-media connectors** (NMC) to reach out to consumers are receiving a great deal of attention today. Whether marketers call them buzz, grassroots, community, or cause marketing, these techniques attempt to facilitate word-of-mouth through both live and electronic means.[2] A non-media connector is active in the arena of a given brand or industry. It can either be a professional in a related field or simply a consumer with a passion for a brand, product, or business. Super blogger Steve Johnson, publisher of four blogs with quirky, consumer product themes, is an example of someone who has created a non-media niche. His blogs include one on the latest trends in junk food (http://www.junkfoodblog.com), one that reviews strange and innovative new products (http://www.strangenewproducts.com), one on beer (http://www.bottlewatch.com), and a fourth on beef jerky (http://www.bestbeefjerky.org). With the exception of the beer blog, no traditional media organizations cover these topics with the same focus or with the same casual style. This demonstrates how non-media connectors' personal interest in a product or industry elevates them above suspicion with a consumer. According to Johnson, "The biggest surprise is the amount of targeted traffic you can generate from a blog pretty quickly, much more than from a non-blog covering the same topic."[3]

Marketers using non-media connectors consider the devotion these people have to a product and the size of their social circles. They expect these NMCs to use their own resources to influence their friends, family, and professional and social groups through conversations, blogs, live events, and social media.[4] As relationships develop, marketers can even encourage and support their NMCs by providing content and events exclusively to the consumers in their **sphere of influence**.

<table><tr><td>CHAPTER
OBJECTIVE
2</td><td></td></tr></table>

Word-of-mouth as a Marketing Tool

Incorporating word-of-mouth into a firm's overall marketing scheme presents a challenge not found in other promotional efforts. All other facets of marketing, including media-centered PR, have explicit channels to the consumer. For instance, organizations can reach their target markets through sales promotion and advertising opportunities, using existing marketing channels such as retail stores and advertising media. Similarly, sales-people with expertise in a given industry are able to make contact with potential buyers, while firms can encourage traditional media channels to review and report on their products. No formal mechanism exists, however, for marketers to identify and reach out to NMCs. One could argue that this fact is precisely the reason that this type of marketing is powerful. The people who act as intermediaries for the marketing message appear not to have a stake in the success or failure of the products they extol or condemn. As a result, their message evokes the highest measure of credibility with consumers.

In April 2007 The Nielsen Company conducted its "Online Global Consumer Study" and found that recommendations from consumers are the most trusted form of promotion for people around the globe. According to the study, an average of 78 percent of consumers relies on the opinion of others to help them make buying decisions.[5] Procter & Gamble® Company's introduction of Dawn Direct Foam® is an example of the power of word-of-mouth. While its ads took traditional P&G form, the company crafted a message that the new foam would help make dishwashing more fun for children. It promptly delivered the pitch, along with some coupons and talking points, to its 450,000 mom "connectors"—an army of brand evangelists, called Vocalpoint, which P&G uses to spur discussions about its products. The moms held up their end of the bargain, increasing sales of Dawn by 50 percent in the test markets.[6]

Creating and Sustaining Viral Word-of-mouth

CHAPTER
OBJECTIVE
3

The message that a firm sends needs to be engaging in order to be passed on, regardless of the mix of NMCs it uses. In their 2005 *Business Horizon*'s article, "Controlled Infection! Spreading the Brand Message Through **Viral Marketing**,"[7] Angela Dobele, David Toleman, and Michael Beverland presented the following five solid rules of thumb for ensuring that your message proliferates:

1. *Capture the imagination by being fun or intriguing.* All elements of marketing should follow this rule, but it is especially important if you expect objective, non-paid channels to carry the message.

2. *The message must be based on an easy-to-use or highly visible product.* A product that is complex or difficult to find does not lend itself to word-of-mouth.

3. *Target well.* The NMCs need to have an interest in the message, have an engaged audience, and be able to maintain or enhance their reputation with that audience by delivering the message.

Key Terms

Non-media connector A person who monitors, analyzes, and shares information about a product or industry. An NMC may be paid for her efforts, but she is not employed by a media organization.

Sphere of influence A term typically applied to nations, marketers use this term to refer to the audience that a connector reaches.

Viral marketing A marketing phenomenon that facilitates and encourages people to pass along a marketing message

4. *Associate with credible sources.* A major reason for using Marketing Public Relations is to capitalize on its assumed trustworthiness. The marketer's job, therefore, is to ensure that all sources are respected—especially for word-of mouth efforts.

5. *Combine delivery technologies.* The message should be conducive to spreading over a variety of technologies—including the Web, e-mail, text messages, and even the human voice—and the connectors must also be able to use a variety of these tools.[8]

Concept Case 6.1: **Non-media Connectors**

In order to effectively promote word-of-mouth and engage non-media connectors, The Falcon's Lair needs to be able to explain why it is unique in its marketplace and why the audiences for the NMCs should be interested in the company. Following is a general statement that The Falcon's Lair marketing team uses to introduce itself to NMCs:

"The Falcon's Lair is not a store; it is an experience. A combination of hiking and climbing's best products and people who are passionate about the sport as well as serving others are the Lair's foundation. From the most experienced climber to families that enjoy a day of hiking, we make sure that our customers' fun is extreme, their safety is never in question, and they are always in style."

Questions:
1. Does this statement reflect The Falcon's Lair's positioning?
2. In your opinion, will this statement capture the attention of non-media connectors? Explain why or why not.

The marketing professional's creativity and the product that is being promoted determine the extent to which viral marketing is effective. In order to get a message delivered effectively, however, a firm must have the right connectors in place. For this reason, firms most often look to the following three categories of NMCs:

- *Reference groups*: Formal organizations, such as professional associations, labor unions, and civic groups, or informal social or professional groups that individuals use as the anchor point for evaluating their own beliefs and attitudes. One may or may not be a member and may or may not aspire to membership in a reference group.[9]

- *Experts and opinion leaders*: Industry professionals, self-proclaimed authorities, and others whose position and notoriety make their views valuable to consumers[10]

- *Citizen Marketers*: Hyperengaged consumers classifiable as Filters, Fanatics, Facilitators, or Firecrackers[11]

CHAPTER
OBJECTIVE
4

Reference Groups

Whether buying for personal consumption or for a business, people look to external organizations for cues to assist them in their decision making. The buyer may be a member of the group, such as a trade organization or political party, or may simply view the group as an authority, as is the case with the American Medical Association® and the Better Business Bureau®.

Many consumers are familiar with the American Dental Association® because of the seal that is displayed on various brands of toothpaste and other oral health products. The ADA is also the premiere professional organization among American dentists. To fulfill its mission, the ADA has an oral health awareness program that is targeted to consumers, students, teachers, and media and that provides information to dentists to assist them in managing their practices and providing the best-possible patient care.[12] As a result, the ADA is on the connector list for every company that manufactures oral health goods or services for consumers or dentists.

Some NMCs monitor companies whether or not the firms want that attention. The environmentalist group Greenpeace® is an example of this type of reference group. Greenpeace has many members and also has the attention of the public at large with regard to society's impact on the planet. The organization garners this attention through its efforts with the media and, more recently, through blogs published by "green-minded" people.

Apple felt the effects of Greenpeace's power as a reference group after launching the iPhone®. In October 2007, three months after the iPhone's release, Greenpeace published *Missed Call: The iPhone's Hazardous Chemicals,* a report detailing the toxic materials in the device and their potential impact on the environment.[13] From a marketing standpoint, this report was very unfortunate for Apple. Subsequent publicity will likely tarnish the environmentally friendly reputation that Apple has been trying to build. Apple's Web site shows evidence of this effort to be seen as environmental friendly; a page on the site states: "How we impact the environment is also important to us, and environmental considerations are an integral part of Apple's business practices. From the earliest stages of product design through manufacturing, use, and recycling, we take care to keep our activities and our products environmentally sound."[14] One could argue, however, that Apple will ultimately benefit from Greenpeace's attention, as it continues its efforts to become the first company to design a cell phone that meets that organization's standards.

Exhibit 6.1 Often consumers look to the affluent and the beautiful to model their buying behavior.

Factoria singular fotografia/Shutterstock.

Concept Case 6.2: **Word-of-mouth and Groups**

Families have many choices when it comes to planning their recreational activities. The Falcon's Lair managers have noticed that many of their customers who fall into their "family and recreational hiker" segment got their start while hiking with a group. As a result, they think that they should make an effort to engage these groups in order to build their customer base. Following is a partial list of reference groups The Falcon's Lair is attempting to reach:

- Church groups
- Scouting organizations

(continued)

Concept Case 6.2:   (Continued)

- Social and civic clubs
- Public and private schools
- Summer camps

Questions:
1. Explain what you would do in order to engage these groups and encourage them to spread word-of-mouth.
2. If efforts with these reference groups are successful, are opportunities for involving the media likely to arise? Explain why or why not.
3. Create a similar reference group list for the hardcore hikers and climbers segment and answer questions 1 and 2 relative to that market.

CHAPTER
OBJECTIVE
5

Experts and Opinion Leaders

Although the terms **experts** and **opinion leaders** have similar meanings, marketers often differentiate the two groups. An expert, for example, tends to be a paid professional in a particular field and/or someone who has expertise in one specific area. Doctors, lawyers, professors, and other professionals that you see quoted in news stories are obvious examples. Tom and Ray Magliozzi, better known as Click and Clack, the hosts of the National Public Radio (NPR) show *Car Talk,* are an extreme example. They were do-it-yourself garage owners in suburban Boston when they parlayed a guest appearance on WBUR into national recognition. That recognition currently includes more than 4 million *Car Talk* listeners across more than 600 NPR stations, a weekly column, "Click and Clack Talk Cars," in 335 newspapers, and over 400,000 weekly hits to the *Car Talk* section of the Web site http://www.cars.com.

Opinion leaders, on the other hand, tend to be revered for their views on a broad spectrum of topics. Arguably the quintessential opinion leader of our time, Oprah Winfrey, has been the launchpad for four dozen books at the top of *The New York Times* bestseller list, has boosted the sales of products ranging from Pontiacs to Dove soap, and has been the patron saint of everything from soft-rock sensation Josh Groban to Boudreaux's Butt Paste.[15]

Not all opinion leaders are in the consumer products world, and even fewer come close to the stature of Oprah, but they are still vitally important to MPR professionals. For example, the drugs your physician prescribes likely depend on the behavior of an opinion leader in her personal network in addition to her own knowledge of or familiarity with those products. In fact, according to recent research by Harikesh Nair, assistant professor of marketing at the Stanford Graduate School of Business, marketing to opinion leaders can boost revenues by an average of 18 percent over the revenue benefits derived from marketing to physicians who aren't opinion leaders. As a result, the pharmaceutical industry is a big believer in the role such physicians play in spurring the sales of drugs.[16]

Exhibit 6.2 People will base their opinions about products on the analysis of experts they recognize and trust.

AVAVA/Shutterstock

Concept Case 6.3: **Looking to Experts**

Over the years the staff of The Falcon's Lair has discovered that hardcore hikers and climbers look to experts for information on climbing techniques, performance of equipment, safety, and finding the best places to climb. To promote the store, management is seeking to work with the following people:

- Owners and instructors of local indoor climbing gyms
- Local tour guides
- Nationally recognized climbing expert Don Mellor
- The expert panel at http://www.rock-climbing-for-life.com

The staff of The Falcon's Lair has also found that the "hardcore" segment has little to no respect for people who speak about hiking and climbing, but who don't have experience with the sport.

(continued)

> ## Concept Case 6.3: **(Continued)**
>
> **Questions:**
> 1. Discuss how The Falcon's Lair management might consider engaging each of these experts.
> 2. Explain the benefits and drawbacks of a regional establishment partnering with nationally recognized experts.
> 3. Will opinion leaders be useful in promoting The Falcon's Lair to this market segment? Explain why or why not.
> 4. Create a list of experts and opinion leaders who are suitable for the family and recreational hikers segment and explain why the two lists differ.

CHAPTER
OBJECTIVE
6

Citizen Marketers

Not all non-media connectors are industry professionals or celebrities. In fact, many are **Citizen Marketers,** that is, ordinary people who have a passion for a particular product, industry, issue, or hobby. The numbers and reach of this segment of NMCs have been growing thanks to the ever-expanding availability of the Internet. In their book *Citizen Marketer,* Ben McConnell and Jackie Huba divide today's regular-folks-turned-marketing-mavens into the following four distinct categories based on their behavior:

1. Filters
2. Fanatics
3. Facilitators
4. Firecrackers[17]

Filters

Filters are a human wire service. They collect traditional media stories, blogger's rants and raves, podcasts, or fan creations about a specific company or brand and then package this information into a daily or near-daily stream of links, story summaries, and observations. Most Filters maintain a steady objectivity like traditional newswire services, but some Filters cross over into analysis. Filters are generally not prone to fits of pique or confrontation, and they occasionally produce their own journalistic work.

With some 7,000 readers following along daily, the Hacking Netflix blog is a great example of a Filter. Blogger Mike Kaltschnee began writing Hacking Netflix in November 2004 and has been posting three to five entries per day highlighting the business dealings of the popular DVD-by-mail subscription business ever since. Kaltschnee describes the genesis of the blog by saying,

> I started this site as an experiment in company and community relations, and it's grown a bit bigger than I expected. I'm a fan of Netflix® and wanted to learn more about the company, sharing what I found. Since I'm a "hack" writer and computer geek, HackingNetflix.com was the perfect name. It may have started as a "fan" site, but I've tried to make it more professional and even (shudder) "fair and balanced." I personally still lean towards Netflix a bit, but I think I'm like most journalists who have to set aside their feelings and be objective in their writing.[18]

With a sustained audience of this size, you can bet that NetFlix executives, along with those at Blockbuster and other DVD and video game rental companies, are paying attention to what Mike presents each day.

Fanatics

The true believers and evangelists dwell in the **Fanatics** category. While they may do some Filtering, they love to analyze a brand, product, organization, or person and prescribe courses of action. Fanatics will praise great company efforts, but they will also criticize mistakes and lapses in full view of the world.

For example, Keith (he doesn't disclose his last name) and his F1Fanatic blog (http://www.f1Fanatic.co.uk/) are focused on Formula One (F1) racing. While he does a fair amount of Filtering, you cannot escape Keith's opinions of Formula One races, drivers, teams, and equipment. Because racing is a business that relies on sponsorship, event promotion, and branding of drivers and their teams, an MPR professional in any organization that touches the sport of F1 must be aware of Keith and his fellow

---

Exhibit 6.3 We're familiar with sports fanatics, but fans exist for just about every interest or hobby you can imagine.

Lisa F. Young/Shutterstock.

Fanatics. This is not because their audience is large, but rather because it is highly targeted and will spread the word to those who really care.

Facilitators

Facilitators are community creators who are like the mayors of online towns. They provide a de facto support group for customers of certain products or simply bring fans of a given product together. The TiVo Community forum (http://www.tivocommunity.com) is an example of the former. Founder David Bott created this community to help fellow home-theater enthusiasts get the most out of their TiVo® systems. The community has more than 130,000 members. Several TiVo employees are visible regulars, although the community and the company are not affiliated with each other.

Myvettepage.com is a community for lovers of the Chevy Corvette®. This site is facilitated by MadVette publishing, owners of several other Corvette-related communities, and gives its members a wide array of possibilities for networking with those who share their obsession, as well as resources for finding parts, accessories, and Corvette-related events. Facilitators like Myvettepage.com are an information resource for a niche market segment of people who spend money feeding their Corvette passion and, therefore, they are an ideal venue for stories about related products.

Exhibit 6.4 Just like the noisemakers that give them their name, firecrackers can add some pop to a product's sales by creating a song, animation, video, or novelty that generates a lot of interest, but they tend to fade away just as fast.

Cyrus Bharucha/Shutterstock.

Firecrackers

Firecrackers are the "one-hit wonders" of Citizen Marketers. They typically attract considerable attention because they have created a song, animation, video, or novelty that generates a lot of interest but tends to die out quickly as their creators go on with their other work.

Despite the fact that Firecrackers tend to disappear as fast as they arrive, they can have a measurable impact on a slice of culture or business. In 2005, seventeen-year-old video blogger Melody Oliveria (a.k.a. Bowiechick) used software included with her Logitech webcam to superimpose cat whiskers, a mustache, a gas mask, and some funky hats on her head and face for a video she posted to YouTube.com. In the video she talked about the troubles of young love, but the whiskers, hats, and so on were the part of the posting that created waves of word-of-mouth. Thousands linked to her post, which was watched by about 1.2 million people. The response to this video was so overwhelming that she posted a second video to explain how she created these effects. While giving Bowiechick some fame, the video also fueled a 128 percent increase in sales of the Logitech® QuickCam® Orbit.

For marketers, Firecrackers can have a tremendous impact, both positive and negative, on product sales. However, they rise and fall so quickly that they are hard to find before they disappear, and there is usually nothing left to support once they are gone.

McConnell and Huba point to three commonalities shared by each category of Citizen Marketer:

1. *Personal expression.* Their opinions or journalism are their own and are designed to inform, entertain, or analyze a brand, product, or issue.
2. *Amateur status.* They are volunteers and are transparent about their motives and associations.
3. *Freely given.* Their work is not meant to steal money, time, or attention from the company of their affiliation. Rather they seek to enhance or improve the company or industry in question.

While many connectors—media and non-media alike—meet one of these criteria, they need to meet all three to truly be a Citizen Marketer.

MPR professionals need to weigh how the credibility of any given Citizen Marketer stacks up against traditional media. In addition, they need to understand the audience of the Citizen Marketer and know enough about any given one to make an educated guess about what he or she will do to any message that is turned over to him or her. The categories supply a basic tool for making the most of these connectors. Generally speaking, Filters want raw yet interesting content, while Fanatics want something that supports their position and stokes the enthusiasm of their audience. Facilitators want the ability to connect their audience to the firm or the firm's products in a meaningful way. Finally, Firecrackers are unique in that they are not predictable. A firm does not know when or why a Firecracker will emerge. The best that MPR professionals can do is to be aware of the world of Citizen Marketers that surround their products and support Firecrackers when they surface.

There is a growing temptation for firms to create their own Citizen Marketers, especially ones that appear to be Firecrackers. However, while many consumers enjoy participating in a community built upon the use or adoration of their favorite products, they have become adept at spotting phony Citizen Marketers and tend to look negatively upon them. As with other segments of business today, authenticity and transparency are important to customers.

Blogs

CHAPTER OBJECTIVE 7

Blogs and bloggers are in a unique position that makes them difficult for marketers to classify. They can be Citizen Marketers if they meet the three criteria. They can be non-media connectors if they are independent of any news medium, or they can be an extension of the media itself. Since blog posts can simultaneously act like a media mention, spur word-of-mouth, and increase product sales, marketers need to understand and pay attention to them. We can see an example of the effectiveness of blogs in a paper titled "Does Chatter Matter?" published by New York University Professor Vasant Dhar. Dhar

---

Key Terms

Offline word-of-mouth Information about products spread from consumer to consumer via face-to-face, telephone, or other non-electronic methods

studied how blog posts impacted the sale of music albums and found that, when an album received more than forty legitimate blog posts before being released, sales were three times the average. If the album was from a major label, sales increased fivefold.[19]

Despite the fact that bloggers may seem like professional journalists, not all of them are, and MPR professionals would be wise to understand this distinction. The primary difference between the two types of connectors is the way they embarked on their writing careers. While journalists are usually trained in the craft and have work experience in either print or broadcast media, bloggers are more likely to be subject specialists without any training in journalism.[20] This difference causes journalists and bloggers to react to marketers in different ways. For example, the former are more likely to understand and expect a certain protocol from marketers when they are pitching a story, while simultaneously being held to specific editorial standards by their medium and profession. The latter may not care for or even understand the way journalists and marketers have traditionally worked together and are not held to any standards but their own. However, since some professional journalists blog, and some media host amateur bloggers, there are no hard-and-fast rules for determining a procedure for working with bloggers.

Firms also have to decide whether they would benefit from engaging in blogging themselves. Blogs offer a vehicle for having a two-way conversation with stakeholders, help in maintaining a level of corporate transparency, and may assist in "humanizing" the company. On the other hand, they also require time and resources in order to live up to the criteria laid out by Dobele et al.

Cisco® uses blogs to communicate about issues that are important to its audiences. For example, the company's legal counsel leveraged a blog during the copyright infringement lawsuit over the name "iPhone." According to Jeannette Gibson, director of new media and operations in Cisco's corporate communications department, "There were a lot of unfavorable comments.... But new-media communication is important in terms of transparency. Be open, accept comments, engage, and respond. People may not agree with us, but they appreciate that we have a blog. Bloggers thanked us for blogging." She adds that blogs are generally viewed as authentic: "Companies don't blog—people do.... It's viewed and received much differently than a press release. It's a great complement to traditional communications."[21]

<table>
<tr><td>CHAPTER
OBJECTIVE
8</td><td></td></tr>
</table>

Online versus Offline Word-of-mouth

Spreading word-of-mouth online has had marketers' attention for some time. In fact, a 2006 study by the Keller Fay Group and OMD found that Americans participated in an impressive 245 million online word-of-mouth (WOM) conversations per day. However, the same study found that online WOM only accounts for about 7 percent of total word-of-mouth. Another 3 billion plus **offline word-of-mouth** conversations take place each day, consisting of 2.5 billion face-to-face conversations and 630 million more over the phone.[22] The co-authors of *The Influentials: One American in Ten Tells the Other Nine How to Vote, Where to Eat, and What to Buy*, Ed Keller and Jon Berry explain, "This means that in addition to online WOM efforts, marketers need to engage customer evangelists and influencers where they live, work, and shop by seeding products (product trials), creating in-store events, and providing opportunities for customers to congregate and share their impressions."[23]

Concept Case 6.4: **Customer Evangelists**

The Falcon's Lair instituted the "Best of the Nest Program" to foster word-of-mouth among ordinary people. This initiative includes discounts and promotions for existing customers who refer new customers to the store or who bring their friends to Falcon's Lair events. Customers will also be able to keep a hiking and climbing journal blog on the Lair's Web site free of charge, as long as they update it at least once every ninety days. Customers who don't want to keep a continuous blog can use the "Story Wall," a place where they can post a story about a spectacular hiking or climbing experience that they have had.

Questions:

1. Recommend other elements that The Falcon's Lair can add to the "Best of the Nest Program" to support word-of-mouth. Explain your recommendations.
2. In your opinion, is online or offline word-of-mouth more important to The Falcon's Lair? Why?

 Reflection Questions

1. How do non-media connectors differ from media? (Chapter Objective 1)

2. How does the perspective of NMCs impact the effectiveness of word-of-mouth marketing relative to other types of connectors? (Chapter Objective 2)

3. Discuss the essential elements for creating and sustaining viral word-of-mouth messages. (Chapter Objective 3)

4. Describe the impact that reference groups have on consumers and explain why. (Chapter Objective 4)

5. Compare and contrast experts and opinion leaders and list some examples of each. (Chapter Objective 5)

6. Discuss and explain each of the three criteria that an NMC must meet in order to be considered a Citizen Marketer. (Chapter Objective 6)

7. What are the four types of Citizen Marketers and why should marketing professionals be interested in them? (Chapter Objective 6)

8. Explain how blogs can be tools for either media connectors or NMCs. Can they can be a mixture of both at the same time? (Chapter Objective 7)

9. Will online word-of-mouth ever eclipse offline word-of-mouth in the number of conversations per day? Explain your answer. (Chapter Objective 8)

Key Terms

Citizen Marketer A hyperengaged consumer, not in the employ of any media outlet, freely giving a personal expression of the passion he or she has for a product or an industry (p. 92)

Expert A person with education and/or experience in a particular field, who is, typically, not a journalist (p. 90)

Facilitator A creator or facilitator of a community (usually online) designed either to be a de facto support group for customers of certain products or simply to bring fans of a given product together (p. 94)

Fanatic A consumer who acts like a product evangelist by continuously monitoring and analyzing a brand, product, organization, or person and prescribing subsequent courses of action (p. 93)

Filter A consumer who collects and shares traditional media stories, blogger's rants and raves, podcasts, or fan creations about a specific company or brand and then packages this information into a constant stream of links, story summaries, and observations (p. 92)

Firecracker A consumer who creates a song, animation, video, or novelty that generates a lot of short-term interest in a product. This interest dies out quickly as the consumer goes on with her other work. (p. 94)

Non-media connector A person who monitors, analyzes, and shares information about a product or industry. This person may be paid for her efforts, but she is not employed by a media organization. (p. 86)

Offline word-of-mouth Information about products spread from consumer to consumer via face-to-face, telephone, or other non-electronic methods (p. 96)

Opinion leader An individual whose attitudes, opinions, and behaviors greatly influence a group or society (p. 90)

Sphere of influence A term typically applied to nations, marketers use this term to refer to the audience that a connector reaches. (p. 86)

Viral marketing A marketing phenomenon that facilitates and encourages people to pass along a marketing message (p. 87)

Application Assignments

1. Keep a log of everything that you purchase during one week. Include the price you paid, where you shopped, and who was with you for each purchase. Note each purchase that was influenced by a non-media connector. For three of those purchases, give details on the NMCs involved and a description of how you were influenced.

2. Identify a word-of-mouth (viral) marketing effort. Give details of this campaign and state whether or not you found it to be effective. Finally compare the campaign to Dobele et al.'s criteria.

3. Interview a classmate, friend, or family member in order to collect demographic and psychographic information and to get details on three major purchases that he or she made within the last year. Then do some research and find at least five reference groups that may have influenced those purchases. Discuss your selections with the person you interviewed. Your report will need to include:

   a. A demographic/psychographic report on the interviewee

   b. A detailed description of the three major purchases

   c. At least five appropriate reference groups

   d. The interviewee's reaction to your selection

4. For one of the following industries, identify at least three experts and three opinion leaders. Explain why they have achieved their status, how they are able to influence consumers, and how marketers can benefit from their presence.

   a. Automotive (Retail)

   b. Entertainment

    c. Fashion

    d. Food

    e. Travel

5. Identify three Citizen Marketers and explain how they meet the criteria. State which type of Citizen Marketer each one is and why. Finally, explain the impact you believe each has on the product or industry with which he or she affiliates. (Hint: Technorati's list of blogs is a great place to start: http://technorati.com/blogs/directory.)

 ## Practice Portfolio

This Practice Portfolio can be based on a fictitious company or on a real company that your instructor assigns to you. (If you used a company in previous Practice Portfolio exercises, continue to use that company.) Add your completed assignment to your portfolio to present to prospective employers.

- Write a short statement describing how your product is fun or intriguing and explaining why, in general, NMCs need to share your story with their audience.

- Using the target market you defined in Chapter 4 as your guide, list the types of reference groups you might use to reach your audience. List an example of each.

- Explain how experts and opinion leaders influence your target market during the buying process. Give an example of an expert and an opinion leader whom you believe will influence this audience.

- Devise a preliminary plan for creating online and offline word-of-mouth using Citizen Marketers by explaining how you can get people to spread the message about your product.

CHAPTER **7**

Building a Connector List

CHAPTER OBJECTIVES
After studying this chapter, you should be able to:

1. Describe how the selection of a connector can dictate the makeup of an audience and how that audience perceives a message.

2. Explain the process of identifying individual connector organizations that contribute to meeting your MPR goals.

3. Evaluate individual media and non-media connectors for use in an MPR effort.

4. Identify and navigate several sources to find connectors.

5. Match specific people within connector organizations to your message.

6. List and explain the pertinent data elements of a connector list.

7. Discuss the reasons that a media list changes over time.

8. Explain the process of choosing connectors for a specific MPR campaign.

Ecover®, a worldwide distributor and manufacturer of ecological household cleaning products based in Belgium, wanted to introduce its new fabric softener, Sunny Day, in a fun and interesting way. To do this, the company hired the Clean Agency, which kicked things off by throwing a "laundry launch party." The agency invited the press and consumers and provided guests with concierge-level laundry assistance—that is, people to actually do the guests' laundry for them.

"This event required pulling together a very targeted regional contact list; it was particularly important to get green media," says Kathy Kniss, director of public relations for Clean. "To drive awareness for the event, we tapped new media connectors at *IdealBite*, *VitalJuiceDaily*, *Smart2Bgreen*, and *ApartmentTherapy*."

Kniss continues:

> We also wanted to get some coverage in traditional media.... Papers really have to compete for readership these days so they can win the local advertising dollars and stay afloat. By promoting events in their own backyard, they demonstrate loyalty to local businesses that will hopefully translate into advertising dollars. Therefore, we really had to know the local media market.

The event took place in a relatively small corner of the sprawling Los Angeles region, so Clean pulled contacts from smaller, local papers like the *Culver City News*, *Wave Newspapers*, and *Blue Pacific Breeze*. The public relations team contacted the features departments in order to encourage reporters to attend the event and, ultimately, generate some post-event editorials. Kniss also explains:

> We pulled together planning editors at all the local broadcast news stations.... Knowing that the local CBS affiliate in Los Angeles tends to give coverage to fun, neighborhood events and that the NBC affiliate is more likely to cover more serious breaking news was a tremendous help to us in conducting this portion of our campaign.

As a result of this campaign, Ecover saw millions of **circulation impressions**, and sales of Sunny Day rose 25 percent. "In a down turned economy, this is amazing!" exclaims Kniss:

> Sunny Day continues to land more mainstream shelf space as well, like the seventy-five southern California Ralphs stores it is currently in, in addition to national distribution among natural/health food stores like Whole Foods Market, Wild Oats, etc. And since Ecover doesn't do much traditional advertising, you can be sure that a majority of sales ARE generated through PR and word-of-mouth.

Courtesy of Ecover

101

<table>
<tr><td>CHAPTER
OBJECTIVE
1</td></tr>
</table>

Connectors and their Audiences

Not all connectors (media, bloggers, and those influential people who spread the word about products of all kinds) are appropriate channels for delivering a Marketing Public Relations message. The type of media (TV, print, electronic), the specific outlet, and the individual journalist or non-media connector (NMC) influence the way consumers perceive the message.

Up to this point we have discussed connectors' ability to reach a target market, but we must also consider how an audience reacts to different channels. To illustrate this concept, ask yourself what type of media have more credibility with an audience: national TV news, local TV news, local newspapers, national magazines, or blogs? Hopefully, you realized that you can only answer this question if you know something about the people who make up the audience and the message being sent.

For example, if we look at business news, we find that one-third of people under age 30 get most of their business news on TV; another third turn mostly to newspapers; and 27 percent rely mostly on the Web. By comparison, people ages fifty to sixty-four rely primarily on TV for business news, while most people age sixty-five and older count on newspapers to keep up with what's going on in the business world.[1]

Likewise, people turn to different media types for different reasons. For example, more people turn to the Internet when

---

Exhibit 7.1 Pew Age-News Source Chart shows differences in media consumption by age group.

Web Meets, Exceeds Newspapers as Main Source for Young

Main source of...	18–29 %	30–49 %	50–64 %	65+ %
International news				
TV	65	61	72	77
Newspapers	20	21	26	36
Internet	25	26	15	3
National news				
TV	63	63	74	77
Newspapers	23	26	25	36
Internet	21	19	13	2
Local gov't news				
TV	48	46	39	47
Newspapers	42	50	58	64
Internet	12	7	4	1
Business news				
TV	33	39	51	41
Newspapers	33	30	38	62
Internet	27	25	14	3
Sports news				
TV	65	73	67	74
Newspapers	22	20	39	40
Internet	20	16	8	2
Entertainment news				
TV	62	60	60	64
Newspapers	13	19	29	43
Internet	25	20	11	2
Commentary & opinion				
TV	37	54	69	67
Newspapers	10	19	16	24
Internet	35	17	9	2

Percentages based on people also follow news about each topic, and add to more than 100% because respondents could name more than one main source.

Source: The Pew Charitable Trusts

Exhibit 7.2 People look to different media depending on what they are looking for at a particular moment.

What Features Distinguish Different News Media

	What sets apart...		
	TV news %	News- papers %	Inter- net %
Features of the Medium	37	46	60
Convenient/Accessible/Quick	14	32	39
Like to watch/read/visual	19	5	2
Easy to use/navigate	–	7	25
Coverage and Content	52	42	40
Specific subjects of interest	22	26	5
Has more in-depth coverage	5	12	11
Updated/breaking news	13	–	14
Concise/brief/to the point	11	–	–
Diversity of sources	6	–	10

Based on regular news consumers of each medium.

Source: The Pew Charitable Trusts

they want news quickly, to both TV and the Internet for breaking news, and to newspapers and the Internet when they are looking for in-depth coverage of a subject.

Since there is a multitude of available MPR opportunities for any firm or campaign, a company's connector list needs to be correspondingly diverse in order to span all of the media types that reach its target audience. A recent study by Advertiser Perceptions showed that when consumers are exposed to a broad spectrum of connector types, rather than one medium alone, they are more likely to express an intent to purchase products such as consumer electronics, apparel, automobiles, beer, and toiletries.[2]

Of course, all occasions to garner media mentions or word-of-mouth are not fit for all connector types. Clearly, if your story depends on showing a product in action, television and Internet-based media are going to be your best choice. If you need to include lots of detail, then print may have an edge. For short "news you can use"-type stories that can be translated into a person's everyday life, such as pocketbook issues, health information, and safety tips, radio is a good platform.[3]

Identifying Connector Organizations

CHAPTER
OBJECTIVE
2

Selecting connector types is only the first part of the process of creating a media list. The next step is identifying the individual outlets that can help you meet your MPR objectives. As Michelle Metzger, senior manager of communications for Entrust®, a security software company based in Dallas, Texas, says,

> Remember, if you're going to get the golden egg of this third party credibility, it only helps if it's in a publication or on a broadcast outlet that reaches your target customers or stakeholders.... Want to sell your stock? Make sure all the financial wires and outlets are on your connector list. Need to sell to IT folks? Then have the top reporters from the trade publications on the list. Need to sell tickets to a concert? Target the radio stations that match the genre of music your artists perform.

Before beginning to add connector organizations, remember that the outlets that pick up an MPR story not only bring the story to their audience, but they also influence the message by the way they report that story and by the image they have with the public. For example, *The New York Times* is known for in-depth coverage and is perceived to have an intellectual style, while *USA Today's* coverage is concise and has a style that aims to appeal to the masses. As a result, you need to anticipate not only how the medium will present your story, but also how the medium's reputation will impact the audience's perception of that story. With the understanding of how an individual medium can change the presentation and perception of a story in mind, you need to find connectors and then evaluate them to ensure that they reach your target audience and are appropriate for your message.

Key Terms

Circulation impressions The number of times the story was covered multiplied by the circulation of the publications in which it was covered

The easiest and most effective way to find appropriate connectors is to ask your customers about their media consumption. Inc.com suggests that you ask your customers the following questions:

- To which TV programs, radio shows, newspapers, magazines, journals, and association newsletters do you pay attention?
- What are your professional affiliations?
- What personal interests, such as sports, travel, and hobbies, do you pursue?
- What is on your must-read list?
- What media keep you current professionally?
- Who are your favorite reporters? [4]

To ensure that you uncover non-media connectors as well, be sure to include questions about the blogs your customers read, Web sites they frequent, and social media networks (LinkedIn, Facebook, MySpace, etc.) they have joined. Compiling this list will reveal some obvious connectors and, perhaps, point the way to others to explore. Pay close attention to the connectors that customers mention most often and to those identified by your best customers.

In addition to asking customers, MPR professionals also turn to their colleagues and connectors with whom they have worked in the past for recommendations of connectors for their media list.

Finally, MPR professionals supplement their lists by utilizing any of a number of commercial PR databases, several of which are discussed in "PR Databases and Directories" later in this chapter (see page 108). These resources can range from simple lists of media outlets to complex databases providing detailed information about media and non-media outlets and the people working within them. Many database organizations also provide other services in conjunction with list creation and management, like PR distribution and tracking.

Concept Case 7.1: **Selecting Appropriate Media**

The managers of The Falcon's Lair have decided to concentrate their connector list on print and electronic media. They reason that the experience of hiking and climbing for both hardcore and recreational participants needs to be covered in a fair amount of detail. Therefore, a thirty-second to three-minute story on a broadcast medium would not have the desired impact on the audience. They also agreed that still images of hiking and climbing appear to be exciting to both target markets, while the audience might perceive video of people hiking or climbing to be boring and uninspiring.

Questions:
1. Are the assumptions about print and electronic media and their appropriateness for The Falcon's Lair connectors list correct? Explain why you support or reject these assumptions.
2. What opportunities are the managers of The Falcon's Lair missing by ignoring other connector types? Explain how you think they might take advantage of other types of connectors. Be specific.

Evaluating Connector Organizations

CHAPTER
OBJECTIVE
3

Using customers and colleagues to identify connectors is also an informal way to evaluate those connectors, by giving you a basic idea of the promotional channels that reach your audience and why. In most cases, however, you will want more detail about the connectors on your list and their audiences. You can find the type of information you will need to evaluate a connector from the following three major sources:

- The connectors themselves
- Third-party auditing firms
- PR databases and directories

Finding Connectors

CHAPTER
OBJECTIVE
4

Individual connectors, especially media companies, publish information regarding their audience in a collection of documents commonly referred to as a **media kit**.[5] Companies create media kits to aid in the sale of advertising for a medium, but they are useful for MRP practitioners as well. For example, *Cosmopolitan* magazine breaks down its readership by age, income, education, marital status, and employment. *Cosmo* also uses these demographic factors to compare itself to its top competitors, such as *Glamour*, *Vogue*, and *Elle.*

This type of information is extremely helpful when you are creating a connector list, because it gives you a better understanding of the medium's audiences and offers some insight into other media that touch the same audience. However, you must remember that the numbers provided by a medium are not always verifiable and are often presented in a manner that is favorable to that medium.

Third-party Auditing Firms

Exploring third-party media audits is instructive and likely to provide a more objective look at a medium's audience. Each major media type has at least one **audit bureau** that validates audience data. The most commonly recognized of these auditing services is Nielsen Media Research®, which is known for measuring television audiences. Table 7.1 is a sample of media auditing companies spanning television, radio, print, and electronic (interactive) media.

Most auditing companies provide some behavioral and psychographic information in addition to detailed demographic profiles, but the types of information vary from audit bureau to audit bureau and even from medium to medium. Although these reports are

---

Key Terms

Media kit A package of promotional materials relating to a specific advertising media vehicle, including the rate card, audience statistics, case studies showing success stories, and related materials

Audit bureau An independent organization that verifies audience reach and demographics for media outlets

Exhibit 7.3 This profile shows marketers who are reading just *Cosmopolitan*.

COUNT on
COSMO

Demographic Profile

	Total Adults (000) 18,359 Readers Per Copy 6.91	Total Women (000) 15,315 Readers Per Copy 5.76	
Women	**Audience (000)**	**Comp (%)**	**Index**
Age			
18–24	4,464	29.1	239
25–34	4,603	30.1	174
18–34	9,067	59.2	201
35–49	3,813	24.9	86
Median	31.0		
IEI			
$20,000+	7,227	47.2	121
$25,000+	6,035	39.4	118
Median	$27,247		
HHI			
$30,000+	11,784	76.9	106
$40,000+	10,193	66.6	106
Median	$57,940		
Education			
Attended/Graduated College+	9,749	63.7	117
Employment			
Total Employed	11,012	71.9	124
Full–Time	8,404	54.9	125
Marital Status			
Single	6,450	42.1	191
Married	6,305	41.2	76
Div/Wid/Sep	2,559	16.7	70
Other			
Women w/ children	8,391	54.8	125
Working women w/ children	5,802	37.9	132
County			
A/B	11,358	74.2	104
C/D	3,957	25.8	90

COSMOPOLITAN

Source: Hearst Magazines.

compiled primarily for advertising purposes, they are equally useful for MPR. The challenge for the MPR professional, however, is that most audit bureaus charge for this information. As a result, small companies or PR agencies may not be able to access the reports they need. Fortunately, companies included in an audit report have copies of these reports and will usually post them to their Web sites or are willing to share them if asked. (Hint: To obtain an audit statement, you'll often have to look into the "Advertising" or media kit section of a medium's Web site or speak to an advertising rep.)

Non-media connectors that do their work both electronically and face-to-face often escape the view of auditing bureaus, which means that you have to do your homework before adding these outlets to your list. A combination of surveying your customers, speaking directly to the connectors, and spending some time with the connector's claimed audience is the best way to ensure that a channel truly reaches a specific audience. A few ways to confirm the audience of a non-audited NMC include the following:

- If the NMC blogs or has another form of Web presence, ask for its Web traffic data.
- Visit the interactive area of the NMC's Web site (if it has one) and see how many people are leaving comments. In addition, try to get a handle on the

Exhibit 7.4 Here *Cosmopolitan* compares its readers to those of its competition.

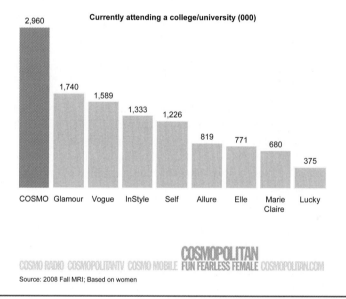

Source: Hearst Magazines.

profile of the visitors and explore the kinds of comments or dialogue that is present.

- If the NMC sells information products like books, CDs, or DVDs based on its area of expertise, ask the connector for sales numbers and a demographic profile of its customers.
- If the NMC publishes a newsletter based on its area of expertise, ask for sales numbers and a demographic profile of its subscribers.
- If the NMC delivers speeches, gives seminars or regularly attends events, ask for a listing of this activity and verify it by attending some events or checking with event hosts.

These connectors tend to have a smaller audience than outlets that are externally audited, but the savvy MPR professional is not daunted by audience size or the rigors of evaluating these channels. If the MPR professional chooses them properly, these NMCs can

Table 7.1

Audit Bureau	Media Audited	Website
BPA	Print	www.bpaww.com
Nielsen Company	Television	www.nielsenmedia.com
Nielsen-Netratings	Online	www.nielsen-netrating.com
Arbitron	Radio	www.arbitron.com
Commscore	Online	www.comscore.com
Audit Bureau of Circulations (ABC)	Print	www.accessabc.com

be highly targeted and productive. As Susan Payton, managing partner for Egg Marketing & Public Relations of Orlando, Florida, explains,

> Bloggers have recently been added to the media lists we prepare for clients, and here's why.... Most of my clients will never get on *Oprah* on the front cover of *Entrepreneur Magazine*. But their chances for great online coverage through blogs are very high. Bloggers are always looking for material (sometimes even daily). By sending them a press release, pitch, or product to review, we're making their work easier.

PR Databases and Directories

There are many resources available to assist MPR professionals in creating a connector list. These resources range from basic to exhaustive in the amount of data that they provide, and the price to acquire them ranges from free to quite expensive. The following are samples of such resources:

- *Blog Catalog*: Blog directory, http://www.blogcatalog.com/directory (Free)
- *Burrelles Luce*: On-demand media monitoring, research, distribution, and evaluation services, http://www.burrellesluce.com
- *Business Wire*®: News distribution service, http://www.businesswire.com
- *Cision*: On-demand media monitoring, research, distribution, and evaluation services, http://www.cision.com
- *Marketwire/Media Hub*: On-demand media monitoring, research, distribution, and evaluation services, http://www.marketwire.com
- *Media Contacts Pro*: Downloadable database, http://www.mediacontactspro.com
- *Mondo Times*™: Media directory, http://www.mondotimes.com (Free)
- *News Link*: Media directory, http://www.newslink.org (Free)
- *Podcast Zoom*: Podcast directory, http://www.podcastzoom.com
- *PR Newswire*: News distribution service, http://www.prnewswire.com

Exhibit 7.5 Auditing statements provide marketers with an unbiased source for evaluating a medium.

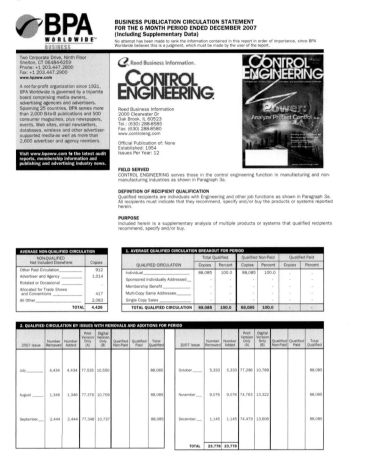

Source: BPA Worldwide and Reed Business Information.

- *PR Web®*: News distribution service, http://www.prweb.com
- *Technorati*: Blog directory, http://technorati.com (Free)
- *USNPL*: Media directory, http://www.usnpl.com
- *Vocus®*: On-demand media monitoring, research, distribution, and evaluation services, http://www.vocus.com
- *Yahoo® Directory/News and Media*: Media directory, http://dir.yahoo.com/News_and_Media (Free)

Using these tools and others like them is essential for the modern marketing professional. The tools, however, cannot replace experience and relationships. Only you will know your story intimately enough to know how you want it to be portrayed and to which audience. Over time you will also know which connectors will be interested in a topic and which will not. Databases, systems, and services make the creation and management of a connector list easier, but they are not a substitute for critical thinking. According to Kip Patrick, senior communications officer at Pew Charitable Trusts:

> While databases remain invaluable tools in the media relations arsenal, these sources should serve only as a first step in creating a useful media list. . . . Solid practitioners are familiar with the outlets they are trying to reach and are regular readers of the reporters they want to target. Certainly there are times when a wide distribution list is necessary (a national product launch, for example), and the PR person may not know every contact on a list. However, these instances should be the exception, not the rule.

CHAPTER
OBJECTIVE
5

Drilling Down to the People Level

Selecting a media outlet is not the final step in creating a connector list. The list is not complete until you have recorded specifics about individuals to whom you plan to target your message and with whom you hope to create lasting relationships. This means getting to know both the people who produce the content and their work. As Alissa Pinck, vice president and general manager of JS^2 Communications in New York, says:

> You need to go beyond the beat. . . . For example, someone might come up (in a database) as a food reporter. However, when you read their pitching tips, you see that they don't cover food at all—they cover housewares. This is helpful both because you can eliminate the wrong contacts and add the right ones.

Andrew Dumont, vice president of tatango.com, a technology company based in Bellingham, Washington, recommends starting small:

> If you are new to PR, start with the smaller media contacts to learn what editors look for; don't go straight for the *Wall Street Journal*. . . . It's very important to pick the right editor for your story. Know what an editor has covered before so when it comes time to make a pitch, you can refer to previous articles done by that editor that relate to your company.

Getting the connector list right at the people level saves time when you are pitching connectors and following up on pitches, because it limits the numbers of pitches and follow-up contacts you need to make. It also shows respect for the connectors by decreasing the chance that you will send them a story idea that is of no interest to them.

CHAPTER
OBJECTIVE
6

The Elements of a Connector List

The more thorough a media list is, the more effective it will be. It is a tool for managing relationships and helps ensure that you are getting the right message to the right audience. Therefore, it is important to be certain that your connector list has the right elements for your firm. Each list should have two parts: the first concentrates on the connector organizations and the second on the people within those organizations.

Organizations

The following are typical items that are included on the organization portion of most connector lists:

- Connector organization name (e.g., *Time Magazine, The Huffington Post*)
- Connector type (broadcast, print, etc.)
- Connector subject (business, art, politics, etc.)
- Audience demographics and psychographics (These will vary by firm and may include age, income, education, or lifestyle.)
- **Reach**[6] (viewership, readership, circulation, listenership, page views)
- Geography (national, DMA, state)
- **Frequency**[7] (quarterly, monthly, weekly, daily)
- Rank in market (e.g., number 2 local news in Philadelphia DMA)
- Lead time (how far in advance the connector needs information in order to include a story in a given issue or broadcast)
- Address
- Web site
- Notes (It is helpful to have an open field to record observations about an outlet that cannot be quantified in another fashion. This is a good area in which to make notes on relationships with a medium and to identify stories the organization has already run for your firm.)

Each of these elements allows you to quickly sort through your list when attempting to find the right connectors for a specific campaign. Most lists will also assist you in formulating your pitch and follow-up with individuals within connector organizations.

Individuals

Each list should include similar information about each journalist, editor, or producer on the list. Elements of this portion of the list include:

- Name
- Address
- E-mail
- Phone

Key Terms

Reach The number of different persons or households exposed to a particular advertising media vehicle or a media schedule during a specified period of time. Also called *cumulative audience, cumulative reach, net audience, net reach, net unduplicated audience*, or *unduplicated audience*, reach is often presented as a percentage of the total number of persons in a specified audience or target market.

Frequency The number of times a person, household, or member of a target market is exposed to a media vehicle or an advertiser's media schedule within a given period of time, usually expressed as an average frequency (the average number of exposures during the time period) or as a frequency distribution (the number of people exposed once, twice, three times, etc.)

- Fax
- Preferred method of contact (phone, fax, e-mail, text message)
- Blog (Even if blogging is not their primary duty, many connectors have a blog. MPR professionals can improve their understanding of a connector by keeping up to date with a connector's blog.)
- Beat
- History (a digest of stories they did or did not cover for you)
- Pitching tips (insight that you have gained from experience or an external source regarding the best way to pitch a story to this connector)

This list is not comprehensive, and MPR professionals typically add items to and subtract items from their list over time. The main point, however, is that the list can be a tool for finding the right connectors for a story and for supporting your ongoing relationship with them. Lists can be kept on paper, in a Rolodex®, on a computer spreadsheet or database, or hosted on the Web by a third-party information company. Regardless of its physical form, a good list will always serve the same purposes.

Concept Case 7.2: **Journalists and Bloggers**

Since most of The Falcon's Lair customer base lives or works in Lehigh and Northampton counties in Pennsylvania (also known as the Lehigh Valley), the Lair's management team has decided to start its connector list by adding journalists and editors from the local newspaper, *Morning Call*. The managers have chosen the following connectors:

- Christian Berg, outdoor writer who also writes the Lehigh Valley Wild blog. Berg covers hunting, fishing, camping, and other recreational outdoor activities, primarily run in the sports section.
- Tyrone Richardson, "Retail Watch" column and blog. Richardson covers the business happenings of retail outlets and may be a good contact for announcing events.
- Jody Duckett, assistant features editor. From exploring the paper's archive, the managers conclude that Duckett often oversees the writing of freelance journalists who produce in-depth stories about entertainment and events.

While the selection of connectors at the local paper seemed fairly simple, the managers are having a harder time with bloggers and non-media connectors. Their gut feeling is that these groups would be a natural match for The Falcon's Lair, but they are not sure where to begin.

Questions:
1. Are there any additional beats, journalists, or editors that The Falcon's Lair managers should have included? If so, name the ones that are appropriate and explain why. (Hint: Explore http://www.mcall.com.)
2. Go to your local newspaper and create a list of beats, journalists, and editors for The Falcon's Lair.
3. Use the Web and the list of resources provided earlier in the chapter to identify two bloggers and two non-blogging, non-media connectors for The Falcon's Lair. Explain why you have chosen each.

List Evolution

CHAPTER
OBJECTIVE
7

As noted above, a connector list is not a static document; in fact, it constantly changes. Since its inception, the media business has been dynamic. Reporters, editors, and producers have been known to change the subjects they cover as well as the media for which they work. Recently, the industry itself has been in great upheaval. Traditional media companies are consolidating operations, while new, non-traditional outlets are springing up all the time. As a result, it is more important than ever for MPR professionals to keep their lists up to date. As Michelle Metzger says,

> Just like the general public they serve, media outlets can be fickle when it comes to their editorial staffs. Inevitably, reporters work their way up the food chain—either at their current outlet or another one....The good news is that if you maintain a good relationship with them while they're on their way up, you can bet they will remember you were a trusted source when they get there. Also, beats are always changing depending on the mood of an audience, so once you have built your list, keep in regular contact with connectors.

Using Your Connector List

CHAPTER
OBJECTIVE
8

Since every MPR campaign has its own set of goals, it will also use a specific set of connectors. That is to say, you will rarely use every connector on your list for a single campaign. One reason for creating a campaign-specific list may be that the story is extremely beat- or industry-focused. In that case, you will not want to waste people's time by pitching them something they are not interested in covering. You also might consider employing only a certain channel to best portray your message. For example, if your story needs to show something in motion to make its point, you will likely include only television and electronic connectors on your list. When you are dealing with breaking news, you will likely employ the television and electronic media again, but this time you are using them for their ability to get out the word quickly rather than for their video format. If you require lots of detail, you may opt for a combination of print and electronic media.

To ensure that you gather the right names for a specific campaign, consider the following six steps for creating your contact list:

1. *Think.* No amount of technology can replace good thinking. Think about what you're trying to say (message) and to whom you're trying to say it (media). Then conduct your list-building based on well-defined criteria.

2. *Consider.* How you are willing to tell your story (i.e., in pictures, in written words, in audio interviews, in television interviews) will determine what types of media you can approach. Is your story visual? Great! You can pursue online, print, television, and possibly radio coverage (assuming the radio station has a Web site). If the story isn't visual (or can't be made visual), exclude television from your list.

3. *Define.* Define the universe of likely media appeal. Consider building an outlet list first and then search within the outlet list for appropriate contacts.

4. *Edit.* Once the software of your choice generates a media list based on your initial good thinking about job role, publication type, etc., it is time to edit the list. Review each reporter's profile to make sure that he or she is indeed appropriate for your list.

5. *Review.* Ask, "Who did I miss?" Did you include a general news assignment e-mail address? If not, go to the outlet profile and look for one. If you find it, add it to your contact list.

6. *Check.* When possible, ask someone else to give your list a final check. A fresh set of eyes can only help.

Remember that your list is your primary tool for managing your relationships with connectors and for linking your story to its audience. Without a well-constructed and up-to-date list, all other facets of MPR execution are starting with a handicap.[8]

An example of good list creation and use is the campaign conducted by Clean Agency for consumer green tech start-up Cyber-Rain. Clean's public relations department outlined a three-tiered traditional outreach strategy that included pulling together contacts from niche media, regional newspapers, and men's magazines.

The focus of the campaign was the introduction of Cyber-Rain's feature product, the XCI smart sprinkler controller, a device that helps homeowners save money on their landscape watering bills. At the time of launch, the XCI was only available online, so reaching online media outlets was a top priority. Using Vocus media services, a Web-based software tool, the public relations team searched relevant keywords such as *tech*, *gadget*, *gizmo*, *cyber*, *IT*, *smart*, and *computer* among online outlets in the database to pull together an initial list of editors, writers, and reporters who might be interested in receiving news about the new product. After a brief round of qualifying the media through phone calls and e-mails, the team had a dedicated list of approximately 100 persons with relevant beats.

Exhibit 7.6 A multi-tiered approach to building a connector list enabled Cyber Rain to launch a new product with lots of media exposure, but not paid advertising.

ShutterStock

"Not only did a strong connector list get us editorial placement on MSNBC.com, NYtimes.com, and Boston.com (*Boston Globe*), we also got a trickledown effect," explains Kniss. "Recognition by the larger media supported our efforts with bloggers who began gathering information to share with their audience."

The trickle down came in the form of blog posts on Engadget, GizmoDiva, and ApartmentTherapy. Kniss notes that these bloggers became new connectors that she added to the company's list:

> We also went after the tried and true method of reaching out to men's magazines. We compiled a mixed list of tech and home contacts among such publications as Men's Journal, Playboy, and Hooters.... Because XCI is a gadget that requires a person to be a homeowner with a sprinkler system already in place, we skewed the target demographic of the magazines to those men aged 35 and older, which, for the most part, ignores outlets such as Maxim and Stuff.

Like the Ecover campaign, Cyber-Rain used no traditional advertising, only PR and word-of-mouth. Kniss concludes:

> We are still calculating impressions now, but they are in the double-digit millions just in the last 10 months. Enough units have been sold in California alone to account for more than 10 million gallons of water saved. Prominent placement in the *New York Times, LA Times, MSNBC, Weather Channel* and *Men's Journal* has certainly helped legitimize the company and make it attractive to venture capitalists, as well as to the BMW design-works group who will be designing their next generation controllers.

 ## Reflection Questions

1. Give examples of how different delivery channels (e.g., media) affect how audiences perceive a news story. (Chapter Objective 1)

2. What are the factors that contribute to the selection of individual connector organizations for a connector list? (Chapter Objective 2)

3. Discuss the criteria used by marketers to evaluate a connector organization and the three major sources of information used in the evaluation process. (Chapter Objective 3)

4. Explain why it is important to identify the individuals within a connector organization and discuss some strategies for selecting these individuals. (Chapter Objective 4)

5. Discuss why audience demographics, reach, and frequency are critical elements of a connector list. (Chapter Objective 5)

6. Describe the limitations of connector list databases and the marketer's role in overcoming them. (Chapter Objective 6)

7. Discuss the factors that contribute to the need to update connector lists frequently. (Chapter Objective 7)

8. Explain why marketers rarely use all of the connectors on their list for an individual campaign, and discuss some rules of thumb for tailoring a list to a campaign. (Chapter Objective 8)

Chapter Key Terms

Audit bureau An independent organization that verifies audience reach and demographics for media outlets (p. 105)

Circulation impressions The number of times the story was covered multiplied by the circulation of the publications in which it was covered. (p. 103)

Frequency The number of times a person, household, or member of a target market is exposed to a media vehicle or an advertiser's media schedule within a given period of time; usually expressed as an average frequency (the average number of exposures during the time period) or as a frequency distribution (the number of people exposed once, twice, three times, etc.) (p. 111)

Media kit A package of promotional materials relating to a specific advertising media vehicle, including the rate card, audience statistics, case studies showing success stories, and related materials[9] (p. 105)

Reach The number of different persons or households exposed to a particular advertising media vehicle or a media schedule during a specified period of time. Also called *cumulative audience, cumulative reach, net audience, net reach, net unduplicated audience*, or *unduplicated audience*, reach is often presented as a percentage of the total number of persons in a specified audience or target market. (p. 111)

Application Assignments

1. Watch a local television news broadcast and read a local newspaper on the same day, noting all of the stories that are covered in both media. Then explain how the connector type (TV versus newspaper) affected the way the story was covered and how the respective audiences perceived the coverage.

2. Explore the business magazines *BusinessWeek*, *Forbes*, and *Fortune*, their respective Web sites, and media kits. Then compare and contrast them relative to the types of stories they cover, their style, and their audience, as well as their reach and frequency.

3. Select one of the topics below and use technorati.com to create a list of blogs that might be interested in covering a story on that topic.

    a. Professor discovers sea sickness cure can be derived from a common industrial waste product.

    b. A major software company and the U.S. Department of Education team up to supply computers to underprivileged school districts.

    c. The American Public Power Association and the Association of International Automobile Manufacturers announce plans to replace 25 percent of the world's gasoline-powered cars with electric-powered cars by 2025.

4. You are the Marketing Public Relations manager for a company that just produced a new combination photo-video camera. The camera uses a new technology that is unmatched in its ability to record sporting events and live performances, as well as to produce studio-quality still photos. The launch of this product is expected to take your company from obscurity to a leader in the market. Create a list of reporters, bloggers, and editors at *The New York Times* that you would include on your connector list and explain why you have included each. (Your instructor may assign your local newspaper or another periodical in place of *The New York Times*.)

5. Find a specific example of changes in the media business over the last decade, and explain how those changes affect MPR professionals in creating and maintaining a connector list.

Practice Portfolio

This Practice Portfolio can be based on a fictitious company or on a real company that your instructor assigns to you. (If you used a company in previous Practice Portfolio exercises, continue to use that company.) Add your completed assignment to your portfolio to present to prospective employers.

- Using one or more of the sources listed in "PR Databases and Directories," in conjunction with material supplied by individual connectors and auditing bureaus, create a comprehensive media list for your company. Briefly describe why you chose each connector.

CHAPTER **8**

The Press Kit and Press Release

CHAPTER OBJECTIVES

After studying this chapter, you should be able to:

1. Explain the elements and purpose of a press kit.

2. Describe the content and purposes of backgrounders, fact sheets, and FAQs.

3. Write an effective backgrounder.

4. Write effective fact sheets and FAQs.

5. Describe the types of supporting material that can be included in a press kit and explain their importance.

6. Compare and contrast traditional versus electronic press kits.

7. Describe the different purposes of a press release.

8. Explain the major elements of a press release and how they contribute to the release's effectiveness.

9. Write an effective press release.

10. Describe a video news release, its purpose, and the controversy surrounding VNRs.

CLASSIC AND CUTTING EDGE *The Learning Channel*

In 2000, when The Learning Channel decided to launch an American version of the British home improvement television show *Changing Room,* there was a lot of skepticism both in the press and the viewing public. The concern was how American audiences would receive a British format. According to Bronagh Hanley of Big Noise PR in San Francisco, "In order to introduce the Americanized version of the show and the unusual concept of homeowners trading houses for a weekend to redo a room in the other's home, we developed a very visual and graphic press kit to introduce the concept, the host, and the designers."

The press kit cover for the U.S. show, *Trading Spaces,* included before and after designs from completed shows and photos of the host and the designers, along with a tagline: "Two teams, two days, $1,000." The press kit itself included a release outlining the show's premise, a fact sheet on the show's format, bios on the host and designers, and glossy photos of the before and after images from the first two episodes. "We also included two of the trademark smocks the homeowners wear on the show to generate buzz," continues Hanley. "We included VHS copies of the first two episodes of the program for pre-air review."

The response from the press was overwhelmingly positive, and calls started coming in immediately with press members even requesting that *Trading Spaces* come to their town. "The demand for interviews with the show's host was incredible and the designers became overnight sensations," exclaimed Hanley.

The press kit and the smocks made their way onto eBay® and fan sites started popping up on the Internet. The press kit and **press release**[1] effectively communicated the show's talent and concepts, as well as generated buzz about a new sensation. The positive results came from the marketers' recognition that connectors had to understand not only the background of the story, but why it was interesting to their audience. In addition, *Trading Spaces*' MPR team equipped the connectors with the tools they needed to engage their constituents effectively.

Through the power of well-executed marketing public relations, supported by a press kit that used both visual and written reinforcement, a new television concept was introduced to the American audience. Subsequently, *Trading Spaces* has joined the ranks of British shows like *Who Wants to Be a Millionaire* and *The Office* that were successfully adapted for the U.S. market.

The Press Kit

In Chapter 7 we discussed the information package known as the media kit. Media companies prepare this kit to inform advertisers about their audience and to give them specifications for submitting ads. However, the term *media kit* can also refer to information that organizations compile for the purpose of informing media outlets and other connectors about their firm, brands, products, employees, and activities. In this book, we will refer to this usage as a **press kit**.

Press kits can exist in paper or electronic forms and can be distributed in person, by mail, via e-mail, or be posted to a Web site. In any case, they serve both as an introduction of a company to a connector and as an ongoing resource for media in their coverage of a firm. Elements of the press kit include the following:

- Documents illustrating the background of the firm and interesting facts about it
- Evidence of previous press coverage
- Support materials, including studies and statistics
- Graphics, such as photos and video

Press kits are primarily produced to support a firm's MPR efforts with the media; they have been a fundamental component of the public relations professional's toolbox for decades. However, press kits can also be useful in working with NMCs. They work well for briefing experts and opinion leaders on a firm, its products, or activities by providing support material as a basis for their analysis and commentary.

According to John Moore, editor of the *Eastern Pennsylvania Business Journal*,

Reporters and editors are always attempting to understand the companies they cover and they often need to know how to approach them. A well-done press kit can provide essential factual background regarding a company's purpose, products, locations and executives. . . . It can also offer important contact information, such as names, addresses, and telephone numbers of key contacts and execs.

Remember that all Marketing Public Relations documents, whether they are a part of the press kit or not, need to be well written and edited. Although deadlines are often tight, MPR professionals need to take their time reviewing what they write before they send it. They should always have multiple people read each piece with an eye on content, clarity, spelling, and grammar before it ever reaches the desktop of any connector. In addition to writing mechanics, tone is important. "Sometimes the people who compile corporate press kits are long on hype and short on facts, and the press kits they produce are much less valuable," cautions John Moore. Regardless of the type of document, it should always be dated and should include contact information for the issuing firm's MPR person/people, as journalists often keep these documents for reference. Furthermore, it is in the MPR professional's best interest to learn and use Associated Press style for writing press releases and associated MPR documents. Certainly, you will discover pieces not written in AP style, but it is considered the industry standard.

Backgrounders, Fact Sheets, and FAQs

Every firm and every MPR campaign has a story behind the story, and connectors will want to know about it before giving you coverage or spreading the word about your product or service. Backgrounders, fact sheets, and FAQs are designed to provide basic information about a company and the topics it is presenting to connectors. As Pauline Bartel, M.A., president and chief creative officer of Bartel Communications, Inc., Waterford, New York, says,

> Especially for complex subjects, these documents are essential. They are an efficient delivery system for the nuts and bolts of the story. From the perspective of the public relations practitioner, they present the facts correctly. From the perspective of reporters, already knowing the who-what-where-when-why-how allows them to drill down deeper during an interview for the quotes and anecdotes that will grace the story.

Each of the three pieces is formatted in a different way to match the different perspectives with which journalists approach a topic. The **backgrounder** is written in prose and is presented as a narrative. It is designed to help all reporters and other connectors who are looking to present their account of the subject in the same form, whether in writing or by word-of-mouth. **Fact sheets** take a different approach to the same information by listing it in bulleted format to help journalists who are not looking to tell a tale, but rather are searching for some details pertinent to a specific subject. Finally, **FAQs** offer a third option; they point out the questions that a typical audience for a given connector might have and supply answers that relate to the firm and its products. Many press kits include all three pieces, while some MPR professionals choose to include a backgrounder and *either* a fact sheet or an FAQ. Regardless of which documents are included, all press kit materials need to be well written and presented in a way that will grab and keep the attention of the person who receives it.

Writing Backgrounders

CHAPTER
OBJECTIVE
3

Backgrounders are narratives about the company, product, or person on which the press kit is focusing. They cover general information and are fact- rather than news-oriented. The object of the backgrounder is to tell the story of the press kit subject in a way that emphasizes the positioning of the firm. Backgrounders include the facts, issues, and perspectives a journalist would find helpful in preparing his or her story. When you write a backgrounder, you must be sure to keep any of your personal opinions brief and to label them as your own. The backgrounder is meant to be a short but substantive "report," offering information, insights, and often some simple statistics about an aspect of the subject being researched by the reporter. They are sometimes referred to as "editorial backgrounders," since they often simply go to the editor to be held in a **subject file** for future reference. When the medium

---

Key Terms

Press release Information of timely value distributed by an organization to promote its views, products, or services

Press kit Information compiled by organizations for the purpose of informing media outlets and other connectors about their firm, brands, products, employees, and activities

Backgrounder Fact-oriented MPR document that takes the form of a narrative about a company, product, or person

Fact sheet A list of facts designed to entice connectors to cover a firm or its products, while supplying them with information to support their coverage

FAQs An MPR document of questions that a typical audience for a given connector might have related to a firm and its products, along with answers to those questions

Subject file A file kept by a journalist or other connector containing information about subjects he is interested in covering

wants to run an editorial about a topic, editors peruse that subject file for relevant facts and figures that help shape their understanding of and opinion about the topic at hand.

"The backgrounder must pass the 'Who cares?' test," says Mark Wright, independent writer, editor, and owner of Mark Wright Communications LLC in Rockville, Maryland. "Any information you offer the media should be interesting, newsworthy, and useful to their readers, listeners, or viewers."[2]

Backgrounder Construction

Most backgrounders start with a simple label such as "Backgrounder" or "Company Backgrounder." Some MPR professionals opt to begin their backgrounders with a headline that describes the main objective of the firm or campaign, accentuates the firm's positioning, and is interesting enough to make the recipient read the rest of the piece. The body of the document should be double-spaced. In most cases, the presentation should flow chronologically from inception of the product or company to the present day. Sometimes, however, working backward in time is more effective. Similarly,

---

Exhibit 8.1 A backgrounder gives a journalist a quick read on a company or product.

BACKGROUNDER
CEDAR CREST COLLEGE   Allentown, PA

Founded in 1867, Cedar Crest College was one of the first women's colleges in the country. Today it remains an independent, liberal arts college for women that combines excellence in scholarship and undergraduate education with an extensive Lifelong Learning program that serves women and men in the surrounding region.

With 16 primary buildings, the campus is located in the beautiful western residential section of the City of Allentown, Pennsylvania. Cedar Crest is approximately 55 miles from Philadelphia and 90miles from New York City in the Lehigh Valley—the third largest metropolitan area in the Commonwealth. Allentown's population is increasing as it becomes home to many families whose members commute to white-collar jobs in New Jersey and New York City. The College is one of six independent colleges in the area that include Muhlenberg, Lafayette and Moravian colleges, and Lehigh and DeSales universities.

The traditional student body includes 850 students, 60 percent of whom are residential students. There are also approximately 950 Lifelong Learning students who study part-time. More than 130 students study in the College's master's degree programs in education, forensic science and nursing.

Educating Women

Relying upon the foundation of the liberal arts, Cedar Crest College has always been at the forefront of educating women to meet national needs as well as preparing them for all aspects of life—intellectual, work, family, personal and community. Through its commitment to the liberal arts, students are engaged in learning to think, write, explore ideas, question, and synthesize information.

Through its programs, students are prepared for the many careers and challenges that living in our increasingly complex society will present them. There is strong data that establishes the distinctive education offered by a women's college. A women's college provides its graduates with a competitive advantage. Given the rapid growth of women in the workplace and the projection of a seven-fold increase in the number of women in senior management roles in the 21st century, the importance of institutions dedicated to women's advancement, success, and leadership is evident.

The College's vision is to serve as a model for the transformation of high-potential freshmen into high-performing graduates and to continue to make a meaningful contribution to the important work of equipping women with the tools they need to succeed in life, excel in work and participate as leaders in their communities. This is an energizing and exhilarating goal.

Excellence in Academics

At its core, Cedar Crest is a liberal arts college, and all students benefit from the strength, values and curriculum of an education in the liberal arts tradition. Cedar Crest has become noted for its strong science programs and the success of its science majors in fields such as biology, genetic engineering, forensic science and biodiversity. The College's pre-professional programs in health and its rapidly growing nursing program make it the most widely respected provider of health professionals in the region.

Its outstanding faculty is committed to creating a cohesive community of scholars and students where many opportunities exist for independent learning, individual exploration and personal growth. There is an 11:1 student/faculty ratio.

Facts At-A-Glance

President:
Carmen Twillie Ambar, B.S.,Georgetown University; M.P.A., Princeton University; J.D., Columbia School of Law

Students:
- 1,800 total full-time undergraduate students
- 850 traditional undergraduate students
- 950 lifelong learning undergraduate students
- 33 states and 31 countries represented in the student body
- 130 graduate students

Academic Programs:
The College's general educational requirements in the liberal arts provide a foundation for intensive study in an academic discipline or pre-professional field. The traditional liberal arts, as well as the professional fields that draw from them, expose students to multiple perspectives on human experience and different fields of knowledge and interpretation. Through their study, students acquire intellectual skills, learn multiple modes of inquiry and explanation, develop cultural, societal and civic knowledge, and establish values grounded in a respect for difference and an appreciation for complexity.

- Over 30 fields of study
- Undergraduate degrees: Bachelor of Arts, Bachelor of Science
- Graduate degrees: Master of Education, M.S. in Forensic Science, M.S. in Nursing
- Certificate programs: CPA, Gerontology, Healthcare Management, Human Resources Management, Nuclear Medicine
- Certification programs: Elementary/Secondary School, Special Education and Public School Nurse

Faculty:
- 90 full-time faculty
- 8 part-time
- 61 adjunct
- 62% are women

Of the regular full-time faculty ...
- 73% possess a Ph.D. or appropriate terminal degree
- 36% are tenured
- The average age is 48 years old

Student to Faculty Ratio:
- 11:1

Campus:
The College's scenic, park-like 80-acre campus is a nationally registered arboretum. The campus contains 16 primary buildings including four residence halls, research laboratories, modern classroom facilities and the state-of-the-art Rodale Aquatic Center for Civic Health.

(Updated March 2009)

Source: Cedar Crest College.

ordering facts by their importance or stating a problem and then describing how the firm or product was created to solve it can be powerful. Regardless of your strategy for presenting your information, be sure to provide some history, along with an explanation of why this issue is important today. State the significance of your topic and back up that statement with facts. In addition, remember to use subheads where appropriate to make for easier reading. While a backgrounder should not exceed four to five pages in length, you should always let the information, rather than the page count, dictate the length of your piece.[3]

Be sure to prominently label the piece "backgrounder" at the top in order to differentiate it from other MPR documents. The label also serves as a reminder to file the piece for future use. Finally, make absolutely sure that current, accurate contact information appears on this and all MPR pieces. A journalist interested in your story *must* have a way to contact you. And, since connectors of all sorts work irregular hours, include a way to contact you outside of your normal office hours.

Formulating Fact Sheets and FAQs

CHAPTER
OBJECTIVE
4

Marketers use fact sheets and FAQs in a variety of ways. They can have a broad focus on firms, business units, or brands or be centered on a single product, person, or event. They can even be based on an individual feature of a particular product, person, or event.

Fact Sheet Construction

Fact sheets often contain similar information as backgrounders, but that information should be presented in a single-spaced, bulleted format. All facts that make up the body must be newsworthy, and they should be arranged with the most interesting and compelling facts first and the mundane yet important facts at the end. The first few points need to motivate the connector to read the entire sheet. They should leave the reader wanting to know more about the subject being presented. Ideally, a fact sheet will entice connectors to report the whole story, while simultaneously providing journalists individual facts that they can weave into related stories.

As with the backgrounder, fact sheets need to be labeled, and good writing and contact information are essential. Unlike backgrounders, however, fact sheets should be limited to two pages. The purpose of a fact sheet is to provide quick, hard-hitting information that will lead the connector to look for more on the subject. If a fact sheet is too long, the connector may never read the important points, or he or she may ignore it altogether.

FAQ Construction

FAQs can supplement or replace the fact sheet, as an FAQ list includes questions about the subject of the press kit that may be of interest to connectors. The answers should illustrate how the firm or its products solve a problem or otherwise bring value to the connector's audience. The construction is almost identical to that of a fact sheet. The major difference is that the FAQ is in question-and-answer format.

Exhibit 8.2 FAQs use a question-and-answer format to inform journalists and the public about a company or product.

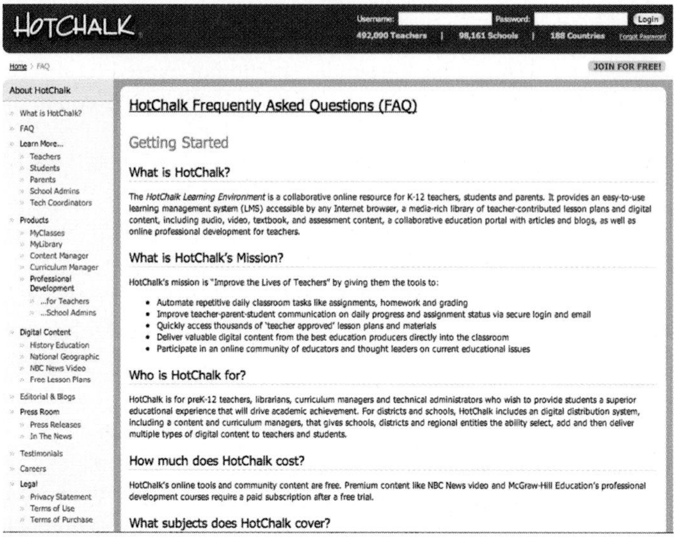

Source: HotChalk.®

Supporting Materials

In addition to backgrounders, fact sheets, and FAQs, press kits often contain extra resources to help connectors understand the story and communicate it to their audience. Photos are one example of press kit support material that can have a great impact on generating media mentions. "Too many people in the journalism field still don't get it," says Mindy McAdams in her blog, Teaching Online Journalism. "Great photography tells a story, and it sells the story too."[4]

The following items contribute to making the press kit more powerful:

Press releases

- News items previously released to the media may be included.
- They should be limited to one to three per press kit.
- Include those press releases that are most current and have the most relevance to the campaign for which the press kit has been assembled.

Company literature

- A press kit may include brochures, product sheets, case studies, or any other type of sales collateral that supports the topic.
- All pieces should be current and have the correct contact information on them.
- All pieces should reflect positively upon the organization and should look and feel professionally done. If a piece does not meet these criteria, leave it out!

Executive biographies

- Since news of executive changes travels fast, any biographies that are included must be up to date. Reporting on an executive who has left a company can be embarrassing both for a journalist and the firm.

- Biographies should be complimentary to the executives but not boastful.
- Photos of executives can be included. Note, however, that some MPR professionals prefer not to use photos to avoid any prejudging of executives' abilities and dispositions based on how they look.

Photos

- Photos that clarify a point in a story or express an emotion better than words work best.
- Photos must be the right quality, format, and size for the medium receiving the press kit. Note that TV, magazines, newspapers, and online outlets all have different requirements. Check these requirements with your connectors to ensure that you provide photos they can use.
- Include information on how and when the photos can be used as well as the appropriate copyright and attribution information.

Expert contacts

- When covering a story based on a firm or product, journalists look for sources outside of the firm to add depth and provide credibility. Supplying journalists with a list of outside experts who are willing to discuss the topic of the press kit saves them time and gives the firm some input as to who will be commenting on the story.

Clippings

- A press kit may include evidence of other times the company or its stakeholders have been covered by the media or other connectors.
- Unless the coverage is historically significant to the firm, all clippings should be as current as possible.
- All clippings should be positive and should reflect the positioning of the firm.
- Clippings often constitute the "In the news" section of an online press kit.

Press Kit Formats: Paper versus Electronic

CHAPTER
OBJECTIVE
6

Throughout most of the history of public relations, the press kit took a physical form that could be handed or mailed to a connector. While this option still exists, marketers rely increasingly on portable media like CDs, DVDs, and flash drives to deliver their press kits, and some marketers simply post them to the Internet. Speed and ease of reproduction have given digital methods an edge over their paper cousins, but many MPR professionals still see a use for the physical form. According to Kathy Kniss, director of public relations at Clean Agency,

> We are on the fence regarding electronic vs. paper press kits. We do both here....For our clients for whom we do more social content creation (blogs, podcasts, tweeting), we have ditched the old press kit model and opted for USB drives emblazoned with their corporate logo or campaign slogan and upload them with multimedia digital files.

Key Terms

Clipping Evidence of the coverage of a firm or its products by the media or other connectors

As Bronagh Hanley of Big Noise PR in San Francisco, California, cautions, "Before sending press kits via e-mail, you should check with the reporter to ensure that he is interested in receiving a large file. All documents should be in Microsoft Word so reporters can cut and paste easily."

In the end, you the marketer, must understand the format that best suits your connectors and the story. If the firm does all of its work virtually, then a strictly Web-based press kit may be the way to go. On the other hand, if the firm participates in several trade shows and other promotional events where connectors are present, that firm would be wise to have a press kit that can be handed out rather than relying on the connectors to download it from the Internet when they get back to the office.

Concept Case 8.1: Getting the Facts Together

In preparing to write a backgrounder and fact sheet, The Falcon's Lair staff has assembled the following list of facts:

- The store is conveniently located, with ample parking.
- The company was founded in 1998 by two hiking and climbing enthusiasts.
- The Falcon's Lair carries only top-quality premium brands of equipment.
- All of The Falcon's Lair employees have been involved in hiking and climbing for at least five years.
- The Falcon's Lair holds classes and seminars to educate beginners to expert hikers and climbers.
- The Falcon's Lair has strategic partnerships with several indoor climbing clubs, as well as with the National Park Service.
- The company has instituted the "Best of the Nest Program," which includes discounts and promotions for existing customers who refer new customers to the store or who bring their friends to The Falcon's Lair events.

Questions:
1. Using both this information and what you already know about The Falcon's Lair, discuss how you would format a backgrounder for the company.
2. In what order would you place these facts on a fact sheet? Is there anything you would exclude? Is there anything else you think you should add? Explain.
3. Write three questions that you feel would be appropriate to include on The Falcon's Lair's FAQs. Be sure to include answers.

CHAPTER
OBJECTIVE
7

Purposes of a Press Release

A press release is information of timely value distributed by an organization to promote its views, products, or services.[5] Also called *news releases*, these documents are the MPR workhorses. Because they are used in almost every campaign, it is vitally important that they be done well. There are many reasons for writing press releases. Regardless of the topic, however, their primary objective is to act as the initial introduction to connectors about the subject that you are promoting, and, thereby, to elicit media mentions and word-of-mouth.

Exhibit 8.3 NVIDIA uses a press release to launch a new product.

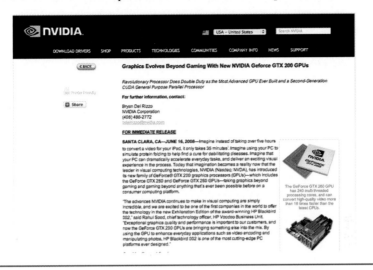

Source: NVIDIA.

Another common use of a press release is to announce a new product or service. This type of press release typically includes a description of the product, a reason for its introduction or explanation of the need that it is filling, and any interesting story behind its creation. An insightful quote from a company executive or an industry expert is always helpful to connectors interested in covering this type of story.

Publicizing the good deeds of a firm and its employees is an effective way to generate media mentions and to help organizations to build a positive reputation with a community or market segment. A smart MPR person will use a press release to ensure that good deeds do not go unnoticed. In fact, media mentions and word-of-mouth surrounding good deeds are so powerful that some large corporations are rumored to spend more money publicizing the fact that they did a good deed than they actually spent on the deed itself.

Reasons to create a press release include the following:

- Release of a new product or service
- Opening of a new business location or relocation of an existing one
- Announcing a special event
- Announcing new personnel or personnel changes/promotions
- Recognition of good deeds performed for the community
- Public appearances by company executives or employees
- Announcement of awards won by organization or stakeholders
- Contest announcements or results (tied in with other promotional activities)
- Announcing the creation of interorganizational partnerships
- Crisis control

Occasionally, MPR professionals want to simply supply information to connectors without being persuasive. In these cases, they write pared-down press releases, known as **media alerts**, to tell reporters about an upcoming event they may want to cover or to give them basic facts about an upcoming news conference.

CHAPTER
OBJECTIVE
8

Elements of a Press Release

The press release has a standard format that public relations professionals follow closely.

1. *Press release label.* A statement labeling the document as a press release or news release appears at the top. Some organizations have special letterhead (paper and/or electronic) just for this purpose.

2. *Release date statement.* Next, the release date statement indicates when you want connectors to release the information to their audience. Typically, you will want the news to go public right away, so the statement will be "For Immediate Release." If you choose to put an **embargo**[6] on the information, you will state, "For Release on (Date)."

3. *Contact information.* Contact information typically follows and includes the name, phone number, and e-mail address of the primary contact at the firm. Some companies choose to save the contact information for the last paragraph of the release or include it as a part of the footer of the document. In any case, contact information is essential and must include a way to reach someone at the firm twenty-four hours a day, seven days a week.

4. *Headline.* The main section of the release starts with a headline and is typically bold and centered.

5. *Sub-heads.* Subheads, placed between the headline and the body, can be used to embellish the headline and segue into the theme of the release.

6. *Body.* The body begins two spaces after the headline and opens with a dateline, the city and state from which the release is generated (in capital letters), and the release date followed by a dash.
Example: ALLENTOWN, Pa., June 23, 2006

If the press release is distributed by a wire service, that organization will add the name of the service in parentheses between the state and the date.
Example: ALLENTOWN, Pa. (Business Wire) June 23, 2006

7. *The lead.* The first two or three sentences of the press release are called *the lead* and need to be attention grabbing. This is where you will win or lose the interest of connectors. The balance of the body includes information on the subject of the press release presented in such a way that the recipient will understand why the story is relevant to his audience.

8. *Boilerplate.* The final paragraph is known as the **boilerplate**.[7] This is a descriptive paragraph about your organization and can include contact information if it is not present at the beginning of the release. It should be the same on every press release you write.

9. Finally, every press release should conclude with the mark "###" centered at the bottom of the page. This signifies the end of the copy.

Producing Press Releases

Simply knowing the format of a good press release is not enough. Each section needs to be carefully crafted in order to maximize media mentions and word-of-mouth while simultaneously assisting connectors in delivering the message to their audience in the way that you intended. MPR professionals need to pay particular attention to the presentation and content of the headline, the lead, the body, and the boilerplate.

Exhibit 8.4 All press releases need these elements.

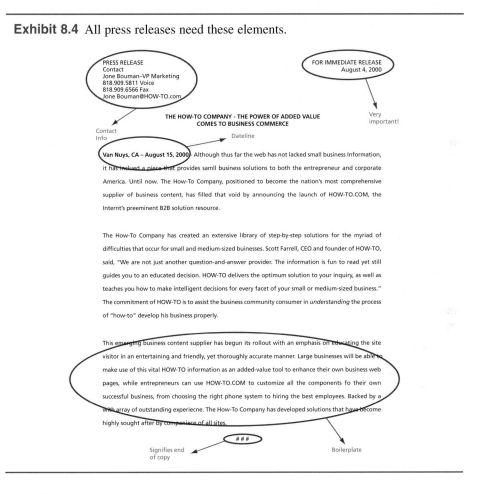

Headline

The headline needs to grab the attention of the reader and make him or her want to read on. A good headline should be short, no more than a single line. According to Alayna

Key Terms

Media alert A non-persuasive form of a press release intended simply to inform connectors of a particular fact

Embargo A heading on a news release indicating that the news is not to be published or reported before a specific date

Boilerplate A short description of a company for editorial use

Tagariello, vice president of communications and human relations at Swiss Re America Holding Corporation in New York City, "Don't make it too wordy—get the name of the company in there if you can, and word it in a way that is most likely to garner a second glance." In addition, a headline needs to make editors believe that the content will grab their audience's attention. The media are obsessed with three topics that they think audiences crave: money, sex, and health.[8] So, use this fact to your advantage when writing headlines, if it is in line with your firm's image and positioning. "The most important part of your headline should come first," says Kathy Kniss of Clean Agency. "Sometimes it's your company's name, a staggering statistic, a location, or even a catchy buzzword. Moreover, headlines should be as informative and concise as possible—they should read like a newspaper headline." To illustrate, she suggests opting for a headline like, "Ecover Drives Home Sustainability with New Car Wash Product," rather than "Ecover Launches New Ecological Car Wash Product."

Editing headlines is an acquired skill that comes with lots of practice. In order to gain experience, read several newspapers and magazines and make a list of headlines that attract your interest. Note what those stories were about, how the headlines were worded, and why they caught your eye. Then try writing your own headlines for the same stories. Try to develop a feel for the rhythm, the use of language, and the impact your words create.[9]

Press releases don't always contain a subheading, but they can; sometimes the subhead can be extremely important. In all cases, the subhead builds on the headline, providing one more reason to read the body of the press release. For example, you can use a provocative headline like "It's a Musical Instrument That Can Kill You!" by pairing it with a subhead like "13,687 People Said They'd Died and Gone to Heaven after Hearing This Instrument for the First Time."[10] The subhead adds clarity and mollifies the overt sensationalism of the headline.

Lead

Leads continue where the headline leaves off. They need to maintain the reader's attention and show the reader why this piece of news would be interesting to his or her audience. Leads should be short—only a sentence or two—free of jargon, and truthful. "With the possible exception of the headline, the lead paragraph is the most important part of the press release and is the first and only shot of grabbing attention," says Molly Lynch, founder and director at Lynch Communications Group, LLC.

Michelle Metzger, head of communications for Entrust, Inc., a security software company based in Dallas, Texas, adds this:

> The first sentence has to grab the reporter. I like to start the releases like I'm telling a story versus the corporate drivel of "Company X, the leading provider of widgets worldwide, today announces it will begin manufacturing bobbles." . . . A better lead sentence might be, "A rare commodity, bobbles help solve a growing problem with consumers, so Company X has decided to offer high quality bobbles to its customers, which make a nice complement to its already market-leading widgets."

"The rest of the paragraph needs to answer the 5 W's and 2 H's: Who, What, When, Where, Why, How and Huh," Metzger continues. "Huh is short for the 'so what,' and should be answered in the opening sentence."

Body

Once the lead is established, the body needs to elaborate on the story and its attractiveness to the connector's audience. While the appropriate tone for a press release varies with the product or service you are promoting, the audience you're targeting, and the media channels you've chosen, MPR professionals agree on a few points that apply to all releases.[11] As Molly Lynch emphasizes, "The body of the press release should be written just as we read newspaper articles, in the style of an **inverted pyramid**, with the key information at the top.... Also, because we're writing in news format, the paragraphs and sentences are simple and short, not long prose, like a college essay."

Exhibit 8.5 Good press releases start with the most interesting, most important facts, and offer the more mundane, but necessary details later.

Inverted Pyramid Writing

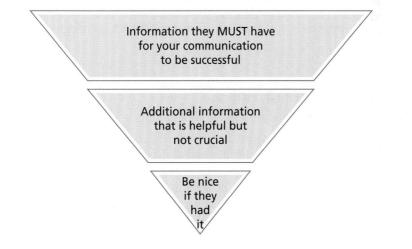

Information they MUST have for your communication to be successful

Additional information that is helpful but not crucial

Be nice if they had it

You should also avoid complicated language, technical terms, and jargon. Even though you may be an expert in your field, the editor, writer, or blogger receiving the release may not be. Michelle Metzger recommends that you:

Stay away from words that are so overused that they no longer have any real meaning. The top picks for this category include words like "solution," "revolutionary," "world-class," "best-of-breed" and, quickly climbing the ranks, "elegant."...Every company thinks it has the best solution and a revolutionary way of approaching a problem. Also, most tech reporters are still nursing snakebites from the last time they

---

Key Terms

Inverted pyramid The concept of presenting information from the general to the specific

wrote about a company that was "revolutionizing" something but ended up closing its doors soon thereafter, so the fact you are touting to do the same scares them a little.

"Cut back on the flowery phrasing and let your strongest points stand on their own," adds Alayna Tagariello. "Use adjectives, but judiciously."

Remember to keep your press release short. You should be able to summarize your news, briefly describe your company, and provide the pertinent contact information in fewer than 400 words.[12] If you prefer to think in terms of pages, strive for a single page if possible, using two pages as your absolute maximum, but only in extreme cases. In addition to brevity, graphics, photos, statistics, quotes from experts or celebrities, and bulleted lists (including: facts, tips, rankings, etc.) greatly enhance a press release and are useful to connectors as they prepare to tell your story. According to Michelle Metzger,

> Quotes are a necessary component of good press releases. They should sound fresh and like an actual human being would speak. Well-written quotes often can be lifted directly from a press release because reporters usually are starved for content in time to meet deadlines.... If you can write a quote they actually might have gotten someone to say in an interview, they can use it without wasting either party's time.

Press Release Writing Tips

Following are some practical tips from PR Web for writing good press releases:[13]

- *Illustrate.* Use real life examples of how your company or organization solved a problem. Identify the problem and discuss why your solution is the right one. Give examples of how your service or product fulfills needs or satisfies desires. What benefits can be expected? Use real-life examples to powerfully communicate the benefits of using your product or service.
- *Stick to the facts.* Tell the truth. Avoid fluff, embellishments, and exaggerations. Journalists are naturally skeptical. If your story sounds too good to be true, you are probably hurting your own credibility. Even if it is true, you may want to tone it down a bit.
- *Pick an angle.* Tie your news to current events or social issues if possible. Make sure that your story has a good news hook.
- *Use active, not passive, voice.* Verbs in the active voice bring your press release to life. For example, "The incident enraged the committee," reads better if changed to "The committee was enraged over the incident."
- *Mixed case.* NEVER SUBMIT A PRESS RELEASE IN ALL UPPERCASE LETTERS. This is very bad form. Even if your release makes it past editors, it will definitely be ignored by journalists. Use mixed case.
- *Correct grammar usage.* Always follow rules of grammar and style. Errors in grammar and style affect your credibility. Editors will reject press releases with excessive errors.
- *Word processor.* Write your press release on a word processor instead of composing online. Writing online will not achieve best results. Take time to do it right. Write, print, proofread. Rewrite, edit.

- *No HTML.* Never embed HTML or other markup languages in your press release. Your press release will be distributed over a wide array of networks. Including such formatting will have a negative impact on the readability of your press release.
- *More than one paragraph.* It is nearly impossible to tell your story in a few sentences. If you do not have more than a few sentences, chances are you do not have a newsworthy item.

Boilerplate

In determining your positioning, you have defined your organization. The last paragraph of your press release is your opportunity to reinforce this message with your connectors and it must be consistent from one press release to the next. Some firms have one boilerplate for the entire organization, while others have boilerplates that are specific to certain company segments, brands, or products. As Molly Lynch says, "The boilerplate gives readers everything they need to know about the company and tells them where to find more information. . . . It's important to keep this clear and consistent with past boilerplates, unless an update or correction is made."

Editing

Before sending out your press release, be sure to check your facts thoroughly and to proofread the release for spelling, grammar, and flow. You should have a disinterested party proofread it as well. If possible, put it down for a day and proofread it one more time before you send it out. "One quick rule of thumb is to let your 80-year-old grandmother read your press release," quips Michelle Metzger. "If she can understand it and grasp why this news is important to the world, then you have succeeded. If her eyes glaze over and she asks you to get her a cocktail, it's time to go back to the drawing board."

This may seem like a trivial matter, but small mistakes can result in big embarrassment for firms and MPR professionals. Let's look at the story of Liz Miller, who became a legend in the public relations world. As communications manager for Jan Marini Skin Research, a skin-care company based in San Jose, California, Miller writes approximately forty press releases a year, e-mailing them primarily to trade publications read by dermatologists and spa owners. One item, which appeared in a trade publication last March, touted special deals on Jan Marini's glycolic-acid products and encouraged readers to call a 1-800 number for more information. When readers dialed the number, however, they got much more information than they expected. Miller, it turned out, had typed in a single incorrect digit and provided the number for a phone sex line. Not surprisingly, she was soon flooded with calls from editors, angry customers, and laughing colleagues. "I told my boss and our CEO that I understood if they had to fire me," Miller recalls. Fortunately, her superiors took pity on her.[14]

Following are some useful tips to use when editing press releases and other press kit materials:

- Consider the point of view of potential editors and journalists as well as their audiences.
- Look for grammar, spelling, and punctuation errors. (Hint: MPR pieces don't always have to follow the rules, but breaking them must be intentional.)
- Determine the goal of the piece and ask if the piece is meeting that goal.

- Break down the piece into its various elements and ask the questions "Why?" and "So what?" often.
- Evaluate the aesthetics of the piece as well as the content. Is it formatted in a way that will look appealing to the audience?
- Make suggestions for improving the piece and give your rationale for each suggestion.

CHAPTER
OBJECTIVE
10

Video News Releases

MPR professionals want their messages to reach an intended audience with their original meaning and intent intact, despite having to work their way through the analysis and interpretation of connectors. So you would expect marketers to be ecstatic when their messages reach the public completely unvarnished by connectors. Over the last few years, however, the use of **video news releases**[15] (VNRs) by television media has caused a stir with the public and has marketers scratching their heads. A VNR is a publicity device created by a firm that is designed to look and sound like a television news story. Marketers prepare a sixty- to ninety-second video, which can then be used by television stations as is or after further editing.[16] However, some VNRs are used unedited, without objective commentary, or without a mention that the VNR was supplied by an outside source. In addition, because firms almost always integrate their own products, services, or professionals into the video, many people feel that the result is an implied endorsement of that firm by a medium.

The watchdog groups Free Press (FP) and Center for Media and Democracy (CMD) have argued that the practice of using these materials without attribution violates the Federal Communications Commission's (FCC) rules that require disclosure of any sponsorship.[17] Sponsors are getting their product or service covered favorably, as if by a legitimate news source, and broadcasters are getting a "news" segment that costs them nothing to produce. As a result of a joint complaint filed in 2007 by FP and CMD, the FCC fined Comcast $4,000 for airing a VNR without disclosure. Officials at CMD state that the organization is not trying to ban VNRs; rather, it is just trying to make sure that the public knows what it is watching. According to Diane Farsetta, senior researcher at CMD, in an October 2007 article in *PR Week,* "At the root is the distinction between reporting and PR materials."[18]

Some marketers have a different opinion and assert that this action was a misinterpretation of the FCC guidelines. In fact, as a result of the wave of public and governmental scrutiny of VNRs, a group of broadcast PR companies banded together to form the National Association of Broadcast Communicators (NABC). NABC's first action was to issue a joint statement with the PRSA supporting the current FCC guidelines. These guidelines require disclosure of sponsorship information of a third-party video only in cases in which the material is political or controversial in nature or if the station was paid to air it. NABC claims that VNRs do not fall into either category. The Radio-Television News Directors Association backed up this position by claiming that the CMD's study of the use of VNRs was biased and inaccurate; the organization even claimed that CMD is unrelenting in its hostility to the principles of free speech.

Producers of VNRs argue that they are valuable to both firms and the media. For example, the Web site of VNR company VideoNewsRelease.net states:

Stations and reporters appreciate a company saving them time gathering video materials. With tighter station budgets, reporters often use "hand out" video—your VNR—to support other material they gather for a story on your industry ... or your company. VNRs eliminate one more roadblock for a reporter working under tight deadlines.

Stations need VNRs. Some will use them as is; some will "cherry pick" elements that you provide and control. It's one more tool in your public relations arsenal.[19]

VideoNewsRelease.net is careful to point out, however, that the VNR must offer something of value to the viewer beyond a company promotion.[20]

Matt Clark of Lotus PR adds,

As a marketer, it is nice to see our VNRs get picked up by media outlets. When they are unedited, it ensures that our client's message gets across.... However, we don't want them to be completely unedited. Media outlets need to have their own editorial control over everything they run. When a media outlet picks up a VNR and puts its own editorial touches on it, it gives the story more credibility. If the public were to find out that some media outlets were running them unedited, there would be backlash and the outlet and product would lose credibility.

There is no question that the VNR is an effective tool for marketers that can also be helpful to journalists. The responsibility of balancing the desire to get a message out with a sense of responsibility to the public falls on the shoulders of the MPR professional. A marketer has an ethical responsibility to ensure that consumers are being served while simultaneously promoting his or her firm and helping to preserve the integrity of his or her media partners.

Concept Case 8.2: **Writing a Press Release**

The Falcon's Lair launched its "Best of the Nest Program" directly to its customers without ever notifying the media. To make up for this lapse, management is working on a press release and has come up with a few possible headlines.

- *The Falcon's Lair Launches "Best of the Nest Program"*
- *"Best of the Nest Program" Has Hikers and Climbers Flocking to The Falcon's Lair*
- *Falcon's Lair Climbs to New Heights as Satisfied Customers Spread the Word*

Questions:
1. Discuss the pros and cons of each headline, and explain which one you feel is best.
2. Write your own headline and explain why it is better than any of the above.
3. Write a lead paragraph that supports your headline and explain why you worded it as you did.

 Reflection Questions

1. Discuss the value of the press kit to the MPR professional as well as to connectors. (Chapter Objective 1)

2. Explain the purpose served by backgrounders, fact sheets, and FAQs. (Chapter Objective 2)

3. Describe the format of a backgrounder and explain the "Who Cares" test. (Chapter Objective 3)

4. Discuss the impact of the organization of the facts on a fact sheet and explain under what circumstances you would choose to use an FAQ instead. (Chapter Objective 4)

5. What are the types of support material typically included in a press kit and what are the specific contributions of each piece? (Chapter Objective 5)

6. Compare and contrast the benefits and limitations of electronic and paper press kits. (Chapter Objective 6)

7. What is the primary objective of a press release and what are some reasons for creating one? (Chapter Objective 7)

8. Describe the format of a press release and explain the purpose of each element. (Chapter Objective 8)

9. Explain the concept of the inverted pyramid and why it is important to press release writing. (Chapter Objective 9)

10. Discuss both the benefits and drawbacks of video news releases and explain your thoughts on how and when marketers should use them. (Chapter Objective 10)

 Chapter Key Terms

Backgrounder Fact-oriented MPR document that takes the form of a narrative about a company, product, or person (p. 121)

Boilerplate A short description of a company for editorial use (p. 128)

Clipping Evidence of the coverage of a firm or its products by the media or other connectors (p. 125)

Embargo A heading on a news release indicating that the news is not to be published or reported before a specific date (p. 128)

Fact sheet A list of facts designed to entice connectors to cover a firm or its products, while supplying them with information to support their coverage (p. 121)

FAQs An MPR document of questions that a typical audience for a given connector might have related to a firm and its products, along with answers to those questions (p. 121)

Inverted pyramid The concept of presenting information from the general to the specific (p. 131)

Media alert A non-persuasive form of a press release intended simply to inform connectors of a particular fact (p. 128)

News release Synonymous with press release

Press kit Information compiled by organizations for the purpose of informing media outlets and other connectors about their firm, brands, products, employees, and activities (p. 120)

Press release Information of timely value distributed by an organization to promote its views, products, or services; also called *news release* (p. 119)

Subject file A file kept by a journalist or other connector containing information about subjects he is interested in covering (p. 121)

Video News Release (VNR) A publicity device created by a firm, which is designed to look and sound like a television news story. Marketers prepare a sixty- to ninety-second video, which can then be used by television stations as is or after further editing. (p. 134)

Application Assignments

1. Search company Web sites to find a backgrounder that you think can be improved. Rewrite the backgrounder. In a separate document, explain what you changed and why.

2. Explore one of the companies listed below and write a fact sheet for that company. (You may use another company with your instructor's permission.)

   a. Costco

   b. Manolo Blahnik

   c. American Eagle Outfitters

   d. Dick's Sporting Goods

3. Go to http://www.businesswire.com and identify a press release issued by a company with which you are familiar. Write a critique of this press release, using tips from the end of this chapter as your guide.

4. Write a press release announcing the introduction of a new master's degree program in Marketing Public Relations at your school. Exchange press releases with a classmate and critique each other's work. Then work together to use what you learned to write a final draft of this press release.

 Practice Portfolio

This Practice Portfolio can be based on a fictitious company or on a real company that your instructor assigns to you. (If you used a company in previous Practice Portfolio exercises, continue to use that company.) Add your completed assignment to your portfolio to present to prospective employers.

- Using chapter material as your guideline, write a backgrounder and fact sheet for your company. In addition, write two press releases for your company. One press release should be for the launch of a new product or service, while the second should announce a special event.

CHAPTER 9

Selling the Story

CHAPTER OBJECTIVES

After studying this chapter, you should be able to:

1. Discuss the concept and impact of "newsworthiness."

2. Explain the goal and persuasive elements of the pitch.

3. Describe and explain the elements of a pitch letter.

4. Define and explain the concept of embargos and exclusives.

5. Discuss the special considerations for pitching a blogger.

6. Discuss the challenges of a live pitch.

7. Discuss how editorial calendars can impact a pitch.

8. Explain the importance of follow-up and observing follow-up protocol.

9. Discuss some tips for getting through the pitching process.

In 1998 Icon Medialab, a one-year-old Swedish Internet/marketing company that was unknown in the United States and only slightly recognized in Europe, wanted media coverage. It turned to international PR expert Priss Benbow of Benbow International PR for assistance: "The company's co-founder called me and said, 'I want articles in *BusinessWeek*, *Forbes*, and *The Wall Street Journal* in the United States and Europe, and I want you to handle media relations exclusively,'" relates Benbow. Understanding that trying to **pitch** an obscure upstart interactive marketing company in an environment where there were literally hundreds of other companies claiming similar technical expertise, Benbow knew that she needed to find the right hook for her pitch. Looking at the target media, Benbow realized that technology and globalization were hot topics; as a result, she felt that a story idea that could bridge the two would have tremendous potential. Fortunately, Icon and its founders had the right mix of experience and recognition in both areas, so Benbow set out to explain to the target media why globalization was an important trend and how the company exemplified the trend, while highlighting some of its global, blue-chip clients.

This positioning and subsequent pitch led to media interviews in thirteen countries and secured $1.2 million of media coverage (based on the cost of purchasing advertising with equivalent audience exposure) in the United States and Europe in one year. Coverage included ABC television, *Adweek*, the Associated Press, *BusinessWeek*, *Forbes*, *Forbes Global*, the *International Herald Tribune*, *Newsweek International*, *The New York Times*, Reuters, *Time*, and *The Wall Street Journal*.

In addition to the fact that Benbow provided positioning that was clearly newsworthy, her pitch letter, in this case an e-mail, was also crafted expertly. The first paragraph highlighted a topic that was in the front of connectors' minds and added some intrigue with the subject line "No Place to Hide." The second paragraph built credibility for the story, while the third illustrated how media might work this idea into their coverage of trends in globalization, technology, and even entrepreneurship.

This effort was an early, yet successful step in building an organization by harnessing the power of MPR. Since this campaign was completed, Icon Medialab has survived the dotcom collapse, has been through a merger, and has continued to be a force in the global Internet marketing consulting field as LBi (http://www.lbi.com).

Shutterstock

Newsworthiness

In many ways MPR is a sales job. That is, MPR professionals need to convince writers, editors, and producers that they have something worth covering, meaning that it is **newsworthy**. But what's worth covering? Typically, a subject must be objective to be interesting to a medium's audience. The audience must also consider it to be newsworthy, so that the medium does not appear to have an ulterior motive for covering it. Ideally, story ideas demonstrate a significant impact on a medium's audience while helping the connectors who cover the story increase that audience by driving viewership, readership, and listenership. Following are some common themes of newsworthy pitches:[1]

- One of a kind
- First ever
- Atypical community service
- Trends
- Unusual applications of products and services
- Celebrities and quirky experts
- Tales of the underdog
- Money, sex, or health issues[2]

Ford employed two of these hooks when it announced that the Mustang AV8R, a one-of-a-kind aviation-themed automobile, would be auctioned off to aid Gathering of Eagles youth aviation initiatives. This effort resulted in positive media mentions for the new generation of Mustangs and helped strengthen Ford's position as a supporter of a key demographic, namely middle-American youth.

Reporting on trends is also attractive to connectors, especially when they can relate a larger trend to the interests or well-being of their particular community. Honda's publicity efforts for the Civic GX, a car that runs on natural gas rather than gasoline, capitalizes on both the rising cost of gasoline and the growing concern about the environment among American consumers.

Conversely, a subject that is *not* relevant to a medium's audience is clearly not newsworthy. This includes any story idea that has a clear sales angle, touts features without benefits, or is too complicated for a connector or an audience to understand.

You also need to think beyond the subject matter of a pitch. Make sure that your story can be thoroughly presented in 500 to 2,000 words in print coverage or as a thirty-second- to four-minute-long segment by broadcast media.

Elements of a Persuasive Pitch

Newsworthiness alone is not enough to get a connector to cover a story. Pitching is the art of getting a connector to commit to covering a story in a way that is consistent with the firm's positioning and the intent of the campaign at hand. Gaining that commitment requires a measure of persuasion in the form of a pitch to ensure that connectors see the value in covering a topic. This requires overcoming the following five obstacles that are routinely in the way of media mentions and word-of-mouth:

1. Credibility
2. Relationships

3. Beliefs and values
4. Interests
5. Communication[3]

Credibility

You must establish that you are a reliable source of information and demonstrate that you, your firm, or the experts that support your story are truly qualified to present material on this topic and are perceived by the connectors' audiences to have some authority or expertise. Journalists and other connectors do not want to get burned by accepting information blindly from those with no relevant credentials. Similarly, they do not want their audience to question the validity of the information that they present.

Audiences (both connectors and consumers) attribute credibility to one of three perceived attributes of the sender: competence, character, and dynamism. Competence refers to the sender's diligence in gathering the story, the accuracy of the facts, and the effectiveness in communication. Character is the receiver's perception of the sender's honesty and integrity. Finally, dynamism is the degree to which the sender puts forth energy or enthusiasm relative to a subject and the degree of charisma evident in communicating a message.[4] As a result, it is essential for marketers to establish credibility that extends from the source of the story to the consumers of that story.

Relationships

When people know, like, and trust you, they are more likely to listen to your ideas and go along with them.[5] While we tend to agree with people we like, we also prefer to disagree with people we dislike. This is the basis of **balance theory**,[6] which asserts that receivers feel uncomfortable, or out of balance, when their attitude toward the sender of a message does not match their attitude about the topic of the message. Understanding this theory leads to the realization that connectors need to like the marketers who are pitching them. In essence, relationships foster balance, and balance creates the right environment for garnering media mentions and word-of-mouth. You should note as well that receivers also find balance in concurrently disliking a sender and a message; while you can assume that a connector who dislikes you and your message will generate some publicity, you should expect that publicity to be negative.

Key Terms

Pitch An attempt to persuade a journalist or other connector to cover a story

Newsworthy A subject that is interesting to a medium's audience, is objective, and will not make the media appear as though it has an ulterior motive for covering it

Balance theory A communications theory that asserts that receivers feel uncomfortable, or out of balance, when their attitude toward the sender of a message does not match their attitude about the topic of the message

Beliefs and Values

The beliefs and values of a connector's audience and medium, as well as her own experience, shape a connector's receptiveness to a message. Therefore, marketers need to discover the direction, depth, and perceived importance of the beliefs and values held by that audience and medium and show the connector how the story they are pitching aligns with them. According to Michelle Metzger of Entrust:

> The most annoying thing you can do is pitch a story about widgets to the fashion column editor....Read, watch, or listen to the media outlets you have determined are the best target and get to know them. It always helps to talk with them "in their world."

Interests

Self-interest is a powerful motivator and a key to strategic persuasion.[7] The pitch is the marketer's vehicle for explaining how covering a story can serve the interests of a particular connector. Ultimately, the pitch is a search for a win-win solution, not an exercise in pressuring an antagonist into surrendering.[8] This philosophy was summed up well by sales guru Zig Ziglar in an article in *PR News*: "You can have everything in life that you want if you will just help other people get what they want."[9] What journalists want are good stories and solid facts. If you don't get the facts straight, you are not serving the connector's interest at all. Remember that when an average person makes a mistake at work, only a handful of people will likely ever know about it. If a *New York Times* reporter blunders, millions of people will know about it.[10]

Communication

Making an effective pitch is a complex process that requires you to reinforce your image of credibility with a connector, while showing him or her that you value your relationship. In addition, you have to demonstrate that you have a story idea that aligns with his or her beliefs and values and provides something of benefit to him or her. With all of these elements in play, you may be tempted to present a lot of information during your pitch. However, volume can obscure your message and can cause misunderstanding, so keep it as clear and concise as possible. Knowing what you are trying to say and saying it precisely and simply are essential components of managing the media.[11]

Not all connectors are looking for every pitch all of the time. So, you must incorporate what you learned about connectors and their organizations in the connector list building process. Specifically, understand when and how each connector prefers to be pitched. The best pitch in the world will be ineffective if it comes at a time when the connector is not paying attention or is working on something else and cannot use the material. Likewise, if the connector prefers to receive pitches via fax and you are sending e-mails, your efforts in formulating your pitch will not be rewarded.

David Strom, editor-in-chief of *Tom's Hardware Guide* offers hints for those who pitch to him: "[T]hink about how you can build a relationship with me; don't just send me a press release.... Have an interesting story prepared, and have every detail ready. If I can trust that you will 'deliver the goods' when you contact me, then I'll give you my time."[12]

The Pitch Letter

Once the MPR documents are prepared and the connector list is assembled, it is time to sell the story. As with any sales effort, the way you sell the idea is as important as the idea itself. The primary offensive weapon for selling an idea for a story is the **pitch letter**. It can be transmitted via mail, fax, or e-mail, depending on the preference of the connector to which it is being sent. A typical pitch letter is used to

- Pitch a story
- Suggest an idea for a talk show segment
- Secure an interview with a certain person about a specific topic
- Position a person or an organization as an expert available for future comment
- Explain why the accompanying press release or press kit is worth a few minutes of an editor's/producer's time.

While many MPR professionals take some creative license in creating their pitch letters, there is a standard format that will help ensure that your letter is both persuasive and thorough. The following checklist is an effective guide to pitch letter writing:[13]

- Attention-getting first paragraph
- An indication that you are familiar with this media outlet and its audience
- Background information and research that supports your pitch
- Description of support elements available and suggestions for other sources of information for the story
- Concluding statement specifying the next step

The Opening

As with a press release, the first couple of sentences of a pitch letter can make or break your attempt to win the connector's attention. There are several recommended opening strategies you can use, such as the following:

1. Using a startling or little-known fact to catch attention is often effective. For example: "Did you know that if a barber commits a felony he can lose his barber's license, but if you are convicted of a felony you can earn a barber's license while in prison?"
2. Double entendres also work well. For instance: "Corporate sponsorship for ski team goes downhill."

Key Terms

Pitch letter A letter, an e-mail, or another written document used to present a pitch

3. Following the style of Geico®, you could start with a question, such as "Did you know that a three-minute phone call could save a consumer hundreds of dollars?"

4. Using intrigue is a great way to get connectors to read on. Be certain, however, that you deliver something truly interesting after setting an intriguing tone. For example: "The secret to a longer life may already be in your refrigerator."

5. There is nothing wrong with cutting to the chase. Don't be afraid to be straightforward with connectors and say something like: "We'll be speaking to the local Rotary Club next week, and the topic we are speaking about will have a direct impact on your readers."[14]

Familiarity with Connector

In its *PR Professional's Credo*, the public relations firm PR-Squared exhorts the PR professional to read several weeks' worth of previous blog posts and/or articles to ascertain whether his or her story would be a good fit for a particular blog or publication. In addition the firm urges the PR professional never to send a press release without being able to demonstrate its concrete relevance to the blogger or reporter.[15] A demonstration of familiarity helps you show how your pitch aligns with the connector's beliefs and values while giving you the opportunity to point out how covering this story serves that connector's audience. You need to know your target media's needs and receptiveness to what you are pitching as well as their specialties and contact preferences.[16] Poor targeting resulting from mistakes in matching story ideas with journalists' needs is the number one reason journalists give for not covering a story.[17]

As a result, mass marketing is out. You will need to draft a different letter—with a different story angle—for every publication on your list.[18] So, use a mass customization approach in which you use the same pool of facts and support material to craft messages that are tailored to individual connectors.

Background Information and Research

Journalists and other connectors are busy professionals with deadlines. They also value objectivity, which means they are interested in backing up ideas and opinions with facts. The MPR professional is responsible for supplying connectors with facts they can use, and the pitch letter is the place to introduce this information and indicate that more is available. As Steve Yoder of *The Wall Street Journal* explained at a PRSA Silicon Valley media training workshop, public relations professionals can help a journalist do his or her job by helping him or her with facts and figures and making sure the journalist has the story right.[19]

An example of a good use of research within a pitch was Now & Zen's efforts to expand its market for its Zen alarm clock, which uses acoustic tones similar to Tibetan bell tolls to gently awaken its users. Along with its PR agency, the company sought to devise a campaign that targeted not just the "cultural creatives" who had been its core market, but also more mainstream consumers. Traditionally, Now & Zen pitched using a spiritual angle, but company managers realized that they needed to supplement that angle with real findings on the product's benefits if they wanted to reach the broader market. As Now & Zen COO David Ratner explains:

> We had science attesting to tangible stress created by the buzzing sound of alarm clocks....By using spiritual-themed pitches for some outlets and more general pitches focused on science and design for others, the agency was able to dramatically expand the number of outlets it could target. The Zen alarm clock received steady coverage throughout the year in both New Age and mainstream outlets.[20]

The agency garnered placement in a broad range of outlets, including *Women's Health, Money, Fit Yoga, Playgirl, Chicago Sun-Times, Newark Star-Ledger, Seattle Times, Fort Worth Star-Telegram, Tampa Tribune, Arkansas Democrat-Gazette, Orange County Register*, and numerous other publications. More important, business increased by 15 percent, and Now & Zen feels that's largely attributable to PR.[21]

Support Elements and Additional Sources

In addition to presenting research, you, the PR professional, should provide additional information, either in a press kit that you made available to the connector before the pitch or as an accompaniment to the pitch letter. If you send the pitch letter as an e-mail, you should send the press kit as a link rather than an attachment, because journalists may be reluctant to open unsolicited attachments. You should also use the pitch letter to alert the recipient to the availability of **B-Roll** footage, audio recordings, or photographs in addition to what is in the press kit.

Supplying connectors with other sources of information and the names of potential interviewees serves to make the connector's job easier and allows you to have some control over the sources used in the story. You need to exercise some caution here, however. If the topic is divisive, and you only provide information that supports your organization's side of the story, connectors might question your credibility.

Action Step

Ultimately, the goal of a pitch is to have the connector commit to covering your story. The pitch letter should let the connector know how to contact you in order to take the next step and/or let him know when and how you will be following up with him or her. The action step, followed by your signature, is the final piece of the pitch letter. Make sure, however, that the connector can contact you the way you indicated, and that you do follow up as you specified.

Key Terms

B-Roll Video footage produced by a firm and supplied to connectors in support of an MPR effort

Exhibit 9.1 Annotated Pitch Letter. Pitch letters need to be customized to the connectors they are targeted toward, but all share these common elements.

(Date) April Meehan, Senior Editor Progress Magazine 433 43rd Avenue New York, New York 10039 Dear April:		
I suggest a feature story on Blanchard Banks of Detroit who, at the age of 64, has just read his first book ever to his granddaughter, Jasmine, age four. "It's a miracle," the silver-haired man explains.		**Attention-getting first paragraph**
Blanchard began life as a farm worker in Mississippi and migrated to Detroit as a young man in 1940. Working in a factory, he managed to get by without reading by meticulously following instructions and occasionally asking someone to "clarify" written communications. When Marks Industries, where Blanchard works, joined the fight for literacy, Blanchard signed-up for the after-work tutoring program offered at his local library. In June he will graduate in a special program to be attended by several U.S. Congressmen.		**Information connecting with medium & its audience**
In the Marks Industries program alone, fifty people have already been able to experience the joy of learning to read. It wasn't easy for Blanchard and the others to admit their reading deficiencies; it wasn't easy to overcome the obstacles of getting enough volunteer instructors, and a suitable meeting place; but the Marks program is making a big difference. In fact there are now plans to expand it into a fifteen-state partnership with local community organizations.		**Background information supporting pitch**
I believe your readers would be inspired by Blanchard's story. There are great photo opportunities here. I'll give you a call in a few days to discuss your interest.		**Support materials (photos) and action step**
Sincerely, Samantha Gerkins		

Source: Reprinted with permission from *How to Write It*, revised by Sandra E. Lamb. Copyright 1998, 2006 by Sandra E. Lamb, Ten Speed Press, Berkeley, CA. www.tenspeed.com.

Concept Case 9.1: **Making the Pitch**

The Falcon's Lair has been trying to get the attention of the mainstream media in hopes of enticing more people to try rock climbing. The managers believe that, if they discuss the health benefits of this sport and position it with just a touch of "extreme," they will have a story that will attract local television stations and newspapers. Here are two initial ideas for an opening paragraph:

"Can something that looks like risking your life actually help save it? Yes, if it's rock climbing. Rock climbing has been shown to build muscle strength and endurance, increase flexibility, and relieve stress. And with a little training it is safe and affordable for everyone."

"Interested in showing your readers/viewers how being at the end of their rope can build muscle strength and endurance, increase flexibility, and relieve stress? It's not another diet or exercise fad; it's rock climbing, and it's fun, safe, and affordable for all."

Questions:

1. Discuss the pros and cons of each paragraph, and explain which one you feel is best.
2. Write your own paragraph and explain why it is better than any of the above.
3. Explain how you would use this letter to build credibility, relationship, and connection with beliefs, and communicate the benefit to the connector.
4. What support information would you include in this letter?

The Power of Embargos and Exclusives

CHAPTER
OBJECTIVE
4

Giving information to a journalist beforehand with the agreement that she will not release it until a certain date is an **embargo**. The idea is to give connectors time to prepare a story before it is announced, with the goal of creating a win-win for the journalist/blogger and the marketer. "I think of embargos as gifts," writes Allen Stern, editor of CenterNetworks, a new Internet blog. "It's a certain level of trust that a PR firm or company has given to a writer. It's the most trust that a company can give out and something that should be respected as such." Many marketers feel that bloggers do not respect embargos and, as a result, have decreased the effectiveness of this tactic. As Stern observes, "I've seen bloggers who post early—whether it's 5 minutes or 30 minutes, it's still early in my book."[22]

As Cece Salomon-Lee writes in her blog, PR Meets Marketing:

Even before blogs, you always risked the possibility of a reporter breaking your embargo. Heck, this happened to me when I worked with a reputable national business outlet before my client launched at a conference.... The article appeared on the Sunday before the conference began and also mentioned a couple of other companies. The saving grace is that reporters were still interested in learning more about the company and in the end I believe embargos are still valid.[23]

Giving a particular journalist or media outlet the right to present a story first is an **exclusive**. In theory, when you give a connector an edge by giving him or her access to a story that his competitors do not have, you can expect him to cover the story in detail and in a way that closely reflects your positioning. Despite the fact that the word *exclusive* implies that you release the story to a single outlet, you can, if you do it properly, give an exclusive on the same story to

---

Key Terms

Embargo Giving information about a story to a connector before the firm wants it released to allow the connector time to prepare his story

Exclusive Giving information about a story to a single connector in order to enhance the firm's coverage in that connector's medium

multiple connectors. The trick is to find connectors in distinctly different markets and let each of them know that you are giving a related story to a noncompetitive outlet.[24]

Pitching a Blogger

While most of what you have read here applies to all connectors, pitching bloggers can be a little different than working with those in traditional media. As Matt Clark of Lotus-PR says, "Blogger relations are very complex and new." He offers the following keys to blogger relations:

- Make sure you do your research and have good reasons for picking your target blogs.
- Engage the bloggers by commenting on their posts and start a true conversation with them before adding them to a media list.
- Make sure the bloggers accept pitches, as many do not.
- Make sure it's okay to e-mail them; some bloggers would rather be contacted through a basic contact form on their site.
- Never send a basic pitch template to them. Pitch letters to bloggers must be very personal.
- Look to extend your relationship beyond just getting a "hit." If you cannot start a strong working relationship, remove bloggers who are not interested in covering your firm from your connector list.

Pitch Live

Some MPR professionals prefer to forgo the pitch letter and contact connectors directly. This contact can take place over the telephone or in person, often at a trade show or professional conference. Pitching a connector "live" requires all the elements of a pitch letter, with the added pressure of having to answer questions on the spot. As a result, if you pitch live, you really need to know the connector and you must be meticulously prepared and have any information the connector might require at your fingertips. When using this method of contact, not only do you need to follow the rules of pitching, but you also need to employ the rules of follow-up.

Mining Editorial Calendars

Marketers do not always have to guess what types of stories connectors want to see or hear. In fact, many media outlets and even some bloggers post editorial calendars that describe the topics that they intend to cover over the course of the year. Over the summer and through the fall, publications begin releasing their editorial calendars for the coming year. This is the time to research your target publications and find out what topics have been scheduled to run beginning in January. The stories that appear to be a natural fit for your company, product, or service are those on which you will want to focus your placement efforts. Since monthly publications can have a lead-time of six months or more, it is never too early to start pitching involvement in stories.

Here is the process you should follow:

1. Make a list of the publications that reach your best audiences/potential customers.
2. If you have a media research service or product—such as MediaMap (http://www.mediamap.com), LexisNexis (http://www.lexisnexis.com), or the like—the next step is easy. Enter your search terms—based on the topic you are pitching—and a list of opportunities will be shown on your computer screen.
3. Find the Web site for the publication you are targeting and search for the section "About Us" or "Media Kit." If you're very lucky, the site will include a section entitled "Editorial Calendar."
4. Once you have located the editorial calendar, scan it for entries that are a match for your market focus, product, or service. Note the issue in which the story is scheduled to run and the deadline date for submitting information and/or materials for that story.
5. If the editorial contact does not appear on the editorial calendar, call the publication and ask to speak with someone in the Editorial Department who can assist you in identifying the correct writer or editor to contact. If you are not able to reach Editorial, try asking the person who answers the phone who the best contact might be. The people who answer the phone sometimes know more than you would expect and can be very helpful.
6. Repeat this process for each of your target publications until you have a list of all scheduled stories for the coming year with potential for your company's involvement.
7. You may find it easier to keep track of your editorial opportunities list if you enter all the information into a spreadsheet, such as Excel. You will easily be able to add, subtract, and sort opportunities as you act upon them.[25]

Follow up, Follow up, and Follow up!

CHAPTER
OBJECTIVE
8

Great materials and a great pitch aren't enough. Media people are busy; if you don't stay on their radar screen, they will forget you. To follow up properly, you also need to be focused in your purpose and to foster your relationship with the connector. Following are some basic guidelines for bridging the gap between making your initial pitch and gaining the commitment of media mentions from connectors:

1. *Follow up promptly* after sending a press release or other material. You should typically follow up within a day or two of the connector receiving the initial pitch. For a time-critical story or one that needs to make the next edition of the news, you will want to make contact within a few hours or less.

2. *Keep following up* until you get a response. Remember, connectors are busy and may be working on multiple deadlines at one time. The fact that a particular connector was not ready to talk when you called or has neglected to return your call does not mean that he or she does not want to hear about your story idea. Don't annoy your connectors, but realize that being a pest is more attitude than frequency.

3. *If they say "no," or it's a bad fit, go away!* Sometimes you simply have to take "no" for an answer. If you aggravate a connector, you increase the chances that he or she will give you negative media mentions or will ignore this and all other story ideas that come from you and your organization in the future.

4. *Keep calls on message.* Your reason for following up needs to be more than simply to ask if the connector received your pitch letter and press kit. You need to be ready to pitch again and get to the next step—commitment.

5. *Be open to alternative ways to get out your message.* For example, you may be pitching an interview with your CEO, but the editor might want to do a feature on your company or product. Go with the editor's preference.

6. *Be polite.* Your mother and your kindergarten teacher told you this many times, and you need to remember it when you pitch. Even though you cannot expect all connectors to be polite in return, you need to keep your composure. Remember that you are likely to have another story you want to pitch to this person some day. In addition, connectors talk among themselves; you don't want to get a bad reputation with a connector's connections.

7. *Be a resource.* What else is the media person working on? Help him or her if you can, even if you will not receive an immediate benefit. You should try to be as helpful as possible throughout every step of the MPR process. When you become a resource to connectors, they start coming to you.

CHAPTER OBJECTIVE 9

Tips for Getting You Through the Pitching Process

The process of pitching and following up is vital in an MPR professional's quest for media mentions and word-of-mouth. While critical thinking and preparedness are essential skills for a marketer's MPR efforts, nothing can replace experience. The following are some tips from famed marketer and author Richard Laermer:

1. Don't bribe journalists.
2. If you're happy with the way a story turns out, don't send a gift thanking the reporter.
3. Strike the word *favor* from your media relations vocabulary.
4. Don't let your boss or colleagues tell you that they'll handle getting the media coverage if you're the one with the connections.
5. Don't believe that whatever you're doing is too important to disclose.
6. Don't miss a deadline.

7. Don't pitch one of your stories that just appeared in a competing newspaper or magazine and pretend you didn't see it or have anything to do with it.

8. Don't break a deal.

9. Never lie.

10. Don't give journalists only one option for using your story.

11. Don't ever believe that you can say anything off the record.

12. Never say that you don't know or that you can't answer a question.

13. Don't leave voice messages and e-mail unanswered.

14. Never be egotistical.

15. Don't play hard-to-get with your answers.

16. Don't make a sport out of getting the upper hand on the media.

17. Expunge buzzwords and jargon from your vocabulary.

18. Simply do not let the media walk all over you.

19. Don't let the media put words in your mouth.

20. Don't think like everyone else, because you'll always be viewed as "regular."

21. Don't shoot down your media opportunities by thinking your big idea isn't doable.

22. Don't miss an opportunity to participate in the larger story.

23. Don't let ornery journalists discourage you.

24. Don't think a news outlet is too small for your great idea.

25. Never go to an interview without an agenda.

26. If you are on national TV, and you feel like making an off-color joke, don't.[26]

 ## Reflection Questions

1. Discuss your view of newsworthiness, and cite some examples of subjects you think are and are not newsworthy. (Chapter Objective 1)

2. Explain why an MPR professional might have different degrees of credibility with different connectors. (Chapter Objective 2)

3. Discuss how the balance theory relates to a connector's relationship with a marketer and beliefs about a topic. (Chapter Objective 2)

4. Describe the various reasons for using a pitch letter. (Chapter Objective 2)

5. List and briefly describe all of the elements of a pitch letter. (Chapter Objective 3)

6. Compare and contrast the purpose of embargos and exclusives. (Chapter Objective 4)

7. Discuss the special considerations for pitching a blogger. (Chapter Objective 5)

8. Explain the challenges of a live pitch. (Chapter Objective 6)

9. If you had a story idea you believed to be ideal for a particular connector, but you did not

see a reference to a similar subject on his or her editorial calendar, would you still pitch the idea to him or her? Explain why or why not. (Chapter Objective 7)

10. Discuss the importance of following up on a pitch and the things a marketer should be aware of when doing so. (Chapter Objective 8)

Chapter Key Terms

Balance theory A communications theory that asserts that receivers feel uncomfortable, or out of balance, when their attitude toward the sender of a message does not match their attitude about the topic of the message (p. 141)

B-Roll Video footage produced by a firm and supplied to connectors in support of an MPR effort (p. 145)

Embargo Giving information about a story to a connector before the firm wants it released to allow the connector to prepare his or her story (p. 147)

Exclusive Giving information about a story to a single connector in order to enhance the firm's coverage in that connector's medium (p. 147)

Newsworthy A subject that is interesting to a medium's audience, is objective, and will not make the media appear as though it has an ulterior motive for covering it (p. 140)

Pitch An attempt to persuade a journalist or other connector to cover a story (p. 139)

Pitch letter A letter, an e-mail, or another written document used to present a pitch (p. 143)

Application Assignments

1. Scan today's news for a story not related to crime, politics, or natural phenomena that has been covered by three or more news sources. Explain why this story was newsworthy and what interest the individual connectors have in it.

2. Search the Web for a current editorial calendar and describe the types of companies and products that this medium is interested in covering. Be specific.

3. Identify a medium that is interested in covering one of the following topics and select a product that you feel would be of interest. After studying the medium's editorial calendar, write the first paragraph of a pitch letter to that connector regarding the product you have selected.

   a. Electric guitars
   b. Personal in-home saunas
   c. Running shoes
   d. Gourmet stoves

4. Search *Business Wire* (http://www.businesswire.com) and find a press release that is of interest to you. Then find a media outlet or blog that is interested in this topic and write a pitch letter to that person or company. In a separate document, explain your approach to writing this letter.

5. Write a script for a follow-up telephone call that you would make to the connector selected in *Application Assignment 4.* Include a list of resources you would have at your disposal for this conversation.

Practice Portfolio

This Practice Portfolio can be based on a fictitious company or on a real company that your instructor assigns to you. (If you used a company in previous Practice Portfolio exercises, continue to use that company.) Add your completed assignment to your portfolio to present to prospective employers.

- Write a pitch letter for each of the two press releases that you wrote for Chapter 8's Practice Portfolio. Using the connector list you created in Chapter 7, target a different connector for each letter.

CHAPTER 10

Social Media

CHAPTER OBJECTIVES

After studying this chapter, you should be able to:

1. Explain what social media are and differentiate between the different types.

2. Describe the function and usages of social networks.

3. Explain the concept of a wiki and its benefits and limitations.

4. Discuss the social media uses of blogs.

5. Describe what makes a podcast or video viral, and explain the difference between MPR and advertising uses of these tools.

6. Discuss the role of bookmarking, rating systems, consumer reviews, and consumer-generated content.

7. Discuss the importance of interlinking a firm's social media efforts, and the potential dangers of social media to firms who use it.

At the young age of twenty-two, Gary Vaynerchuk took over the running of his family business, a liquor store in New Jersey. Over a period of six years (1998–2004), Gary and his father Sasha rebranded the business as Wine Library and transformed it from a local store doing annual sales of roughly $4 million to a $50 million national industry leader.[1] Gary first demonstrated his penchant for entrepreneurship by opening a lemonade stand franchise at age six and by building a successful baseball card business in his teens. However, he had no interest in getting involved with the family liquor business. "My father used to make me go to the store with him and I hated it," Gary explains. "But eventually, I realized that people collect wine, and they are willing to spend some serious money on it. This made me see the connection with my baseball card business. Like baseball card collectors, there's a community of wine collectors out there."

This revelation spurred the renaming of the liquor store from Shoppers Discount Liquors to the Wine Library. While Gary was advocating exploiting this niche, he credits his dad with coming up with the name that fit their new position in the marketplace. The new positioning itself was a good start but was not the engine that drove the Wine Library's explosive growth. The explosion came from Gary's enthusiastic approach to using social media: "We had had a website since the early nineties, but in 2005 I noticed that the Internet had gone social," he says. "It was becoming a two-way conversation, and I knew we could capitalize on it in a way that benefited our business and our customers."

Gary Vaynerchuk is honored to taste some serious white Burgundy with Jean-Marc Roulot, proprietor of one of the most hallowed domaines in the Cote de Beaune.

Courtesy WLTV.com

In February 2006 Wine Library TV (http://tv.winelibrary.com) was born. WLTV is essentially a video blog that is also distributed as a video podcast through iTunes®. It is shot with one camera and is unedited. During each episode Gary tastes and reviews several different wines, but this is not a stereotypical wine critic show; it is neither stuffy nor technical. Gary shoots straight from the hip in a way that is entertaining and educational. His unique approach has caused WLTV to go viral and to have tens of thousands of subscribers. "I was humbled when I had five people subscribing," relates Gary. "With over 500 shows under our belt and more than 90,000 views per day, I am just blown away and truly grateful."

When asked what has made WLTV such a success, he says, "It comes down to two things: content and community. People want to be a part of something and you need to give them something worth coming for."

He continues, "The world wants authenticity, and the Internet is real. People and businesses that leverage social media to follow their DNA (i.e., pursue their passions) will be the next Brad and Angelina and the next Oprah." He even cites Perez Hilton, whose blog has become more powerful in the world of celebrity gossip than *US* or *People* magazines.

When it comes to authenticity, Gary practices what he preaches. This is not only evident in his unconventional style, but in the fact that he pans 60 percent to 70 percent of the wines that he tastes even though he is in the business of selling those wines.

In addition to WLTV, Gary and Wine Library are active in other forms of social media that Gary credits for the business's rapid rise. For example, the video blog solicits feedback from viewers and it is not unusual to see 100 to 200 comments from fans for each episode. Gary is active on Facebook, MySpace, LinkedIn, Viddler, Corkd, and Pownce. Gary and several Wine Library employees are very active on Twitter. He has also started to do some live broadcast using live video stream application Ustream.tv, and encourages people to bookmark and share Wine Library and WLTV content through Digg, Delicious, StumbleUpon, and even good old fashioned e-mail.

When asked if getting into so many avenues of social media is worth it, Gary answers with a definitive "yes":

> An investment of just a few thousand dollars in social media returned more to me than millions of dollars in conventional advertising. Plus, think about how things get spread around. Even if I talk to the fifty best connected people in New York City every day, and they tell all of their friends about me, I still can't top the power of connection with social media. The Internet is a big place and you can't really be overexposed.

The success of Gary's methods is evident through more than just the extreme increases in sales for his business. He is one of the top thirty followed people on Twitter and has grabbed the attention of traditional media. He has appeared on Donny Deutsch's *Big Idea, Late Night with Conan O'Brien, The Ellen DeGeneres Show, Mad Money with Jim Cramer*, and *Nightline.* He is also consulting with the Pennsylvania Liquor Control Board, Procter and Gamble, and Green Mountain Coffee® to help them promote their brands through social media. Gary says:

> I'd like to be remembered as a pioneer in social media the way Lucille Ball or Bob Hope are remembered for being pioneers of comedy. I also envy the members of the CKC (college kid crew) because they are the first generation that will be able to combine the passion that is in their DNA with social media to do what they love and live incredibly successful lives.

What Is Social Media?

The way people communicate has changed drastically over the last decade, and marketing professionals are working hard to try to keep up. **Social media**[2] are often defined narrowly and considered to be synonymous with **social networks** like Facebook and MySpace. While these popular cyber destinations are types of social media, there are other non-network types as well. Think of social media as all sites where participants can produce, publish, control, critique, rank, and interact with online content.[3] As a result, we can include blogs and micro-blogs, video sharing, bookmarking applications, wikis, forums, and opinion sites, as well as social networks. It is the power of interaction that attracts consumers and allures marketers to this space.

Marketers can assume, with reasonable certainty, that anyone who spends time interacting within a specific Web environment fits within the demographic profile of that environment and shares the purchasing behaviors of that group. For example, marketers looking to reach a market segment such as video game enthusiasts (gamers) that is typically difficult to reach via traditional media have a wealth of options to touch this market via social media. Not only do most of the popular games have communities as a part of their online offering, there are Web communities dedicated to gamers and their passion. GamerDNA.com, for instance, professes to reach people who are very difficult to reach outside of their interests in and around gaming. This site specializes in youthful, passionate, digitally connected consumers who participate in many online activities and social media and are among the first to choose games and technology products and tell their friends about them.[4] GameRankings.com serves the same industry, but focuses on gathering and disseminating ranking and reviews more than fostering community. In either case, these sites can be a direct connection between the marketers of video games and their most coveted customers.

So, why should marketers care about social media? The social media study conducted by Cone Inc. in 2008 showed that 93 percent of social media users believe that companies they buy from should have a presence in social media. In addition 85 percent believe a company should not only be present but should also interact with its consumers via social media. In fact, 56 percent of users feel both a stronger connection with and better served by companies when they can interact with them in a social media environment.[5] As a result, marketers should not view a social medium as a connector. Rather the social medium becomes the vehicle for connecting marketers with connectors and, more important for connectors to hook up with each other and spread their opinions to the larger community. For example, the people who frequent Facebook and TripAdvisor.com are connectors, while the sites themselves are not. This mix of social media participants blurs the lines between connector and audience; in any given community an individual may be both a connector and a member of the audience.

Key Terms

Social media Electronic media where participants can produce, publish, control, critique, rank, and interact with online content

Social network A Web-based community designed to promote interaction, discussion, and sharing of content among its users

Exhibit 10.1   Some market segments, like video game enthusiasts, are difficult to reach by traditional media, but are highly involved with social media.

Diego Cervo/Shutterstock.

CHAPTER
OBJECTIVE
2

Social Networks: A Tool of Inclusion

If the term *social networking* is familiar to you, chances are that either Facebook or MySpace are the networks that pop into your mind. If you're a business professional or an adult student, perhaps you've heard of LinkedIn or Gather.com. These sites are among the most popular of social networks but are just a few examples of a universe that consists of literally hundreds of thousands. These networks range in content from those whose purpose is strictly for socialization or networking to networks that focus on highly specific products, issues, or lifestyles. Examples of the latter include Cork'd (http://www.corkd.com) for wine enthusiasts, Streetball.com (http://www.streetball.com) for those embracing the "basketball Hip-hop lifestyle," and Care2.com (http://www.care2.com) for environmental/social activists. A social network probably exists for any product a marketer can hope to promote. In addition, Web sites like Ning.com (http://www.ning.com) allow you to create your own social network for free.

Despite the fact that targeting a specific audience through social networks is fairly easy, using them effectively can be a challenge for marketers. The mere fact that a marketer is showing up in a social network can send up a red flag among the community members. Rick Murray of Edelman Digital describes marketing with social media using a cocktail party metaphor: "If you walk in with the loudest clothes, you're going to get kicked out, and no one is going to pay attention to you," he said in an interview published in *Advertising Age*. "Blend in, and once you do, make sure you add value."[6]

Marketers must identify themselves as such, while they prove their worth to the network. As Gary Vaynerchuk pointed out, the proof comes by creating outstanding content and fostering a community. This holds true whether you are participating in an existing community or creating one of your own.

MPR on Public Social Networks

Facebook CEO Mark Zuckerberg was quoted in *USA Today* as saying, "Pushing your message out to people isn't enough anymore; you have to get into the connections and conversations." In the same article Jeremiah Owyang, an analyst at Forrester Research explains, "Traditional marketing is distorted and endorsements are now passed from trusted customers to prospects, not directly from the brands themselves."[7]

Dunkin' Donuts' utilization of a Facebook fan page is an example of marketers making good use of social networking. The presence of more than 175,000 fans (as of October 2008) on Dunkin's page is evidence of a sense of community. Many of these fans actively participate on the page by posting comments to the **wall**, creating and moderating discussion threads, participating in polls, and posting photos of themselves and friends enjoying Dunkin' Donuts' products and facilities. In addition to the content contributed by fans, the page contains updates from the company on products and specials, as well as a calendar of events and photos and videos produced by the firm.

According to David Tryder, manager of interactive and relationship marketing for Dunkin' Donuts,

> Social networking provides an entirely new way for Dunkin' Donuts to engage with our consumers, and we embrace it as a way to participate in the online conversation among our brand loyalists, as well as with those who are not as familiar with us yet....Facebook presents a highly cost effective opportunity to connect with consumers in a way that traditional advertising cannot. With Facebook, we can share, listen, respond, and educate—there is so much flexibility and opportunity to interact in a casual, authentic way....

Consumers appreciate this and want this from their favorite brands—these are the same people who are recording their television programming and fast-forwarding through commercials, so if you expect to engage with your brand's fans within social media, you must understand that approaching it in a traditional way isn't going to be effective. Brand marketers covet their most efficient and effective marketing tools—consumer

Exhibit 10.2 Dunkin' Donuts harnesses the power of Facebook to connect with their customers through a public social media channel.

Robert Sullivan/Getty Images, Inc.–Agence France Presse

Key Terms

Wall The space on a social network page where friends, fans, or contacts can write a message to the owner of that space

brand ambassadors, who truly understand their brand and its core value proposition. Word-of-mouth marketing hasn't changed much, but the opportunities that enable it have grown significantly, and we intend to explore all of those opportunities side by side with our consumers. What has changed is that social media has allowed brand ambassadors to move from spreading the word about our products from a one-to-one basis to a one-to-hundreds, or even one-to-thousands. Additionally, this has allowed our culinary team and brand managers to connect with customers in a meaningful way without the expense of conducting focus groups. This starts a conversation that is honest, straightforward, and genuine.

Of course, connecting a company with a community can have its challenges. Tryder points out that the Web is the Web, and there is some risk involved. Particularly when it comes to getting publicly posted comments that aren't positive. But that's part of the cost of participating in the conversation, If a company is prepared and willing to be proactive, these risks can be managed. He cautions that there is no blanket answer or magic formula, and each company has to look at social media relative to how they effect the connection to its customers.

Molson Coors Brewing Company experienced some of the potential downside of social networks after creating a photo contest on its Facebook fan page. The campaign encouraged college and university students to post pictures of themselves partying on campus. While received well by students in the target audience, the schools and community at large were quite upset. "The contest was misinterpreted as promoting irresponsible drinking," said Ferg Devins, a vice president at Molson Coors Brewing Co. The company withdrew the contest following pressure from Canadian universities and prompted Devins to comment, "The whole realm of social media—there's lots to learn. It's really a new area. We're probably groundbreaking and leading in a lot of things we've been doing."[8]

Creating Your Own Social Network

While public social networks have the greatest name recognition with the average consumer, mission-specific social networks are actually most abundant. In fact, as of April 2008, the do-it-yourself social network platform Ning.com was hosting more than 230,000 social networks and was growing at a rate of 1,000 new networks per day.[9] While quite a few of these networks are personal or cause- or hobby-related, many of them deal with products and businesses. As a result, marketers should pay attention to Ning's Web site, where the company explains that a social network can be used to:

- Raise awareness
- Connect events with attendees
- Inspire and educate
- Share insight and provide support
- Share tricks of the trade
- Create community for customers

Of course, most marketers can ignore Ning's suggestions for using social networks to create your "Wed-site" (i.e., Web site for your wedding) or to make your pet happy. However, marketers do need to pay close attention to the suggestion that social networks can create community with customers. In fact, if we include prospective customers in this audience, we have gotten to the essence of social networking in marketing. Marketers need to change their mind-set and realize that they cannot simply translate their mainstream media advertising efforts into success in a social network. In contrast to the traditional advertising notion that frequency of *message* leads to achieving marketing goals, frequency of *contact* is actually more likely to be the winning formula for this medium. In this format consumers want firms to speak to them.[10] According to Matt Dickman, vice president of digital marketing at Fleischman-Hillard in Cleveland, Ohio, "You have to add value to each interaction and use the naturally viral nature of the community instead of forcing it."[11]

Concept Case 10.1: **Social Climbing**

The Falcon's Lair management has always believed that the sense of community that exists between the customers and staff is the cornerstone of the company's success. Combining this with the fact that the Lair's clientele ranges from typically tech-savvy teens to "forty-somethings," the managers feel confident that they can successfully venture into social networking. Therefore, they have decided to create both a Facebook page as well as their own social network as another way to add value to The Falcon's Lair brand.

Questions:

1. What will these social networking efforts have to accomplish in order to be successful?
2. Explain some specific things that The Falcon's Lair managers should include on these sites to help them bring value to their customers.
3. Can you recommend some specific Facebook pages or social networks that might act as examples for the Lair's management team? Explain why you like the sites you are recommending.

Wonderful World of Wikis

CHAPTER
OBJECTIVE
3

It has been the first stop for term paper writing students across the globe and the bane of professors almost since its inception. In addition, some of its virtues are also its vices. The subject in question is, of course, Wikipedia. Wikipedia is the online encyclopedia that anybody can edit; it is responsible for the creation of the term **wiki**. The essence of the wiki is to provide a repository for content of any sort that can be edited, added to, or updated by the community of those interested in the subject. While Wikipedia effectively covers any subject, other, smaller wikis are popping up all over with a seemingly endless array of subject matter, including those with business and promotional intent.

Key Terms

Wiki A repository for content of any sort that can be edited, added to, or updated by the community of those interested in the subject

Exhibit 10.3 Wiki-based collaboration can be an easier and more efficient way of working together.

Shutterstock

Wikis can be useful tools for promoting a business, especially where a community can be built around those with a passion for a specific topic. Think of social networking as content built around a community, while a wiki is a community built around content. The key success factor for a wiki is its innate ability to foster group collaboration by allowing a group of people to work on the same document rather than having them share multiple versions of the work in progress.

The success of a wiki depends on building active, sustainable participation. Wiki participants must see that the software is simple to use and does not require them to spend lots of time figuring it out. As use of the wiki grows in your organization, make sure that people feel comfortable trying new, unexpected ways of using it.[12]

A good example of a non-Wikipedia wiki that works by building community around content is the Muppet Wiki. It describes itself as "a collaborative encyclopedia for everything related to Jim Henson and the Muppets. The wiki format allows anyone to create or edit any article, so we can all work together to create a comprehensive database for Muppet fans." With more than 17,000 articles posted about Jim Henson and his puppet progeny, it is clear that this wiki supports the Muppet brand without any overt selling or advertising. "The most important thing, which a lot of people don't recognize, is that you have to treat your (wiki) contributors like they're people," Danny Horn, co-founder and community manager of the Muppet Wiki, reminds us. "You have to welcome them, help them, and encourage them. People who work on wikis are doing the most outlandish thing—spending hours adding to a site without getting paid or even having their name attached to their work. People who host wikis should never stop telling their contributors how beautiful and amazing they are."[13] This is especially important when you realize that the contributors are your connectors and will help you support the interest of the noncontributing members who make up approximately 80 percent of the wiki community's visitors.

Of course, there is a downside to wikis, in that completely open collaboration can lead to the addition of material that is either incorrect or misleading to the community. Erroneous data can originate from well-intentioned community members who were not diligent in their fact checking, but it can also stem from those with malicious intent hoping to deceive or discredit the wiki and its members.

CHAPTER
OBJECTIVE
4

Blogs Big and Small

Up to this point our discussion of blogs has centered on finding and pitching bloggers with the intent of having them cover a story. While blogs do sometimes act like traditional media, they also have a social component in that the audience can interact with them, primarily by responding to blog posts. Therefore, firms can take advantage of additional media opportunities by creating blogs that supply content and foster community and by participating in the interactive side of blogs that are relevant to the firm's business and audience.

Create Your Own

"For any organization, a blog is part of a long-term customer evangelism strategy," says Ben McConnell in his blog, Church of the Customer. "Since blogs are easy to set up and pay for (some are free), launching a blog should be at the top of your to-do list."[14]

McConnell offers several reasons why all businesses should blog:

1. Blogs fan the flames of customer evangelism. Their personal nature helps humanize you and your organization.

2. They function as an instant-feedback mechanism. Most blogs allow readers to respond to your posts or link to them on their own blogs. These features provide almost real-time feedback on ideas and issues that strike a chord or highlight new or existing problems. A blog can help reveal a little problem before it becomes a big one.

3. They compel you to share your knowledge more often. A blog is about sharing what you know, think, and believe; search engines index your ongoing knowledge-sharing, making it easier for customers and prospects to find you.

4. Blogs facilitate the spread of buzz. Honest, informative, or thought-provoking posts about issues important to customers and prospects tend to be spread more often.

5. They allow you to have more simultaneous conversations than would ever be possible in person.

6. Most blog service providers offer good-looking templates to use if your existing Web site design is embarrassing or nonexistent.

7. They help position you as a knowledgeable expert in your industry.[15]

McConnell goes on to say that authenticity is essential because people want to communicate with people. While customers know they are in a dialogue about a brand or product, they do not want obvious sales techniques. He also cautions marketers not to have a thin skin. Some of the feedback received through a firm's blog might be hard to take, but you need to hear all types of customer opinion, not just the good stuff.[16]

Gretel Going at partner Channel V Media in New York City offers the following tips for creating and maintaining a blog for a business, brand, or product:

- *Identify your editorial platform and underlying message.* You want your voice to be accessible and to speak directly to your audience.

- *Don't simply talk about yourself.* Educate and engage readers with topics for which your product or brand can authoritatively offer thought leadership.

- *Be prepared to give away what was once considered proprietary information.* In order to be useful to readers, you have to entice them with applicable content, such as research, industry stats, or best practices used by your company; hoarding your intellectual property in the online space does not do you any good.

- *Identify your buyers' personas and make sure your message caters to their needs.* You might find that your audience is so diverse that you need to have more than one blog. On the other hand, the audience may be so niche that you can really home in on one specific message.

- *Make friends with likeminded bloggers* and be sure to leave comments on their sites in order to align with the industry as a whole and to increase your visibility. You should also link to other bloggers who have a similar perspective and support your ideals.

- *Update regularly (with blind faith that this will work).* If your blog is engaging, easy to find, and useful to your target audience, they will come. Regular updates also raise your status with search engines such as Google.

- *Respond to comments to build a community of active readers.* This step is like the online version of going to a bar "where everyone knows your name." Those who make comments on blogs often pride themselves on their contributions to sites they hold in high esteem; reward this type of interaction with consistent responses and dialogue. Others will likely follow.

- *Check your tracking and your key words regularly* in order to understand how new readers are finding you and what problems they're trying to solve—and be sure to address those problems in upcoming posts.

- *Make sure your homepage is accessible from your blog.* While you do want to separate the two in terms of content, you also want to create a positive association between your persona and message and the brand, product, or service you're ultimately promoting.

Participate in the Blogosphere

Chances are that multiple blogs exist that both cover topics of interest for any firm and reach the firm's audience or some subset of it. These blogs should already be on the firm's connector list. Therefore, firms should monitor and even participate in such blogs. If you choose to participate in the **blogosphere**,[17] you need to behave like a member of the community, rather than a salesperson, and you need to offer something of value rather than a sales pitch. If you use this approach correctly, then you and your firm will become valued members of the community. You can also build your credibility with the blogger, should you want to approach him about covering a story. According to Robyn Tippins, the community manager of Yahoo! Developer Network and chief blogger of Sleepyblogger.com (http://www.sleepyblogger.com):

> I applaud marketing/PR people taking part in online discussions. This exposes the fact that marketers are real people, with real opinions. Of course, I'm talking about professionals who give their own opinion and not one they are paid to pretend to have.... If marketing professionals are pretending to like something merely because that something is made by their firm or one of their clients, then all of our online discourse becomes suspect.

Micro-blogging

Have you ever used the status update function on Facebook or LinkedIn? It is the place where you answer the questions "What are you doing right now?" or "What are you working on?" If you have used it, you have no doubt noticed that this post is logged to your profile for all of your friends and contacts to see. Perhaps you have even heard of Twitter, the application that is dedicated to status updates and allows members to follow their friends' and colleagues' changing states. Since members are only permitted to post 140 characters per entry, some have taken to calling Twitter and its competitors (such as Pownce and Jaiku) **micro-blogs**. While many an old-school marketer has dismissed micro-blogs as a waste of time, some firms are putting them to good use: "Twitter is a great way to get customer service feedback. It is instantly accessible to customers to vent about a current situation that they are having," says Jaqueline Wolven, founder of Moxie Marketing and Public Relations. "If a firm monitors Twitter using a tool like Tweet Scan, it can search for the company and respond to clients instantly.... For example, when a **tweet** is posted about losing luggage, the customer is unhappy with JetBlue, JetBlue sees it, and responds directly to the customer offering solutions."

Zappos.com, the Internet shoe retailer, makes a different use of Twitter. The company CEO, Tony Hsieh, tweets, Zappos encourages its employees to tweet, and the company has created a special Web page (http://www.twitter.zappos.com) that consolidates all public mentions of Zappos into one community-friendly page that even includes access to a Twitter tutorial. Through these efforts Zappos.com is successfully using Twitter to put a human face on the company and to engage with customers more deeply.[18]

Video Sharing and Podcasts

CHAPTER OBJECTIVE 5

Informational videos and podcasts are yet another weapon in the marketer's arsenal. In April 2008 ComScore reported that 71 percent of the total U.S. Internet audience, or 134,471 million users, viewed online video. In addition, they found that in that month viewers watched an average of 82 clips with 228 minutes of video viewing.[19] Video and audio podcast availability and use are also on the rise. As acceptance of these media grows, they become more valuable to marketers. There is a fine line, however, between an MPR use of videos and podcasts and their use as advertisements. In order to be MPR, the use must be a clear effort to provide information to an audience without an overt sales pitch. It may be entertaining, and ideally would lead to increased brand awareness or sales, but as soon as it looks like it might be a commercial, it becomes advertising rather than MPR.

Nonetheless, videos and podcasts need to be interesting and provocative enough to get passed from consumer to consumer, or, in other words, go viral. Mark Rogers of Dolcinema.com notes that you need to answer two questions before adding video into your marketing mix: "Do you have content that is provocative, compelling, funny, sexy,

---

Key Terms

Blogosphere A collective term encompassing all blogs and their interconnections. It is the perception that blogs exist together as a connected community (or as a collection of

connected communities) or as a social network.

Micro-blog A status update application that logs entries to a common Web site, or a

multi-user blog with restrictions on entry length

Tweet An entry onto the micro-blog Twitter

enticing or outrageous?" and "Will your content start a conversation?" If the answer to these questions is yes, then you are ready to start thinking about the use of video. Rogers suggests the following:

- Make your campaign creative, consistent, and cohesive with the brand's image.
- Commit to being part of an online conversation and cultivate your network.
- Create content that can be easily shared and downloaded.
- Find the **hook** that will make your message resonate with the target audience.

Gary Vaynerchuk's use of video podcasts in the opening case is a good example of an MPR use of these tools. Another is Home Depot's how-to videos for all types of home improvement projects on Blip.tv. While the presenters are usually clad in Home Depot aprons, each video focuses on helping customers complete a project on their own, thus fostering the company's positioning of "You can do it. We can help."

CHAPTER
OBJECTIVE
6

User-generated Content: Bookmark, Review, Rate, and Co-create

Since the interaction of firms with consumers, consumers with firms, and consumers with each other is what makes social media so powerful, marketers need to have an understanding of the various ways that consumers add to this conversation. Contributions can range from simply bookmarking the Web address of something interesting, to rating or reviewing products or services, to ultimately contributing content to an electronic community, forum, or Web site.

Bookmarking

Social bookmarking sites are one of the driving forces in the democratization of digital media. These sites work by allowing members (membership is usually free) to submit their favorite site to the larger community. The site then tracks the number of people who submit a given item and post the most popular items to its home page. Members are also able to add comments to the posts and, thereby, interact with those of similar interests. The notion of democratization stems from the fact that the media consumers decide on the main stories to be presented by the site, rather than an editor working for a specific media outlet. Bookmarking sites also serve to aggregate popular news and other media into one place.

In October 2008 eBizMBA.com ranked the thirty largest social bookmarking sites using a combination of inbound links, Google page rank, Alexa rank, and U.S. traffic data from Compete and Quantcast.[20] The following are the top ten:

1. Digg.com
2. Buzz.yahoo.com
3. Technorati.com
4. Del.icio.us.com
5. Propeller.com
6. Stumbleupon.com
7. Reddit.com

8. Mixx.com

9. Fark.com

10. MyBlogLog.com

Marketers can take advantage of social bookmarking by adding buttons to their blogs and other Web content that submits their sites to bookmarking sites.

"This can do nothing but good things for your website," says Liane Bate in her April 28, 2007, article for the online magazine American Chronicle (http://www.americanchronicle.com). "If everyone gives your post a Digg, think of all the links in Digg you will have pointing back to your site. This will certainly increase your traffic when someone goes onto Digg looking for a post on a topic that interests them."[21]

Exhibit 10.4 The ability to instantly share links across social media is one reason it is such a powerful MPR tool.

Shutterstock

Ranking and Reviews

Another area where consumers can interact with a firm or its products is with online ratings and reviews. BizRate.com is an example of a site where consumers can rate products they have purchased and post reviews of both the products and the seller. The site then makes these ratings available to the shopping public. Angie's List is a similar application that focuses on service industries such as electricians, plumbers, and even medical doctors. Similarly, Amazon.com allows customers to rate review the books and other products they have purchased and even includes the ability to post a video review.

Although good ratings and reviews can clearly benefit a firm by building a positive image and increasing sales, the possibility of negative reviews has made some companies wary about participating in such a process. This can be a dilemma for marketers since Internet forums are emerging as an alternative to mass media as a source of information. These forums are replacing society's traditional reliance on the "wisdom of the specialist" with the "knowledge of the many."[22]

Consequently, an ethical predicament arises when negative customer reviews about a firm's products or the products of its business partners appear in a forum that the firm owns. Some marketers contend that they have a moral responsibility to keep all comments, good or bad, available for all to see, while others believe that negative comments build credibility, as long as they don't outnumber the positive comments. Still other marketers feel that they have a duty to protect the brand and reputation of the firm and its business partners, so they feel compelled to remove negative commentary. This debate is likely to continue for some time; the philosophy for managing such forums will depend on the point of view of individual firms and marketers flavored by the opinions and preferences of their stakeholders.

Key Terms

Hook A creative ploy to garner attention or interest in a subject

Co-created content Web content resulting from a collaboration of a firm and one or more consumers

Co-created Content

The Fiskateers example in Chapter 3 demonstrates how firms can encourage customers to produce material that is useful both to the firm and to their fellow customers. A collaboration of this type is commonly known as **co-created content** and is becoming an accepted practice for turning your best customers into product-evangelizing connectors.

Another example occurred in 2006 when the band The Barenaked Ladies reached the end of its contract with Warner Music. The band members decided to revert to the band's independent roots by experimenting with new ways of reaching out to their fans through cyberspace. "The main thing is just shifting the focus to the fans and letting them decide how they want to consume the music," said song-writer and guitarist Ed Robertson.[23] The band members conceived a contest in which fans downloaded the raw tracks for one of five of the band's numbers, remixed them any way they wanted, and posted them back to the band's Web site. The contest resulted in interpretations that vary from country to reggae to waltz. The band selected five of the best remixes and repackaged the winners in one CD, with proceeds from the sales of that CD going to charity.[24] The contest not only drew the fans serious enough about the band to post remixes to the band's Web site, but it also drew countless other fans, while garnering the attention of new and traditional media outlets alike.

Connecting the Dots of Social Media

CHAPTER
OBJECTIVE
7

The Barenaked Ladies not only capitalized on co-created content, but they spanned the spectrum of social media by avidly sharing music and videos on their Web site, hosting a message board (discussion forum), blogging, maintaining a Facebook fan page with more than 23,000 fans, and having their own YouTube channel. As was the case with Gary Vaynerchuk and the Wine Library, the band members made a clear effort to tie all of these elements together into a community with many neighborhoods. Benjamin Leis of Blizz Marketing & Public Relations, a firm that specializes in marketing to college-aged consumers, offers these tips:

> To make the most of social media, I update my Facebook status to reference my new blog posts so it will then show up in the news feed of all of my friends, and I do the same thing on Twitter. . . . In addition, I use the Blog Networks application on Facebook to recruit fans to my blog. I also reference influencers within my blog content so that those same influencers turn around and post the link to my blog post in their own social media spheres, which drives traffic to my blog.

Social media and its various and growing iterations present a unique opportunity for marketers to find and communicate with consumers in ways that are faster and more personal than ever before. However, the great challenge within this opportunity is to be certain that you are reaching the right audience, through the right channel, at the right time, and keeping up with the changing social media habits of your target consumers. In addition, the speed at which your promotional message travels and the fact that social media can create permanent records of your message can exacerbate Marketing Public Relations missteps as profoundly as they can summon success.

Concept Case 10.2: **Melding Social Media**

With The Falcon's Lair staff contributing to its blog regularly and a growing fan base on its Facebook fan page, the managers of The Falcon's Lair have decided to try to take their social media efforts to the next level. Creating videos, podcasts, and wikis are high on their list. They are even considering a ratings and review section on the company's Web site to rate both hiking and climbing gear and hiking and climbing locations. A few staff members are enthusiastic about becoming active on Twitter, and they plan to brainstorm ideas about instituting a co-created content contest.

Questions:
1. Since the managers of The Falcon's Lair have limited time and money they can dedicate to completing these social media projects, they need to prioritize. Describe how you would prioritize these activities and explain why.
2. Explain how you can connect the different social media elements that The Falcon's Lair management wants to use so that they support one another.
3. Conceive and describe a co-created content contest that would benefit The Falcon's Lair and its customers. Explain how it would work and its benefit to both parties.

 Reflection Questions

1. Compare and contrast social media with traditional media. (Chapter Objective 1)

2. Discuss the characteristics of the four levels of engagement found in people using social media and explain marketers' potential approaches to each. (Chapter Objective 1)

3. Differentiate between social networks and social media. (Chapter Objective 2)

4. Explain how marketing via a public social network differs from using a firm-created social network. (Chapter Objective 2)

5. Describe the concept of a wiki and discuss some possible uses of wikis in an MPR context. (Chapter Objective 3)

6. Why should firms blog and what are some examples of blogs that you feel are especially effective at promoting a product, brand, or firm? (Chapter Objective 4)

7. Discuss the benefits and potential pitfalls of marketers participating in the blogosphere. (Chapter Objective 4)

8. Discuss your interpretation of how a video or podcast that meets the criteria for MPR differs from one designed for advertising purposes. What are some examples of each? (Chapter Objective 5)

9. Compare and contrast the value of user-generated content and firm-created content to both firms and consumers. (Chapter Objective 6)

Chapter Key Terms

Blogosphere A collective term encompassing all blogs and their interconnections. It is the perception that blogs exist together as a connected community (or as a collection of connected communities) or as a social network. (p. 164)

Co-created content Web content resulting from a collaboration of a firm and one or more consumers (p. 168)

Hook A creative ploy to garner attention or interest in a subject (p. 166)

Micro-blog A status update application that logs entries to a common Web site, or a multi-user blog with restrictions on entry length (p. 165)

Social media Electronic media where participants can produce, publish, control, critique, rank, and interact with online content (p. 157)

Social network A Web-based community designed to promote interaction, discussion, and sharing of content among its users (p. 157)

Tweet An entry onto the micro-blog Twitter (p. 165)

Wall The space on a social network page where friends, fans, or contacts can write a message to the owner of that space (p. 159)

Wiki A repository for content of any sort that can be edited, added to, or updated by the community of those interested in the subject (p. 161)

Application Assignments

1. Conduct a "social media self-audit" by listing all the different social media that you participate in regularly. Discuss how these social media are interconnected (for example, Twitter may act as your Facebook status update), and describe the values that each medium brings to you.

2. Search Ning.com for three firm-created social networks and evaluate them based on how well they raise awareness, connect events with attendees, inspire and educate, share insight and provide support, share tricks of the trade, and create community for customers.

3. Go to technorati.com and find and evaluate a firm-created blog using the criteria outlined in the chapter by Gretel Going of Channel V Media.

4. Identify a firm that participates in multiple forms of social media. List all of those forms; describe how they are connected, and explain how the firm and its customers benefit from this effort.

Practice Portfolio

This Practice Portfolio can be based on a fictitious company or on a real company that your instructor assigns to you. (If you used a company in previous Practice Portfolio exercises, continue to use that company.) Add your completed assignment to your portfolio to present to prospective employers.

Conceive and describe a concept for promoting your company using one of the following:

- A social network
- A wiki
- Co-created content

CHAPTER 11

Events

CHAPTER OBJECTIVES

After studying this chapter, you should be able to:

1. Differentiate between self-produced and third-party events.

2. List and explain the factors that lead to an event's MPR success.

3. Describe how a marketer can select and participate effectively in a trade show.

4. Discuss the value of a firm's use of or participation in seminars and conferences.

5. Explain the process for selecting, planning, and executing community or cause-related events.

6. Describe the important elements of press conference preparation.

7. Explain the ways that marketers can accommodate different media types at press conferences.

G ood event marketing campaigns usually reflect the client's core values. In the summer of 2006, TBA Global Events created a campaign that reflected its client's *cone* values. For the "Random Acts of Cone-ness" campaign, TBA, which is based in Woodland Hills, California, helped Ben & Jerry's introduce its new waffle cone with a three-city sampling program in Chicago, New York, and San Francisco. According to Sean Greenwood, Ben & Jerry's Grand Poobah of Public Relations, "This was a great way for us to share our values of social activism and having a good time, while at the same time raising awareness about our products."

Ice cream-maker Ben & Jerry's is famed for its socially responsible operations and its lighthearted marketing, two messages that TBA keyed in on with the campaign. For example, the "Cone Samaritans" not only handed out cones in busy downtown "cone zones" but also distributed the treats at firehouses, police stations, and children's hospitals. And while some consumers were lucky enough to be handed a cone, others had to work to win one, either by showing their prowess with Hula Hoops or by riding a branded scooter.

Even such a straightforward campaign brought challenges. The summer's record heat required TBA to maneuver a total of nine 24-foot freezer trucks through congested downtown streets. Also, the campaign included a "Cone-O-Gram" option, which enabled consumers to have a cone delivered to a friend or coworker within city limits. The problem: Many deliveries were slated for high-security office buildings. "Some friendly smiles, quick thinking—and a great deal of cone bribes—went a long way,"

Courtesy of Ben & Jerry's

TBA management says. "Our messengers managed to work their way into even the most secured buildings in New York, Chicago, and San Francisco."[1]

"We used street teams of 15 to 30 in each city, and even used street performers," relates Greenwood. "This was just a regional effort, but the size of the market and the response of the people and the media made this campaign really strong."

"Cone Samaritans" distributed 50,000 full-sized samples per market and created national awareness and buzz through coverage on ESPN, CNN, national and local newspapers and industry trade magazines.[2] Specifically, the street team's activity along Wacker Drive in downtown Chicago generated news coverage on Chicago's network affiliates. Similarly, while spreading "cone-ness" in New York, Sean Greenwood and the new product had appearances on ESPN's morning show and on CNN's *American Morning* with Soledad O'Brien and Miles O'Brien.

When all was said and done, Ben and Jerry's and TBA were able to create an event that linked with the image of the company, engaged the company's intended audience, created buzz and a media presence, and gave the public a nice take-away—an ice cream cone.

MPR Approach to Events

CHAPTER OBJECTIVE 1

When thinking of events in an MPR context, distinguish between marketing an event and using events to market a product, brand, or firm. While a firm or marketer can use MPR to accomplish the former, this chapter concentrates on the latter. We can classify events in several ways, with the two major categories being self-produced and third-party events. **Self-produced events** are events a firm conceives and coordinates, while **third-party events** are put on by an external organization that invites firms to partner with them. Self-produced events have the distinct advantage of being tailored to the firm's products, customers, and overall mission. They do, however, consume a considerable amount of the firm's time and money. Conversely, third-party events can be less of a drain on a firm's resources since another organization has the role of event manager. The downside is that multiple firms typically participate in third-party events and they end up competing for the attention of the event's participants. In addition, the purpose of the event is less likely to align with the marketing goals of any specific firm.

We can also classify events by geographical region, industry, audience, or type. Types include:

- Trade shows
- Conferences
- Seminars
- Community events
- Charity events
- Press conferences

So, with the exception of the press conference, the MPR purpose behind these events is to create a nonthreatening environment to facilitate face-to-face contact with customers and connectors and help perpetuate awareness of the firm in a world that is growing increasingly impersonal. Note that merely paying to be a sponsor of a third-party event in exchange for signage at the event or having the firm's logo on the event's promotional material is akin to advertising; for this activity to be MPR, the firm has to bring something of value to the event participants and strive to become part of the event's community. An event's ability to create a high level of engagement with that audience will ultimately foster media mentions and the spread of the firm's message via word-of-mouth. In addition, a well-planned and executed event will support other areas of a firm's marketing mix by strengthening brand awareness and even stimulating product trial or producing qualified sales leads.

Planning and Executing Successful MPR Events

CHAPTER
OBJECTIVE
2

While each type of event is unique, using the following rules of thumb always contributes to an event's success:

- *Select events carefully.* Similar to the process of choosing connectors, be sure that the topic of the event aligns the firm's mission with a definable target audience.
- *Link the image of the firm and the event.* Remember that people attend events because they have an affinity for the topic of the event, not for the company or companies sponsoring it. The more closely you can align that topic with the perception of the firm, the better off you will be.
- *Engage the audience.* Meet people, shake hands, and move around to make sure that the people in the firm are meeting the people in the audience. Also, seize any opportunity to speak to the audience or an interested segment of the audience.
- *Create a presence.* Use advertising-type marketing vehicles to make the firm, its participation in the event, and its message stand out. Remember, if this is your only initiative within an event, you are really advertising rather than conducting MPR. However, signs, ads, and even people in branded clothing can enhance how the participants perceive the firm's involvement in the event.
- *Have a takeaway.* Have something to give event attendees that will remind them of your firm, brand, or product, but make sure that it will really be a reminder. It should be something that they will use or see when they are thinking about your firm. Takeaways that attract non-prospects or that people will bring home to give to their kids are a waste of time and money.
- *Tell the connectors before the event.* Pitch the media and fire up your social networking activities to let your stakeholders know about the event and why it is important to them. Supply them with content that is newsworthy and can be spread from person to person.
- *Tell the connectors during the event.* Give the media access to the happenings of the event, and demonstrate its meaning and value to them. By the same token, you need to reinforce the significance of the event to the participants and give them a reason to feel satisfied that they came.
- *Tell the connectors after the event.* Send a recap to the media and include photos, videos, and testimony from happy participants. Send thank-you notes to the participants, reminding them why the event was important and encouraging them to spread the word about what they have learned or experienced at the event.

Following these guidelines should give you a good start on planning your MPR event. The following segments address the nuances and tactics for specific types of events.

Trade Shows

Trade shows are periodic gatherings at which manufacturers, suppliers, and distributors in a particular industry, or related industries, display their products and provide information for potential retail, wholesale, or industrial buyers.[3] From this definition you can see that they are sales-oriented events where the primary goal is for firms to meet potential buyers. Despite their bias to the sales portion of the marketing mix, however, trade shows can provide ample opportunities to garner media mentions and spur word-of-mouth if the firm chooses the right shows and employs the right MPR strategy.

Selecting a trade show requires the marketer to look closely at the attendees. First, are the attendees really potential buyers? If they are not, then a firm probably has little reason to invest in attending that particular show. You certainly will not get any support from the firm's sales department if buyers will not be present. Additionally, the presence of the right buyers leads to the attendance of the appropriate media and others who will spread the word.

Exhibit 11.1 Tradeshows offer a central location for buyers in a given industry to see all of the latest products and to meet with vendors.

Peter Kovacs/Shutterstock.

Exhibit 11.2 IH-M&RS Buyer Profile

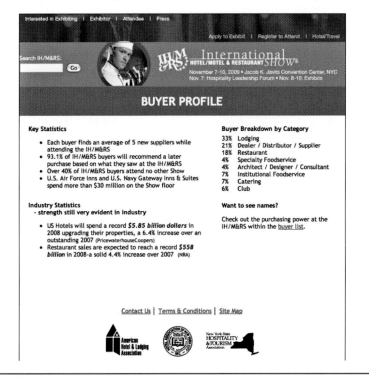

Source: International Hotel/Motel & Restaurant Show.

Information on attendees and a list of media who typically attend a trade show are usually available from the trade show management company. For example, if your firm sells products used in the hotel, motel, or restaurant industries, you might be interested in participating in the International Hotel/Motel and Restaurant Show (IH/M&RS). As illustrated in Exhibit 11.2, the IH/M&RS publishes a profile of attendees, including both the projected number and a breakdown of the companies and industries that the attendees represent, as well as some useful statistics on their buying behavior.

In addition, you can search the show's exhibitor list (see Exhibit 11.3) to find a list of media who participate in this event.

Once you select the trade show you are going to attend, your next step should be to pitch your connectors. Your connector list should include the media that are participating in the trade show as well as the media and bloggers you would normally pitch for a story about the products or services you plan to display at the show.

Once the time for the trade show arrives, you need to prepare press kits for the show in hard copy form (that is, paper), electronic media like a CD or flash drive, or a combination of both. These kits should have multiple distribution points. You should make a point to visit the exhibits of all media outlets at the

Exhibit 11.3 IH-M&RS List of Exhibiting Media

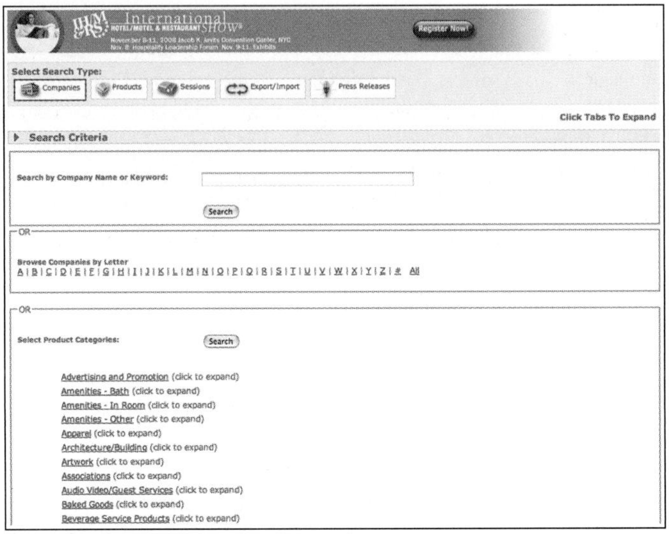

Source: International Hotel/Motel & Restaurant Show.

show, to speak personally with each editor, and to give each a copy of the media kit. You should also have several copies of the media kit in your **booth** at all times; you should instruct anyone manning the booth to give one to any potential connectors who visit during the course of the show. If an MPR professional is not going to be in the booth at all times, you need to train the other firm members working the show in the basics of recognizing a connector and presenting him or her with a media kit.

Typically, trade shows have a **press room** where all exhibitors are invited to drop off press material that will remain available to all media involved with the show for the duration of the event. Almost all media outlets use press rooms, but only a fraction of trade show exhibitors take advantage of this service. The trade show management company can usually give you a good estimate of how many press kits you need to bring to the press room, but you should check from time to time to ensure that your press kits don't run out. As Mike Thimmech, director of marketing communication and lead generation for Skyline Exhibits, says:

> Trade shows are a great focal point for the industries that they serve in that they bring firms, buyers, and the media together face-to-face.... They are live networking events, and the most skilled marketers will keep an eye out for the press, whether on the show floor or at a reception.... Keep in mind that they are looking to report on new products and industry trends, and they are hungry for good quotes. Be prepared.

After the show, be sure to follow up with all connectors who picked up a media kit or had any contact with your firm at the show. They may be interested in your reaction to the show, as well as success stories that you have, customer testimonials, and photographs from the show. Make sure that you have documentation of these elements in addition to your original press kit available to e-mail or download.

In recent years some marketing professionals have questioned the effectiveness of trade shows, citing declining attendance. While there is conflicting evidence on trends in trade show turnout, buyers clearly no longer need to wait until trade show time to see the latest and greatest products. Advances in communications technology and transportation allow prospective customers to see products online, instantly, and to receive a demonstration or sample within a few days. These facts do not necessarily signal the end of the value of trade shows, but they do clearly indicate the need for marketers to plan and execute their participation well.

Seminars and Conferences

CHAPTER OBJECTIVE 4

Producing seminars and participating in conferences are good ways for marketers to interact with their audience by giving them something of value. That value typically takes the form of information. As a point of differentiation, you can consider a **seminar** to be a self-produced event where a firm arranges to have an expert in its industry conduct an informational session for its audience. The expert can either be someone from within the firm or a noted outsider. Seminars can last as short as an hour, but may be as long as several days. We sometimes refer to longer seminars as workshops. **Conferences**, by contrast, are gatherings of people who either are members of a particular industry or profession or who simply have a common interest and come together to share information on a topic. In addition to networking with their peers, conference participants have the opportunity to attend presentations, demonstrations, and panel discussions led by experts in the field of the conference's focus. Within these sessions firms can find opportunities to promote their products by providing useful content to the audience. Seminars and conferences used for MPR purposes should:

- Be educational or informative to the intended audience.
- Never be a disguised sales pitch.
- Position the organization or someone within it as an expert.
- Give the members of the audience a reason to remember the firm, its products, and its people.

Gene Dickison is President and Chief Investment Officer for MtM Financial Group, LLC. According to Dickison:

> As a financial advisor I must fashion a system that will allow my prospects to experience, evaluate, and grow to trust me in as non-threatening a setting as possible....Seminars are a near perfect setting for prospects to maintain a safe distance and yet see me up close and very personally. Inviting current clients

Key Terms

Booth The exhibit or other area occupied by a firm on the floor of a trade show

Exhibit 11.4 Experts in many fields offer educational seminars to help educate customers and potential customers in a manner that builds the expert's credibility while bonding with the customer.

allows those relationships to deepen and gives them the opportunity to invite their friends to meet me—perfect word-of- mouth.

In addition, providing exceptional content within the seminar setting creates a favorable impression on those in attendance. Great content is important because it encourages media attention; a seminar that is no more than an infomercial isn't newsworthy. As a result of our seminars focused on educating and informing our audience, we have received tens, perhaps hundreds, of thousands of dollars of free publicity from our seminar efforts.

As with all events, conferences and seminars should be newsworthy to the firm's connectors, so you must be certain to inform connectors of these events before, during, and after they occur. In addition, you should be sure to support their reporting efforts with the written and visual material that they need to compose great coverage of your story.

CHAPTER OBJECTIVE 5 Marketing with Community and Cause-related Events

From time immemorial companies have supported community initiatives and charitable causes. For almost as long, consumers have been skeptical about whether the motivation for this support is rooted in the desire to do good or just a desire to promote the firm.

In reality, the bulk of firms' community and cause-related efforts are designed to serve both the public and their bottom line.

Marketers also need to understand the modern definition of *community* when it comes to event marketing. We can define communities as groups of people in the same geographic area (state, city, neighborhood), but they may also be any group with an affinity for a common topic or cause. The group can range from environmentalists to automobile enthusiasts. For example, grassroots marketing centering on automotive lifestyle events saw new life in the late 1990s and really took off after 2000, with events like General Motors' Auto Show in Motion, Taste of Lexus, and Mercedes' C-Spot events.

The Mercedes event was a sixteen-city tour designed to promote the entry-level C-Class model line to younger buyers through an orientation to the panache of the Mercedes-Benz brand and firsthand experience with the performance of its products. What made the C-Spot event unique, according to Michelle Cervantez, vice president of marketing for MBUSA, was its targeted use of experiential marketing:

> Another of our goals in the C-Spot Tour was to create awareness and aspiration among future buyers. So what we wanted to do was to present the C-Class models in their element, so to speak. If you entered the event, looked around at the products, services and lifestyle, and you felt as though you had stepped into your weekend, then there's probably a Mercedes in your future. That's the message we wanted to send.[4]

Erich Gail, executive vice president of Automotive Events, believes that automakers are transitioning marketing dollars into experiential-marketing events in order to connect with consumers on their own ground. This belief is illustrated by the fact that Automotive Events had nearly doubled its 2007 revenue, from $8.5 million to $15 million, at the end of the third quarter of 2008.[5]

Companies can demonstrate their community activism and philanthropic nature in many ways. In this segment, however, we will concentrate on event-based efforts. Planning and executing such efforts requires following these steps:

Select position-centered event. As with most events, the marketer has to choose or design the event carefully to ensure that the audience is a segment of the public with whom the firm wants to create, maintain, or repair a relationship. Regardless of whether the event is to be self-produced or you are participating in a third-party function, you need to be sure that the community issue or charitable cause aligns with the firm's positioning in order for the event to contribute to the company's overall marketing strategy.

Set goals. Once you choose the event, you must set objectives for it as well. MPR goals for such an event can include spreading word-of-mouth by directly interacting with the attending audience by fostering media coverage. In either case, newsworthiness for this type of event hinges upon the event's relevance to the audience it claims to be serving.

Determine format. If you are planning to produce the event yourself, you need to consider your audiences and goals to determine a time, place, and event format that will work for you. Event formats include:

- Lectures and speeches
- Discussion panels

- Community forums
- Social events such as parties, concerts, balls, and dinner dances
- Auctions or contests
- **Work events**

Find the right venue. While thinking about format, you must also consider holding the event in a place that enhances your message, that is convenient for your guests and media, and that might actually draw some attention on its own merits.

Invitation list. Once you have decided upon the format and venue, it is time to create an invitation list. This list is essentially a list of media and non-media connectors who will reach out to the firm's target audience. In addition to the connectors, you should also think about inviting people whose presence alone might help draw media coverage or spread word-of-mouth. (However, you need to be careful that the image of any noteworthy people you invite is in line with your message.) Following invitations should be a traditional wave of press releases, pitching, and follow-up that highlight the importance of the event to the target audience and society at large. Furthermore, be sure to include information about the venue itself and special guests, if either is significant to the story.

Meet and greet. During the event, make sure that your organization's people are out with the crowd meeting people and building relationships. This is a great time to put names with faces and to get feedback about the event. All of the firm's employees should be schooled in presenting its message, because each conversation will be an informal pitch to spread word-of-mouth or vie for a media mention.

Prepare a takeaway. Your guests should leave with something fun or useful that will make them think of you at a time when they would most likely think about your product. If the item is something that attendees will keep where others can see it, or if it is something they will show off, even better.

Recap. As with other events, you have the opportunity to pitch connectors one last time when the event is over. Thank the influencers who will spread the word about your event and give them some incentive to tell their friends. This incentive can take the form of sales promotions, such as product samples or coupons they can distribute, or it can be as simple as sharing photos and stories about the event that they can show to their friends. As for the media, tell them about the significance of the event one more time, and give them the photos, videos, testimonials, and access to attendees in order to make their job easier and their story more interesting.

Community and charity events require marketers to be sincere in their efforts as well as to employ all of the elements of MPR in order for them to be a success. Cause-related marketing can give a company's products low-cost exposure, increase the product's ability to win customer support, and break through the advertising clutter in the marketplace. This type of marketing can also generate favorable customer attitudes toward the sponsoring firm and increase favorable purchase intentions toward the firm's brands.[6] In effect, firms can do well by doing good.

Concept Case 11.1: **Community Events**

After some deliberation over the selection of an appropriate partner, The Falcon's Lair management has decided to team with Wildlands Conservancy (http://www.wildlandspa.org), a local environmental advocacy group, to conduct educational hiking tours for elementary school students. The tours will be led by an experienced Falcon's Lair employee and a naturalist from the conservancy. The leaders will teach the students about the basics of hiking technique and safety, as well as the importance of preserving our natural spaces.

Questions:

1. In your opinion, is this a suitable MPR event for The Falcon's Lair? Explain why or why not.
2. Explain what The Falcon's Lair needs to do in order to effectively leverage this effort into the creation of word-of-mouth, with appropriate media mentions.

Planning and Executing Press Conferences

CHAPTER OBJECTIVE 6

Before you plan a **press conference**,[7] you should be very clear about your goals. However, whatever your organizational goals are, remember that you have to have something newsworthy to announce, reveal, or talk about.

Setting Up a Press Conference

- State a good reason for holding a press conference. Good reasons include the fact that the news you are going to reveal has not yet been covered by the press, or there is an emergency, or you are about to reveal an important new issue.
- Decide what message you want to deliver through the media.
- Work out the location of the press conference. Find an appropriate place that is convenient and has the facilities you need. Where you choose to have a press conference depends on your needs and the specific circumstances of

---

Key Terms

Work events Events where attendees actively participate in an activity such as building a house for someone needing shelter, filling sandbags for flood-prone communities, etc.

Press conference The convening of representatives of the media by a person or organization to explain, announce, or expand on a particular subject

your situation. Dramatize your position by choosing a good backdrop. For example, the Ukrainian chapter of Greenpeace held a news conference, which was dedicated to the tenth anniversary of the explosion at the Chernobyl nuclear power plant, on the steps of the Chernobyl Ministry Palace. At the conference, Greenpeace activists revealed results of a study they had recently completed. About thirty media outlets covered the event.

- Be ready to provide technical assistance for reporters, such as phones, microphones, additional lighting, and so on.

- Set the date and time of the press conference, taking into account reporters' deadlines. Usually the best days of the week to get news coverage are Tuesday through Thursday. Check to see that no competing news events are already scheduled at the time of your conference.

- Invite the media. Send a press conference advisory to appropriate local media outlets at least a week before the press conference. Follow up with a phone call two days before the press conference to make sure that everyone on your connector list has received the advisory and to remind them about the event.

- Invite guests. Make phone calls and send written invitations to prospective guests you want to have at the press conference, such as other members of your group, allies, and friendly politicians.

- Prepare your speakers to deliver your message. Generally, it is good to have just one or two speakers during a press conference so people don't talk on top of each other or mix the message. Rehearse with the speakers to make statements brief and clear and usually no longer then ten minutes. The spokespeople should be experienced in the subject so they will be able to respond to questions after the statement.

- Let the press know that the speakers are available after the press conference. Prepare speakers with thirty-second answers for radio or TV and quotable, simple messages for print reporters. Help speakers practice with a video camera or tape recorder.

- Choose a **moderator** for the press conference. You will need a person to control the process and keep reporters on the subject. If someone goes off subject, the moderator can return the focus by saying such things as: "That's an interesting point, but we are here today to discuss...."

- Prepare background materials. Be sure to have press kits available that are specific to this event.

- Practice roles with the members of your group. It's important that everybody understand his or her role in the event. Think about what will happen all the way through the press conference and how it will look to reporters. The key question to ask is "What if...?" (What if reporters ask a non-spokesperson member a question? What if your opponents show up and heckle?)

- Prepare visual aids. Charts, big maps, pictures, or other props will help get your message across. However, remember that slide shows are difficult for TV, radio, and print reporters to use.

Exhibit 11.5 Press conferences connect people and firms directly to the media—face to face.

Cyrus Chang/Shutterstock.

Making Your Statement

Think through how you can get your message across through the setup of the press conference. You can maximize your impact differently, depending on whether you expect TV, radio, or print reporters to come.

Television: Visual Impact
Ask: "How can we set up our press conference to give reporters a good picture?"

- Seat speakers at the front close together so they all fit in the picture.
- Seat people in the audience who clearly fall into your target market close to the speakers so they are in the picture as well.
- Display posters or banners with your firm's name and logo on them.
- Bring props. Anything that illustrates your point and that will grasp the attention of reporters and their audience will work.

Key Terms

Moderator The master of ceremonies or facilitator of a press conference

Radio: Audio Impact
Ask: "What sounds would be of interest to radio reporters?" and "What can we do to make things technically suitable for broadcast?"

- Provide uncluttered sound with good acoustics and a minimum of background noise.
- Have designated, well-prepared speakers so everyone is not talking at once.
- Have a prepared statement so you can make the main points clearly but do not sound like you're reading it! Practice making a statement from notes.
- Have only the designated spokesperson(s) speak to the media during the press conference.
- If you have people or equipment that make interesting sounds, demonstrate them at the conference.
- If you're holding the press conference at a rally or event with a lot of people and noise, set up a quiet space away from the action for interviews.

Print Media: Verbal Impact
Ask: "What would we want if we were newspaper reporters?"

- Provide a press kit with background material.
- Pass out copies of press releases.
- Use simple, powerful, quotable lines when speaking.
- Don't say anything that you can't back up with facts. If something is not a proven fact, but you are sure it is true, preface the statement by saying such things as, "in my opinion" or "we believe..."
- Don't bring up anything you are not prepared to discuss. If you are asked questions that you don't want to talk about, say, "We're not ready to discuss that matter at this time," or "Our group has not taken a position on that issue."

Starting the Press Conference

Be ready to welcome TV reporters at least fifteen minutes prior to the beginning of the conference, as they usually need time to set up their equipment. Meet everyone at the door and ask them to sign a guest book you have already prepared (noting that you may need their addresses for the next event). Give them your background material and a copy of the press statement. Start the press conference as close to on-time as possible, and certainly no later than ten minutes after the scheduled time, to respect those who arrived promptly.

Running the Press Conference

The moderator begins by welcoming everyone and briefly introducing the speaker(s). Remember that statements should not be longer than ten to fifteen minutes. After the speakers are finished, ask for questions and make sure answers are simple, brief, and pointed. (Speakers should be coached beforehand to ensure that questions are handled properly.) A little bit of humor will enliven the press conference as well. Good visual aids make your story more interesting, so be creative.

The moderator should end the press conference before it drags out too long. After your important points are made, step in and conclude the proceeding. Thank everyone for coming and offer additional information that is available from your office. Thank the attending connectors for keeping readers, viewers, and listeners informed about this important community problem.[8]

Concept Case 11.2: **Press Conference**

Having prepared press materials for the "Best of the Nest" program, The Falcon's Lair has decided to hold a press conference. The managers have booked climbing expert Don Mellor to speak about the value of good equipment and proper training for climbers at all levels during the conference. The Lair's president will then explain the "Best of the Nest" program. They have their connector list together and expect to have reporters from print and television media in attendance, as well as a few customers who blog about hiking and climbing.

Questions:
1. Discuss the venue options for this event and select a place. Explain your reason for choosing this venue.
2. Prepare the statement that the Lair's president will deliver to the audience.
3. Explain how you would assist the different connectors in their coverage of this event.

 Reflection Questions

1. Compare and contrast self-produced and third-party events. (Chapter Objective 1)

2. What are some factors that contribute to an event's MPR success? (Chapter Objective 2)

3. Explain how marketers can decide whether a particular trade show is right for them. (Chapter Objective 3)

4. Discuss the value of using seminars and conferences as a marketing tool for the firm and its target audience, as well as the criteria to ensure there is value for both parties. (Chapter Objective 4)

5. What is the process for selecting, planning, and executing a community or cause-related event? (Chapter Objective 5)

6. What are the key elements of press conference preparation? (Chapter Objective 6)

7. Explain the ways marketers accommodate different media formats at press conferences. (Chapter Objective 7)

Chapter Key Terms

Booth The exhibit or other area occupied by a firm on the floor of a trade show (p. 177)

Conference Gathering of people from a particular industry or profession or who simply share a common interest who come together to share information on a topic (p. 179)

Moderator The master of ceremonies or facilitator of a press conference (p. 184)

Press conference The convening of representatives of the media by a person or organization to explain, announce, or expand on a particular subject (p. 183)

Press room A room at a trade show where exhibiting firms can leave press materials for the use of members of the media attending the show (p. 178)

Self-produced event An event conceived and put on by an individual firm to serve its audience with the intent of promoting its products (p. 174)

Seminar A self-produced event in which a firm arranges to have an expert in its industry conduct an information-al session for its audience (p. 179)

Third-party event An event created and managed by an organization that opens it up to other firms for participation (p. 174)

Trade show Periodic gathering at which manufacturers, suppliers, and distributors in a particular industry or related industries display their products and provide information for potential retail, wholesale, or industrial buyers (p. 176)

Work events Events where attendees actively partici-pate in an activity such as building a house for some-one needing shelter, filling sandbags for flood-prone communities, etc. (p. 182)

Application Assignments

1. Your company manufactures a sports energy drink that is sold through health food stores and upscale gyms and spas. Use http://www.tsnn.com to find three trade shows that are appropriate for your firm. Research each show further and explain why it would be appropriate for your firm, including a discussion of attendees and media.

2. Your company is releasing a new automobile that runs on water, will eliminate the country's dependence on foreign oil, does not pollute, and is affordable. A special mineral that makes this automobile possible is only available in the earth of the pristine areas of Colorado and Utah, and its mining will effectively industrialize 25 percent of the forest land in each state. The company's CEO has asked you to announce the launch of this car by having a press conference. In prepara-tion for this you will need to:

   • Create your connector list using resources discussed in Chapter 7.
   • Decide on a venue and explain why you have chosen it.
   • Write a press release announcing the press conference.
   • Prepare your statement and/or presentation for the press conference.

Practice Portfolio

This Practice Portfolio can be based on a fictitious company or on a real company that your instructor assigns to you. (If you used a company in previous Practice Portfolio exercises, continue to use that company.) Add your completed assignment to your portfolio to present to prospective employers.

Select a community or charitable cause that aligns with your firm's MPR goals and explain how you would produce such an event. Be sure to:

- Select an event format and explain why you have chosen that format.
- Decide on a venue and explain why you have chosen it.
- Describe, in detail, whom you will invite to the event (remember both target audience and connectors).
- Determine which members of your firm will attend the event, and explain what they are expected to do while they are there.
- Explain what you will prepare as a takeaway for those attending the event. Be sure to differentiate between what you give to members of the target audience and what you give to connectors.
- Discuss your strategy for recapping the event.

CHAPTER 12

Experts and Interviews

CHAPTER OBJECTIVES

After studying this chapter, you should be able to:

1. Explain the value of creating experts within the firm.

2. List and describe the different publishing opportunities and basic strategies for using them.

3. Discuss how speaking engagements can be used as a marketing tool and some basic strategies for selecting and conducting them.

4. Explain how a firm creates and uses expert sources.

5. Describe the preparation for an interview from an MPR perspective.

6. List and explain the elements of a successful interview.

"Making the simple complicated is commonplace; making the
complicated simple, awesomely simple, that's creativity."
–*Charles Mingus*

David Becker is CEO of Philippe Becker Design, Inc., a privately held branding,
packaging, and design agency based in San Francisco, California. The company
has twenty-two employees and just under $5 million in revenue. In 2007 and 2008,
Inc. Magazine named Philippe Becker to its list of the top 5,000 fastest-growing
private American companies. It serves clients globally, including Clorox; Disney;
Forbes; Gap; Hewlett-Packard; IDEO; Meade-Johnson; Safeway; SanDisk; Starbucks;
T-Mobile; Wal-Mart; Whole Foods Market; Williams-Sonoma, Inc.; and Wrigley.

Becker attributes the firm's success to his decision to build relationships
with journalists and editors in respected publications in order to raise the profile
of the agency and to position himself and his company as thought leaders:

> Thought Leadership is important because it raises a company's visibility and
> credibility which helps increase sales....Business experts become thought leaders
> when they understand their industry deeply, share lessons they have learned, are -
> objective and non-partisan, and speak the truth about challenges and opportunities.

Further, Becker believes that demonstrating his expertise can also contribute to the
greater good of the profession.

Understanding that Marketing Public Relations is a process rather than a
transaction, Becker set out to build consistent, long-term relationships with
members of the media. He used a combination of interrelated MPR activities
to capitalize on the synergies between them in order to achieve a sum that is
greater than the individual parts. These
activities included establishing media
relations leading to published articles
and mentions about the agency,
arranging speaking engagements,
distributing press releases, writing
bylined articles, and submitting
for and winning awards. As a result
Entrepreneur Magazine, *PR Week*, and
The San Francisco Business Times
have all published feature articles
about the agency or its president.
Additionally, an article in *Les Echos*,
a leading French business publication,
featured the agency's work and it was
mentioned on the Web sites of *The
New York Times*, *Reuters*,

Philippe**Becker**   look / deeper   **what**   / to connect
how
philosophy

We create, design and build brands
for new products, emerging categories
and evolving brands—for start-ups to
the Fortune 100.

We also have a knack for translating
business objectives and challenges
into design that people connect with,
understand, pick up, talk about or
maybe even love.

(and what brand doesn't want to be loved and understood)

© 2009 PhilippeBecker. All rights reserved. / 612 Howard Street, Suite 200, San Francisco, CA 94105 / T 415 348 0054 / F 415 348 0063 / Site Map

Courtesy of Phillipe Becker Design Inc.

and *Forbes Magazine*. Over four years the results of these efforts yielded forty feature stories and thirty-six media mentions, which resulted in half a million to a million dollars' worth of press coverage (relative to purchased advertising), decreased **sales cycle**, and improved quality and quantity of sales leads. Ultimately, Becker believes the company had a 5 to 10 percent increase in sales revenue per year directly attributable to MPR.

Creating Experts for Marketing Purposes

From the beginning, this text has discussed how the power of Marketing Public Relations emanates from the fact that its results appear as news from trusted sources rather than as advertising or salesmanship. Consumers crave expert opinion, so the media is always looking for credible contributors whose expertise is in line with the subject matter of their particular medium. The thoughts and opinions of experts from CEOs of Wall Street brokerage firms to owners of small middle-America industrial businesses are in demand by consumers and the media.

Since every firm combines the ability of its people with its assets to either manufacture a good or provide a service, we can conclude that each has one or more experts on staff to facilitate the production of that product or service. As a result, all marketers and firms have the opportunity to position such experts as thought leaders in their field. Applied properly, positioning a company leader as an industry expert can generate considerable payoffs and deliver a huge boost to revenue without cutting into the company's bottom line.[1] Marketers have many avenues for positioning their firm's **thought leaders**;[2] these include writing bylined articles, white papers, case studies, and even books; speaking in front of interested audiences; and acting as a source of information and interviews for journalists.

Regardless of the vehicle used to showcase a thought leader, using experts as part of an MPR strategy should follow these tenets offered by Ken Lizotte, author of *The Expert's Edge: Become the Go-To Authority People Turn to Every Time*:

- **Be Authentic.** Offer ideas that you can sincerely stand behind. If you are a sales expert, offer ideas for effective selling that you've developed or at least investigated yourself.
- **Don't Self-censor.** You might worry that your ideas are not original enough or that they've been said or written about before. No matter; many ideas are "evergreen" and can be put out for people to hear and learn again and again.
- **Say It Your Way.** Don't try to sound like someone else, such as a mega-famous thought leader. Nobody needs to hear about your "seven habits of highly effective people." Make up your own way of communicating your ideas; don't copy from someone else.
- **Persistence Is Everything.** Put your ideas out there wherever you can and watch the chips fall where they may. Submit speaking proposals to 100 meeting planners, not just to one. Submit your articles to 100 publications, not just one

article to one. Submit your book proposal to 20 publishers. Then follow up as much as possible. Don't wait for the phone to ring!

- **Look to the Future.** Don't just write or speak about what you know. Instead, predict trends, analyze new developments, and speculate about the implications of what's currently going on. The true thought leader helps LEAD the way. Decide where the road is going and beckon your followers to join you on a journey.

Getting Published

CHAPTER
OBJECTIVE
2

While being published has historically meant applying ink to paper, it now includes writing for Web-based media as well. In either case, written works benefit from the implied endorsement of the medium that publishes them. They are also durable, meaning that they have an extended life where they can be used for MPR purposes and to support other elements of the marketing mix, such as sales and direct marketing efforts. For example, when a company executive writes a book or gets an article published in a prestigious journal, that publication is newsworthy. As a result, it provides ample reason for the firm's marketers to reach out to connectors in pursuit of media mentions. Additionally, sales and marketing staff can distribute copies of the book or reprints of the article via mail or e-mail or by handing them to prospective customers to help them differentiate the firm from its competitors by highlighting the firm's recognized expertise in the field.

Articles

Articles can be an effective tool in a firm's quest to position itself and its people as thought leaders. Of course the subject of the article must be in line with the company's positioning, and the medium in which it is to be published must reach the right audience. Many publications, both print and online, actively solicit articles from interested and qualified outsiders. Search the Web sites of the media on your connector list to find such opportunities, as these publications include submission guidelines that explain the content they are seeking as well as directions for formatting the article.

Marketing professionals often refer to these written pieces as "bylined articles" to illustrate the importance of the **byline** (the line of text that identifies the author). Obviously, the audience needs to know that one of the firm's experts penned the article. However, some of the firm's experts may be too busy to write an article or simply may not be skilled essayists. In such cases, it is normal practice for marketing professionals to work with the expert to craft articles together. The marketer can participate by gathering information, wordsmithing, and drafting the final work. Professional ethics, however, dictate that the mind and works of the expert receiving the byline *must* be the source of the content.

Key Terms

Sales cycle Time between initial contact with a prospective customer and the completion of a sale

Thought leaders People or firms whom an industry or a consumer group recognize for contributing a new way of thinking and/or original perspectives to their field

Byline The line of text indicating the author of an article or other published work

Exhibit 12.1 Publishers have specific guidelines for submitting articles, which MPR professionals should adhere to when preparing a submission.

Source: TFH.com

As the emphasis on MPR has grown among marketers, firms often include a bylined article strategy as a part of their overall marketing plan. For example, the database marketing firm Merkle, in conjunction with its public relations firm, the DPR Group, set a goal to create and raise awareness of the company's products and services through consistent positive media exposure to position the company and its executives as industry experts and thought leaders. To accomplish this goal, DPR worked with Merkle experts to determine possible topics for bylined articles and developed an article outline based on Merkle's input. The PR firm then created a connector list and a specialized pitch for each of the targeted editors. Once a pitch was accepted, the firm developed a draft article that Merkle approved and submitted it to the specific publication or Web site. As a result, DPR (and Merkle) successfully placed articles in dozens of publications and Web sites, including *DM News*, *Fundraising Success*, *Target Marketing*, *Direct*, and *Advancing Philanthropy*. The company has received feedback that its customers, partners, employees, and others noticed and read the articles, which raised their awareness of the company and the expertise of its executives.[3]

A bylined article is typically between 500 and 2,500 words in length, depending on the subject and the needs of the medium. If article length, format, and topics of interest are not available on the medium's Web site or in its media kit, call and ask for more details. In fact, a phone call is a good way to begin a relationship with an editor or a blogger that lasts beyond a single article. In addition, if the publication or blog has posted an editorial calendar, you, the marketer, can use it to get a feel for the type of content that the outlet is seeking. Remember that any phone calls you make, cover letters you write, or e-mails you send are effectively pitches for your article. As a result, you need to follow the standard rules for pitching introduced in Chapter 9. Keep in mind that editors prefer articles that:

- Tie into larger trends
- Are about money
- Include celebrities
- Focus on the unusual
- Excite with sex and scandal
- Introduce new and innovative ideas
- Provide tips and "how-to" information

According to Ken Lizotte, "Pitch your ideas to relevant trade or business publications.... You can locate them via a directory of trade and business publications found in any public library, or by searching the Web, or (sometimes the best tactic of all) by asking your clients what they read!"[4]

Make sure that the draft you send to the editor or blogger is well written. If it is not well written, the recipient is more likely to reject the article and it will also diminish your chances of getting another opportunity with the outlet in the future. Alternatively, the editor might choose to rewrite your piece drastically, thereby risking a change in tone or content. Occasionally an editor or blogger may publish the article without reviewing it, and any mistakes that you have made will appear for the entire world to see. Last, never present a disguised sales piece as an article. The editor will almost always reject it. If it slips by the editor and the audience picks up on it, both you and the editor will be disgraced.

Write a Book

Let's face it, being the author of a book lends credibility to a source. Just think about the pitching process. Pitching an editor about "Jane Doe, author of *My Struggles in Sausalito*," is likely to get more press and interview opportunities than just pitching "Jane Doe." Nonetheless, writing a book is an enormous undertaking that needs to be planned and executed as well as any other MPR activity. The book must be on a topic that is of interest to both connectors and audience; it has to be well written by someone with at least a modest level of verifiable credentials; and then it has to reach the marketplace.

Traditionally, reaching the market meant finding a publisher who was willing to take a chance on turning a marketer's words or the words of a firm's experts into bound pages of ink, paper, and glue. Today, other alternatives, such as self-publishing or electronic publishing, have become viable options. Each of these alternatives has its own level of risk and reward.

Traditional Publishing Using a traditional publisher gives the author the additional authority of the publisher's imprimatur, as well as assistance in editing, marketing, and distributing the book. Traditional publishers, however, require a formal proposal and have a lengthy vetting process that ultimately rejects more proposals than it accepts. If you pursue the traditional publishing route, choose the publishers carefully, so that your topic and style line up with the publishers' past offerings and audience. Also, be certain that your proposal matches the guidelines set forth by each individual publisher, is impeccably written, and clearly illustrates why they should bother to market your book.

Elizabeth Gordon, owner of the management consulting firm Flourishing Business in Atlanta, Georgia, and the author of *The Chic Entrepreneur: Put Your Business in Higher Heels*, is a great example of someone who used a book to position herself as an expert, thereby invigorating her business. The book was released in May 2007 and spent seventeen consecutive weeks on the Amazon bestseller list. "The publication of my own book has certainly opened many doors in terms of speaking engagements," says Gordon. She has also been interviewed by *Entrepreneur Magazine*, Airtran's *GO Magazine*, *The Dallas Morning News*, and the Associated Press and has a weekly radio show/podcast on which she interviews experts and successful entrepreneurs. "As the host, I am naturally seen as the expert, and this way I can build relationships with other experts and expand my network of others like me," Gordon continues. "The book and the radio show, along with traditional PR and media relations, have positioned me as an expert in my field and have been one of our primary marketing strategies."

Exhibit 12.2 Experts like Elizabeth Gordon have written books that support their business ventures.

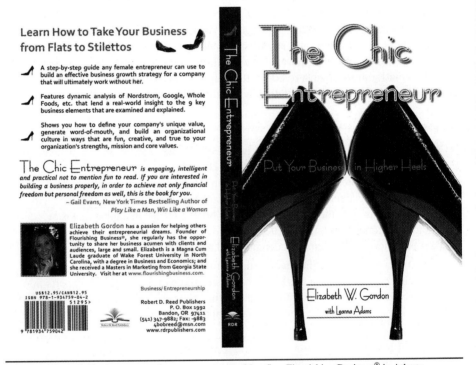

Source: Elizabeth Gordon, owner of management consulting firm Flourishing Business® in Atlanta, Georgia, and the author of *The Chic Entrepreneur: Put Your Business in Higher Heels*

Self- and Electronic Publishing Self-published and electronically published books, on the other hand, don't have the constraints of materials published by a publishing house do, but they also lack the market endorsement and support that comes with such a partnership. Sometimes, however, the freedom to publish something on your own time that addresses the concerns of a very specific audience can be a strong MPR tool. Additionally, the stigma attached to self-publishing is beginning to fade. "The perception that self-publishing means an author isn't good enough for a 'real' publisher is disappearing," says Brent Sampson, chief executive officer of Colorado-based Outskirts Press Inc. Sampson also believes that people who want to establish themselves as experts in their field are good candidates for self-publishing and that a successfully self-published work can get the attention of publishers by demonstrating that the author has established himself or herself with an audience and is willing to do the marketing.[5]

Regardless of whether a book is self-published or released by a publishing company, the marketer must parlay its release into MPR opportunities, such as media interviews and speaking engagements, which will, in turn, drive the image of the firm's brand.

Case Studies and White Papers

Case studies are short-format articles that take a problem-solution approach to a particular issue based upon the expertise of a professional or organization. A company can self-publish them either as a part of its Web site or sales literature. However, a company realizes the greatest MPR value when a media outlet publishes the case studies instead. A typical case study describes a problem or challenge faced by an industry or segment of consumers and explains a possible solution and how to implement it. In addition, it should illustrate the benefits of the solution in terms of money saved, ease of implementation, and the time required to complete that solution. The firm's product or service may be part of the solution, but the case study cannot overtly sell that product or service. The author should also strive to include alternatives to his or her own products, if they exist, in order to ensure a measure of objectivity in the piece.

Once the study is published, it can then take on a life in other areas of the marketing mix, such as being posted on the firm's Web site or appearing as part of its printed sales literature. It can also be useful as a part of the firm's media kit to provide additional background about the company and its products to journalists and to reinforce the perceived newsworthiness of the firm.

White papers[6] are similar to case studies, but they are strictly factual. There should not be even a hint of selling in them. The PR purpose of a white paper is to position a person or organization as an expert and to gain exposure in influential circles. The topics for white papers can be problem-solution; a new discovery or theory; or a new application to an existing product, service, theory, and so on. White papers are unique in that they take technically complex information and translate it into a format that helps buyers make educated decisions without selling to them. A March 2007 Knowledge Storm/Marketing Sherpa survey found that 75 percent of technology industry marketers use white papers in their marketing mix, 71 percent of technology industry buyers read white papers before making a purchasing decision, and 57 percent of buyers pass white papers along to their colleagues.[7] This last statistic is evidence that white papers have the ability to spread word-of-mouth; they also add credibility to your press kit and pitching efforts.

Blogs and Podcasts

As we have discussed, blogs and podcasts can be a part of a company's or industry's social media environment. They can also be powerful tools in a firm's efforts to position itself and its people as experts. Like much of new media, blogs and podcasts are fast and easy to set up and cost little more than the time of the person who manages them.

Both vehicles give the company's professionals a recurring platform for sharing their expertise with an audience. Their use can be a bit tricky, however, within the framework of establishing personalities of authority, because they need a recognizable audience. As a result, marketers need to use other MPR tools first to promote the blog or podcast before they can use it to claim authority or expert status. Success comes from getting traffic and establishing a reputation. Here are some basic rules of thumb that you, the marketer, should follow: stay on message; publish at regular intervals (some are published several times a day, while others are published as little as once a week); link to other blogs that share the audience and subject matter; and submit blog posts to **news aggregators** like Digg, Fark, and Boing Boing.[8] Once the blog or podcast begins to get some traction with an audience, be sure to mention it in all of your pitches. In addition, be sure to give it a presence in other areas of the marketing mix, such as linking to it from the firm's Web site, mentioning it on sales literature, and ensuring that salespeople tell customers and prospects about it. You can even replace the music that callers listen to while they are on hold with a mention of your blog or snippets from an audio podcast.

<table>
<tr><td>CHAPTER
OBJECTIVE
3</td><td>

Speaking

</td></tr>
</table>

Opportunities for speaking engagements abound. Every metropolitan area has at least one chamber of commerce, local chapters of trade organizations, Rotary clubs, Kiwanis clubs, and more. These groups are always on the lookout for speakers for the programs that they present to their members and the public. There are also countless national trade associations and conferences that count on expert speakers to attract an audience to their events. The American Society of Association Executives (ASAE) alone has more than 10,000 members, many of whom regularly produce events that have speaking opportunities embedded in them. Ken Lizotte recommends that you, the marketer, "Search out calls for speaking proposals, especially at organizations of which you are either a member or which you frequent." He also recommends that a firm makes it known on its Web site that its experts are available for speaking engagements and that the site lists relevant speaking topics and includes a calendar of past, present, and future engagements. He further suggests that you distribute any articles written by the firm's experts to everyone who attends a speaking engagement and that you remember to emphasize again that the firm's speakers are available for future speaking gigs. "Exposure breeds further exposure, thereby growing your speaking assignments exponentially," reminds Lizotte.

As with most elements of MPR, speaking is a part of a cycle. When you arrange a speaking engagement, you must inform connectors about where and when the talk will take place, let them know why it is newsworthy, ask them to inform their audience before the event happens, and encourage them to cover the event itself. During the day of the speech, you should support the connectors covering the event with press kits and provide access to the speaker. When the event is over, you should send connectors a recap of the event, including access to photos, videos, and written transcripts, along with a pitch on why they should still tell their audience about the engagement. In addition, you should copy any press **pick-up** (with permission of the publisher) for use in future press kits, on the firm's Web site, and as sales collateral.

Despite the great value in using a firm's experts to make presentations, all experts are not necessarily good public speakers. As a result, you need to assess the ability of any given expert to make a good presentation and provide training if necessary. In the

Exhibit 12.3 ASAE is an organization of business and professional associations with over ten thousand members. Many if not most of these associations regularly look for experts to address their membership on topics relevant to them.

ASAE & The Center for Association Leadership

event that an expert cannot speak effectively in public, you must consider an alternate means of using this person's expertise. For example, have someone else present the material, have the expert write instead of speak, or make a video recording of the expert to remove the live audience from the situation and allow for editing.

Being an Expert Source

Regardless of whether they are targeted at journalists for the purpose of garnering media mentions or at individual influencers with the intention of spreading word-of-mouth, the vast majority of MPR activities involve the marketer reaching out to connectors regarding a specific topic. In other words, these activities involve pitching a story or idea of some kind. However, occasionally a reporter or another connector may be looking for information that you have but are not currently pitching. As a marketer, you should never miss out on a promotional opportunity, so you need to reach out to all of your connectors to let them know what kind of help you can provide should the need arise. We call this activity **source filing**. It is simply making an effort to establish yourself as an expert with connectors in a way that will get them to keep your information on file

CHAPTER
OBJECTIVE
4

Key Terms

News aggregator Internet-based platform that compiles news stories based on either the tagging of the story by its user community or at the discretion of an individual person or organization

Pick-up Evidence (press clipping, video, etc.) of a media mention

Source filing Initiating communication with a connector to inform him or her of the availability of a subject matter expert as a resource for future stories

for future use. Without any specific way to follow up, you have no real way of knowing when your effort will pay off. When it does, however, the payoff can be significant.[9]

When you create your connector list, be sure to profile the connectors in a way that you can understand and sort the topics that are of interest to each of them. This is pretty straightforward for most marketers, but many tend to forget the need to diligently assess the true value of all of the people and information possessed by the firm. If marketers do any source filing at all, it tends to revolve around the firm's executives. However, a wealth of knowledge is buried in the depths of the engineering, research and development, operations, finance, and yes, even sales departments. The MPR professional's duty is to dig up this treasure trove of wisdom and match it with the connectors who are interested in it. As Ryan Short of MODassic Marketing in Dallas, Texas, says:

> Our client's engineers and sales staff had an enormous amount of expert knowledge. However, they were previously uninvolved in the PR efforts. We changed that....We began working with the engineers and sales staff to develop original content rather than press releases and we targeted select publications and studied their existing articles and editorial....Providing an editor with a story makes his job a lot easier. In one instance we set up a lunch meeting with an editor and our client's sales staff. This was purely a get to know you meeting and the conversation often had nothing to do with our client's business or PR....It was all about developing a relationship. This editor enjoyed the free lunch and not being pitched to death. The editor continues to e-mail the sales people for quotes to this day.

To help foster expert/reporter relationships, author and marketing guru Peter Shankman launched Help-A-Reporter (http://www.helpareporter.com) in March 2008. HARO, which connects journalists with the sources they require using a social media platform, has a growing stable of journalists from around the world who use the service on a daily basis. This free service grew to more than 40,000 members before the end of 2008.[10] This is just the first of what will be many attempts to merge source filing with social media. The marketers who master the use of these tools are likely to be the ones who excel at MPR.

Concept Case 12.1: **Expert Advice**

The Falcon's Lair employees live for hiking and climbing. Everyone from the owners on down participates in one or both of the activities. Some are experts in climbing techniques; others are equipment specialists; and a few possess an amazing knowledge of all of the best hiking and climbing sites within 100 miles of the store. Additionally, almost all of the management and staff have expressed an interest in either writing or speaking about their area of specialty.

Questions:

1. Explain the types of publishing opportunities that may be available for The Falcon's Lair's MPR efforts and give some examples.
2. Find some local and national speaking opportunities for The Falcon's Lair's experts and suggest some themes.
3. Write a pitch for source filing purposes that positions the Lair's management and staff as expert sources for connectors. It can take the form of a letter, an e-mail, or a telephone script.

Interviews: Preparation and Practice

Regardless of whether you have been source filing or pitching a specific story, your "bite" from a connector will often come as a request for an interview with someone from the firm. At times, you will simply need to handle a few questions; at other times, the connector will express interest in a lengthy interview with a company executive or expert. Whether the interview is to be with you, a company executive, or one of the firm's experts, your job as the marketer is to ensure that the interview is aligned with the company's MRP goals and that the interviewee is prepared. Additionally, the interviewee needs to represent the organization in a way that is consistent with the company's positioning and goals and needs to present himself or herself in a positive light.

Prepare

The following steps should help you or an interviewee prepare for the interview:

- Work with the connector to get a clear understanding of what he or she is looking for.
- Never assume anything in prepping for an interview.
- Avoid surprises by communicating with the journalist ahead of time.
- In addition to asking the interviewer about his or her goals for the session, investigate the interviewer and his or her medium in order to understand the style of the journalist and media outlet.

Research of this sort will let you know whether to expect difficult or embarrassing questions. In addition, you will learn if data is important to the medium and journalist or if that person prefers the information to come in the form of stories and anecdotes. At this point in your preparation, you may find that the connector requesting the interview is not right for your firm. Alternatively, you may conclude that he or she should be speaking to someone in the firm other than the person he or she requested. It is much better to determine this fact before, rather than during, the interview.

Once the interview topic is secured, it is time for the interviewee to get a firm grasp on the message. You need to work with the interviewee to compile three to five points that will give both the questioning journalist the content he or she is seeking and support the firm's position relative to the issue at hand. Make sure the points can be made clearly, and prepare an agenda for the interviewee to use. Even though the interview will follow the questioning of the connector, having an agenda should help to keep the interview on point and away from subjects you do not want to discuss. In addition, make sure that the interviewee is armed with some or all of the following support material:

- *Facts and statistics*: You can see an example of being prepared and on target with facts and statistics in the September 2008 interview of Julia Stewart, CEO and chairwoman of DineEquity Inc., by Kai Ryssdal for American Public Radio's show, *Marketplace*. Ryssdal's first question was simply, "How's business these days?" Stewart responded,

  Business is good. If you think about it, on the IHOP side we have had 22 consecutive quarters of same store sales and life continues to go well. The guests love our limited time offers, and the day to day business of coming to IHOP for breakfast, lunch, dinner and late-night...it's all good. And on the Applebee's side; it's work in progress on the turn-around, but we're meeting all of our objectives in terms of the actual turn-around.[11]

While the average person might have stopped after the first sentence, Ms. Stewart had a point to make and some facts and statistics to back it up, and she got right to work. This answer set the tone and shaped the agenda for the rest of the interview.

- *Quotes*: An interviewee can clarify a point and lend some credibility to his or her argument at the same time by using the words of well-known people. If a recognized expert from outside of your firm has said something that can help make your case, use it in the interview. For example, if your CEO says, "Warren Buffet says this industry is growing faster than any other, and I believe him," she will be much more effective than if she says, "I believe our industry is growing faster than any other."

- *Stories*: For countless generations human knowledge was passed down from mouth to ear in the form of stories. Stories stick in people's minds and are adaptable. On her blog Conversation Agent, marketing consultant Valeria Maltoni writes:

Storytelling is the backbone of our ability to remember and transmit information by compressing it into manageable chunks.... We are able to edit the information we receive to suit our needs. We edit to make it simple and concrete. As we do that, we tend to recall and include the pieces of information that match our worldview and, by doing so, we rewrite some of what we hear to suit our thinking.[12]

Therefore, if you can weave a story into your interview, do it. The story will make the interview more memorable and will get adapted to align comfortably with the attitudes of those who see, hear, or read the interview.

Practice

Practice does make perfect, regardless of whether you are the one being interviewed or you are preparing someone. Anticipate a full range of questions and practice answering them. Be sure to include easy questions, hard questions, and questions the journalist might be using to bait the interviewee into saying something provocative or controversial. Think about how to respond to opening small talk and how you want to close the interview. These last points are especially important if the journalist is recording the interview for broadcast or Internet distribution.

The interviewee needs to practice by answering questions from you in the way he or she would answer them in the actual interview. If the journalist plans to record the interview on video, videotape the practice session as well to assist in analyzing the interviewee's body language as well as his or her spoken answers. Posture and facial expressions can sometimes say more than words. You'll want to know in advance if the person being interviewed has a propensity to slouch, look overly serious, or act excessively jovial when discussing serious topics.

Exhibit 12.4 Interviews are a great way for firms to create relationships with journalists and make a connection with customers, but you must be prepared.

Haihong Zhao/Shutterstock.

Executing the Interview

Understanding the goals of the interview from the perspective of the firm and the connector, along with being well prepared and rehearsed, are critical factors in interviewing success. Regardless of preparation, however, the actual interview is usually the most nerve-wracking for the marketer and the interviewee. Here are some tips for you to give the interviewee before the event:

Relax! You're prepared.

Remember, Physical appearance matters.

- Dress in line with your message, positioning, and the style of the medium. If the interview is about a formal subject and the interviewer is from a formal organization, business attire is likely appropriate. Watch the videos of the annual addresses of Bill Gates of Microsoft and Steve Jobs of Apple to see how physical appearance communicates the positioning of a firm. (You can find these videos by using Google to search for the CEO's name along with "speeches and keynotes.")
- Body language says as much as your words. Don't be so rigid that you come across as robotic, but don't be so casual that you seem sloppy or disinterested.

CHAPTER
OBJECTIVE
6

- Remember that physical appearance matters even if the interview is not being photographed or videotaped. You can influence journalists by appearance as much as any other audience member can. (Phone interviews and Web chats are obvious exceptions to this rule.)

Connect with your interviewer. Much relies on this connection; the better you hit it off, the easier the interview will be.

Stay on message.

- Don't let the journalist steer you off course; stay on your agenda.
- Use **bridging** to stay on point by answering questions that get off topic by saying something like, "That's a great question, but what you really need to focus on is…"
- Use language to accentuate your main points. Use verbal signposts such as "this is important," or "a critical thing to remember is."

Casual, conversational confidence is the mark of an expert.

- Stay loose, even under fire.
- Exude confidence in the area of your expertise.

Make sure that your prepared answers do not seem prepared.

Use short, sweet, and simple speech.

- Keep your responses short, but make sure they have some content; avoid "yes" or "no" answers at all cost.
- Leave the tech talk and jargon at the office. Simple answers play better.

Be enthusiastic.

- Journalists don't want a boring interview; if you bore them, they won't call back.
- If you are informative and entertaining, you'll be a success!

Stay positive

- Don't argue.
- Don't get defensive.
- Don't blame.

Don't say, "No comment."

- Hopefully, you will know in advance about any questions that could get this response; be prepared to answer meaningfully.
- If a question raises a legal issue, say, "My attorney has counseled me against speaking about this issue, but what I can say is…"
- If you don't actually know the answer, say so and offer to get back to the journalist after doing some research or suggest an alternate source.[13]

Preparation, practice, and execution of a well-selected interview make the hard work of pitching a story and positioning the firm as a reliable expert source pay off as a solid media mention and potential word-of-mouth. In addition, good interviews beget good interviews; if it goes well, you are likely to get called back by the interviewing connector and by others who have seen, heard, or read the interview.

Concept Case 12.2: **Interview Time**

The source filing and other MPR activities have paid off. A national outdoor magazine has requested an interview with one of The Falcon's Lair's owners for an article titled, "The New Face of Hiking and Climbing Today."

Questions:
1. As the marketer in charge of the Lair's MPR, discuss what you would do as soon as you are informed of the national magazine's interest.
2. Once you have a handle on the journalist's goals for the interview, explain how you would prepare.
3. Describe the conversation you would have with the Lair's owner right before she begins the interview.

External Experts

Most of this chapter discusses the use of experts that come from within the firm. Recognize, however, that you can use external experts to your benefit as well. Chapter 6's discussion of reference groups and opinion leaders provides a basic framework for understanding this group and how you can identify and utilize them. However, you need to note that partnering with an external expert for mutual benefit is different from employing a paid expert endorser. The former is an MPR effort while the latter is closer to the realm of traditional advertising and promotion.

In addition, recognize external experts when they do exist, because media or other connectors are likely to recognize them, even if the firm does not. So, when this situation arises, be sure to ask yourself the following questions in order to find a strategy that will best complement your MPR strategy:

- Should you simply avoid commenting in areas well covered by others?
- Should you try to find areas of potential cooperation?
- Should you ignore the existence of other experts and let the media bring them up?

As with all other elements of MPR awareness, a proactive approach will ensure that external experts enhance the firm's image rather than detract from it.

Key Terms

Bridging An interview technique that allows an interviewee to address an interviewer's question and move on to a topic that aligns with the interviewee's goals for the interview

Reflection Questions

1. Explain why all firms have opportunities to use experts in their marketing efforts and why doing so is powerful. (Chapter Objective 1)

2. What is the value of publishing bylined articles, and what are some factors that make an article appealing to editors? (Chapter Objective 2)

3. What are the purpose and format of a case study and its value to a company's overall marketing mix? (Chapter Objective 2)

4. Discuss the sources of speaking opportunities available to experts and how marketers need to support them. (Chapter Objective 3)

5. What is source filing and how does it differ from other MPR activities? (Chapter Objective 4)

6. What are the marketer's responsibilities in selecting and preparing company experts for interviews? (Chapter Objective 5)

7. What are the elements of a properly executed interview? (Chapter Objective 6)

Chapter Key Terms

Bridging An interview technique that allows an interviewee to address an interviewer's question and move on to a topic that aligns with the interviewee's goals for the interview (p. 204)

Byline The line of text indicating the author of an article or other published work (p. 193)

Case study A short-format article based upon the expertise of a professional or organization that takes a problem-solution approach to a particular issue (p. 197)

News aggregator Internet-based platform that compiles news stories based on either the tagging of the story by its user community or at the discretion of an individual person or organization (p. 198)

Pick-up Evidence (press clipping, video, etc.) of a media mention (p. 198)

Sales cycle Time between initial contact with a prospective customer and the completion of a sale (p. 192)

Source filing Initiating communication with a connector to inform him or her of the availability of a subject matter expert as a resource for future stories (p. 199)

Thought leaders People or firms whom an industry or a consumer group recognize for contributing a new way of thinking and/or original perspectives to their field (p. 192)

White paper An educational report made available to the public that expounds on a particular industry issue (p. 197)

Application Assignments

1. Write a case study for *one* of the following new products:

   - Nuclear Knee Savers: High-tech running shoe insoles
   - The Lie Pod: MP3 player–sized device that can determine if someone is fibbing to you
   - The Language Lozenge: In mint, cherry, and chocolate, put one of these dandy candies in your mouth and your English words will come out as Spanish, French, or Italian.

Write a serious case study, but please have some fun with this. Consumers, editors, and producers don't like boring PR material. Be creative!

2. You are the MPR manager for a company that makes one of the products described in Application Assignment 1. CNN's Anderson Cooper plans to interview your CEO next week in a segment he is doing about CEOs of companies that make product innovation a priority. Explain what you would do to help your CEO prepare for this interview.

Practice Portfolio

This Practice Portfolio can be based on a fictitious company or on a real company that your instructor assigns to you. (If you used a company in previous Practice Portfolio exercises, continue to use that company.) Add your completed assignment to your portfolio to present to prospective employers.

- Write a case study for one of the products or services that your company provides.
- Choose a connector from your list and explain how you would prepare one of your company's executives or experts for an interview with this connector. Include the following:

    a. A written description of the connector and her medium to give the interviewee an understanding of the style and tone of the interview
    b. A list of ten likely questions and their answers
    c. A summary of facts, statistics, quotes, and anecdotes to be used during the interview

CHAPTER 13

Crisis Management

CHAPTER OBJECTIVES

After studying this chapter, you should be able to:

1. Define crisis in a marketer's terms.

2. Explain how new media contribute to escalating and defusing a crisis.

3. List and describe the elements of a crisis plan.

4. List and explain the rules of crisis management.

5. Describe post-crisis marketing and learning opportunities.

As illustrated in T. L. Stanley's December 11, 2006, Advertising Age article that follows, the World Diamond Council (WDC) clearly realized in advance that the issue of "blood diamonds" was one that could hurt the image and sales of diamonds. The quickness with which the organization addressed the potential crisis that a movie with the popularity of "Blood Diamond," starring Leonardo DiCaprio, could cause the industry was an indication that the WDC was conscious of the issue and prepared to face a scenario that rapidly elevated the public's awareness of the origins of conflict diamonds. WDC's MPR efforts included informing the media through more than ten press releases on the subject in 2006 and establishing Diamondfacts.org, along with its work to educate retailers in the proper way to communicate with customers about blood diamonds in preparation for the launch of the movie. Also, while there is no evidence that the two parties were in discussion, the public statement by Warner Brothers announcing that they and the WDC were "on the same page" was a coup for the diamond industry.

Gem sellers launch blitz against "Blood Diamond"; DeBeers, others build PR effort to counter movie's harsh take on industry.

The action thriller "Blood Diamond" is kicking up more than Oscar buzz.

The Warner Bros. movie, premiering Dec. 8, has thrown the diamond industry into spin control. The World Diamond Council trade group has launched an estimated $15 million public-relations and education campaign to combat the movie's images of diamond smuggling from war-torn African countries.

Much is at stake for both sides. The film makes its debut during the heaviest selling season for the $60 billion-a-year worldwide diamond industry, and the U.S. accounts for nearly half of diamond-jewelry purchases. South Africa-based DeBeers, which markets more than 40% of the world's diamonds, has been front and center in the PR efforts.

For Warner Bros., a studio that's suffered this year from duds such as "Lady in the Water" and "Poseidon," "Blood Diamond" represents an Oscar contender and a potential bright light at the box office.

Watchdogs think a powerful Hollywood film that's well-received could be the diamond business' worst nightmare, causing a boycott of the gems that movies and TV shows for years have glamorized.

World Diamond Council executives said they don't think that will happen. "We welcome the opportunity to talk about what's been accomplished in reducing the number of conflict diamonds to less than 1%," said Carson Glover, WDC spokesman.

The WDC created a website, DiamondFacts.org, that touts recent reforms that claim to have taken most conflict diamonds out of circulation. A conflict diamond, or blood diamond, is so named because proceeds from its sale fund wars against legitimate governments. That rather innocuous definition doesn't include the civilian human-rights violations that typically surround the conflict-diamond trade. Industry watchdogs agree that progress has been made but say the percentage of conflict diamonds remains far higher than WDC estimates.

Igor KaliuZhnyi/Shutterstock

209

The WDC, flexing its own brand of star power, enlisted Nelson Mandela to talk about the economic benefits of diamond mining for the African population. Some 65% of the world's diamonds come from African countries. The group hired crisis-management firm Sitrick & Co. to direct its educational efforts, including full-page ads in U.S. newspapers such as the Los Angeles Times, The New York Times and USA Today.

Anticipating a wave of questions, the WDC has given retailers packets of information for themselves and for customers, detailing the fight to take conflict diamonds off the market via the U.N.-backed Kimberley Process.

The film, set during Sierra Leone's civil war in 1999, stars Leonardo DiCaprio as a soldier-turned-smuggler who's chasing a rare pink diamond.

Ed Zwick, the filmmaker, has steadfastly refused to change the film or add a disclaimer the WDC has requested saying that voluntary reforms have stamped out most conflict diamonds. Studio executives say the film is a fictionalized account set at a time in history when conflict diamonds were more common.

Warner Bros. executives decided to release the movie at holiday time, when serious Oscar-bait films often crowd the schedule, because it's a heavy-traffic time at the multiplex. The fact that it's also the biggest diamond-buying season did not affect the release date, executives said.

The movie doesn't intend to stop people from buying diamonds, but rather to get them "to ask questions and be informed," a Warner Bros. spokeswoman said. "We're on the same page with the World Diamond Council about education."

This isn't the first time the issue of conflict diamonds has come up in entertainment. Kanye West won a Grammy for his music video "Diamonds of Sierra Leone," and several prominent members of the hip-hop community have made a documentary called "Bling: A Planet Rock" that's expected to air on VH1. The History Channel has a separate documentary called "Blood Diamonds" airing in December.

Source: Reprinted with permission from the Dec. 1, 2006, issue of Advertising Age. Copyright, Crain Communications, Inc. 2006.

CHAPTER
OBJECTIVE
1
Crisis for Marketers

Crisis management and crisis communications are business disciplines unto themselves, as they span the workings of the entire firm. They are a course of study that includes but is certainly not limited to marketing. Since an organization's future can ride on how well it manages a crisis, crisis management may be one of the MPR professional's most critical skills. Because crisis management is so complex, however, this chapter merely scratches the surface of this important subject.

For marketers, a crisis can take a multitude of forms:

- It can be an instance when a company's product actually does harm to the person or property of a customer. Examples of this type of crisis include the case of seven people dying as a result of ingesting cyanide-laden Tylenol capsules in 1982 and the increased number of rollover accidents in Ford Explorers in the late 1990s and early 2000s that was attributed to a particular model of Firestone tires.

- Crises can also emanate from situations in which customers or publics discover that their perception of a company, its brands, or products are not in line with reality. In 2005 and 2006, for example, BP (formerly British Petroleum) suffered a fatal refinery explosion and a pipeline leak while in the midst of repositioning itself as an environmentally and socially responsible energy company with its "Beyond Petroleum" campaign. Subsequent cuts in production and employee allegations of inadequate maintenance and inspection practices[2] exacerbated the impact of these events.

- The behavior and practices of the people within a firm can create predicaments for marketers as well. For example, in 2002, marketers at General Electric had to respond to publicity surrounding an affair and subsequent messy divorce of recently retired CEO Jack Welch. The media frenzy surrounding Welch brought up questions about his lavish retirement package and seemingly extravagant personal expenses that GE picked up during his tenure. In addition, the timing of this crisis increased the likelihood of Welch and GE being painted with the same brush as other embattled CEOs and their companies, such as Bernie Ebbers of WorldCom and Kenneth Lay from Enron.[3]

Historically, firms have taken either a passive, defensive, or reactive approach to dealing with crisis. The passive approach assumes that the problem will eventually go away if the company simply ignores it, while the defensive approach involves the company defending itself from a weak, unanalyzed position. The reactive approach, on the other hand, consists of management drawing up a plan based on an issue after it arises. A fourth mode of addressing a crisis, the preemptive approach, requires a firm to identify potential issues before they arise and either eliminate the potential problem or construct a plan for dealing with it if it does come to pass.[4] In this chapter we will focus on using the preemptive approach, and outline some rules that apply to crisis MPR both in the preemptive and reactive response modes.

The Role of New Media in a Crisis

CHAPTER
OBJECTIVE
2

Arguably, word of rats in a restaurant's kitchen would be a Marketing Public Relations nightmare, whether it happened today or in the 1930s. The difference is that the damage that such an infestation caused in the 1930s would be limited by the number of people who witnessed it and how vehemently they told others about what they saw. If the restaurant's proprietors eliminated the problem soon after patrons discovered it, no physical evidence would linger and the rumors would likely fade over time.

Today, however, the environment is a bit different, as in the case of a 2007 incident in which rats overran a Taco Bell restaurant in New York City. According to the franchise owners, they recognized the infestation problem and began construction in the basement of the store to resolve it. Unfortunately, the work in the basement drove the rats into the retail portion of the building. The city's department of health cited the eatery, but that was just the beginning.[5] The bigger MPR crisis stemmed from video—an amateur video followed by footage from a news organization—showing a multitude of rats scurrying around the restaurant floor while people looked on in disgust. The videos made national news, the blogosphere, and YouTube, and even today you can still find the story on the Internet. While

Igor Norman/Shutterstock.

Exhibit 13.1 New portable Web-enabled technology allows consumers to share a story with the world, regardless of whether it is good news or bad.

diners from both decades would likely be equally repulsed by restaurant rats, the news of their presence spreads faster and farther and stays around much longer today than it would have in days gone by. "This story will live on the Internet for all time," said Stephen Fink, president of Lexicon Communications, in an article in the February 26, 2007, edition of *Advertising Age*.

To make a difficult situation worse, today's media and technology environments not only speed events into crisis status but can create a perceived crisis so that a marketer may not be able to tell immediately whether the feedback he or she receives accurately reflects the sentiments of the true market or just a small set of vocal outliers. Unfortunately, the cries of a vociferous minority can turn a crisis from perceived to actual as stakeholders who may have been apathetic toward the incident become concerned over the public response.

A common source for such crises is the missteps and miscalculations that other areas of the marketing mix, especially advertising, perpetrate. A notable example is the "Baby Wearing" ad campaign that Motrin ran in late 2008 to target mothers of newborns who carry their babies on their person. Motrin's goal seemed to be to increase sales to this demographic by tying the phenomenon of baby-wearing to its popular painkiller. However, the tactic backfired for Motrin as many moms felt that the company was condemning baby-wearing and the backlash hit cyberspace hard.[6] Negative responses appeared fast and furious on blogs, Twitter, and YouTube. The makers of Motrin had an MPR problem on their hands, which had started out as what they felt was a harmless advertisement. Motrin's experience reinforces the need for firms to understand the dynamics of the new media side of MPR, have a plan, and be ready to react to situations arising from all corners of the firm.

On the flip side, new media can help firms deal with MPR crises with increased speed and agility—at least in reaching out to consumers and connectors who are plugged in. The use of new media, in fact, was a part of Ford's response to the MPR crisis caused by a request for financial assistance that General Motors, Chrysler, and Ford made jointly to the U.S. government in 2008 to help them weather the great economic downturn of that year. Ford went into crisis-communications mode by assembling a digital push, anchored by a Web site, TheFordStory.com (http://www.thefordstory.com), to differentiate itself from GM and Chrysler. It also launched campaigns on several Web sites, including Google and its YouTube video site, various blogs, Facebook, and Twitter, in an attempt to make its case for a bailout as quickly and widely as possible. In an article in *The Wall Street Journal,* Ford's global digital and multimedia communications manager, Scott Monty, said, "The auto makers in general have gotten a black eye in the media, and we didn't feel like we were getting a fair shake.... With digital media, it lives on for a long time. It's picked up in Google searches, people pass it along and share messages they care about with blogs and their social networks of choice."[7]

Creating a Crisis Communications Plan

CHAPTER
OBJECTIVE
3

Crises are inevitable. According to Oxford-Metrica, in the years between 2009 and 2014, 83 percent of companies will face a crisis that will negatively impact their bottom line by between 20 percent and 30 percent. Ill-prepared companies can find themselves not only mired in their crisis but in their poor public position on the crisis as well.[8] Crisis plans are not a luxury for any company. The purpose of a crisis communications plan is to create a mechanism that allows the company to assess a situation and clearly communicate to stakeholders both the magnitude of the crisis and what the company intends to do about it. The plan creates a structure for analyzing a crisis and creating a plan of action that can be implemented swiftly. In moments of crisis, time is of the essence, and organizations with a plan will likely be better equipped to respond quickly and logically to any situation that arises.

In a 2008 article in *Marketing News*, Chris Gidez, U.S. director of the risk management and crisis communications specialty group for Hill & Knowlton Inc., points out that firms need to take into account that the communications challenges are just a by-product of a business crisis, and that they need to have a sound business response accompanied by a very effective communications plan.[9] A crisis plan should be so simple that anyone who can read can understand it. Since crises rarely appear exactly as anticipated, a plan should not be centered on the perfect scenario in which only a trained communicator is in charge of the execution. As bench strength (having more than one person who can do any given job) is the secret to great athletic teams, it should be the secret to your crisis plan as well. This means having people from multiple levels and functional areas within the firm involved in crisis planning and trained for crisis response.

These are the four steps you should follow to create a successful MPR crisis communications plan, according to crisis communications expert Gerard Braud:

1. ***Vulnerability audit***: Create a report based on interviews with people in your organization in which you ask them what might go wrong and why. Your interviewees should range from top executives to managers to line employees, and you should ask them a few simple open-ended questions, including, "What do you think might go wrong here that would result in a crisis?" You'll want to consider likely crises and worst-case scenarios, delve into bizarre possibilities, and, as illustrated in Table13.1, rate each one on the likelihood of occurrence and on the impact it would have on the firm.

   When looking at the scenarios, you should also consider that a crisis is not always a fire or explosion but may be something internal, often referred to as a *smoldering crisis.* According to the Institute for Crisis Management in Louisville, Kentucky, a slowly developing internal crisis (such as one stemming from employee controversy or mismanagement) is twice as likely to happen as a sudden crisis (such as a natural disaster or catastrophic product malfunction).

   In preparing your plan be sure to make an extensive list of the scenarios that people identified, and then rank their probability of occurrence. Deal with the top ten most likely to occur first, and then proceed down the list accordingly.

Table 13.1 Vulnerability Audit

Vulnerability Title	Vulnerability Description	Likelihood of Occurrence	Potential Impact on Firm
Product malfunction	Product sold to a customer malfunctions in such a way that it causes significant harm to the customer's person, property, or to other people.	Since the firm sells hundreds of products from hundreds of suppliers, the likelihood of this occurring is high, despite the reputation of and our relationship with our suppliers and our periodic testing of incoming merchandise.	Media accounts and word-of-mouth could create a public perception that the firm sells inferior products or encourages customers to buy products that they are unable to use resulting in a loss of sales.

2. *Creating the heart of the plan*: The heart of the plan is the part of the plan that coordinates notification of key leaders during a crisis, as well as notification of the media, employees, customers, the community, and other key stakeholders specific to your organization. "The heart of the plan tells you each step to take in the communications process from the time the crisis begins until it ends. It keeps people on task and focuses on rapid communications," says Gerard Braud. "A huge problem in crisis communications is decision paralysis, in which executives and leaders fail to communicate in a rapid, timely manner. For example, says Braud, in the case of the shootings at Virginia Tech in April

of 2007, the first statement was not issued until 2 hours and 11 minutes into the crisis. The first statement about the initial two shootings at 7:15 a.m. went out at 9:26 a.m., 11 minutes after the next twenty-nine people were killed. This is decision paralysis. Had that first statement gone out within one hour of the onset of the crisis, it may have prevented the next twenty-nine deaths.

Each plan should have two sets of statement templates. The first is a very basic fill-in-the-blank template often called "the first critical statement." Your plan should dictate that even if all of the facts are not known about a crisis, the most basic facts should be communicated within one hour of the onset of a crisis. The second statement will be a more detailed statement, described in step 3. This more detailed statement will likely be issued during the second hour of the crisis. In addition, the heart of the plan should list the members of a crisis management team, as well as the appropriate spokesperson(s) and media contacts. Despite the fact that people leave and change positions within a firm, people should be named with multiple ways to contact each of them. "Not listing names is a fatal flaw of many crisis communications plans," says Braud. "Even though people change roles, firms need to realize that the crisis communications plan is a living document and someone should be reviewing and updating contact information on a monthly basis."

3. *Scenario statements*: Go down your list of possible crisis scenarios identified in step 1 and write out what you would say to your critical audiences in the event that each of these situations happens. These are essentially templates that will be modified and updated on the day you need them. Include fill-in-the-blank sections that allow you to add the "who, what, when, where, why, and how" followed by a complete script that you or a spokesperson can say verbatim during the crisis. There are many "true-isms" you can write today so valuable time is not lost writing them on the day of the crisis. The statement may include multiple-choice options for listing the number of injured or dead, or a list of various agencies that may respond during a crisis. Braud suggests that you write it all out on a clear sunny day, then before the final statement is issued, you simply edit out the choices that do not apply and use the ones that do apply.

Once written, these templates must be submitted to members of the crisis management team for pre-approval, so they can be used rapidly without further permission on the day of the crisis. These statements should be placed in an appendix of the plan. When needed, the same statement is issued simultaneously to all media, employees, customers, and other key audiences. For example, as the statement is read to the media it can simultaneously be sent via e-mail to all employees and customers, with a copy simultaneously posted to the Internet for all to see.

4. *Testing*: A crisis communications drill lets all parties become familiar with the plan and ensures that it works as intended. Even the best plans have flaws that

---

Key Terms

Scenario statements The portion of an MPR crisis plan that maps out the "who, what, when, where, why, and how" of specific potential crises

Vulnerability audit An exercise for identifying and documenting potential MPR crises for planning purposes

a practice drill can expose and correct. Executing the plan in a drill can reveal potential personality conflicts with leaders or responders. Conflicts and leadership failures can then be addressed in an evaluation session following the drill, so that they are not repeated on the day of a crisis. A drill also allows you to test the quality of your spokespeople as well. Videotaping their performance can help develop their skills. All potential spokespeople should also receive annual media training.

Many organizations have emergency response plans for coordinating police, fire, rescue, and EMS during a crisis. The security director or risk manager should schedule regular emergency drills. However, many fail to include communications in these drills. As a result, many responders and managers become overwhelmed when the media demands interviews during an actual crisis and employees and their families make demands for information. The drill can be either a tabletop (having those involved run through their reactions to a scenario in a conference room setting) or a real-time drill. In either case, it should include both role-players portraying members of the media who show up on-site with cameras and an off-site team that works to overload switchboards with phone calls.

The key is to have everything pre-written and blessed by legal and corporate leaders well in advance of the crisis, so you will be able to communicate quickly and effectively on the day of the crisis. Speed of communications can save lives.[10]

Concept Case 13.1: **Crisis Plan**

The Falcon's Lair management team and staff have always been a close-knit group of noncontroversial people who strive to put their customers first. The Lair has never had any crises, so no one has ever considered planning for one. With a rash of lawsuits appearing in the news, and some sensational press coverage surrounding them, the Lair's managers begin to wonder if, despite having good people and selling top-quality products, the business might at some time be susceptible to an MPR crisis. At a staff meeting someone suggests that the store's reputation could be ruined if one of its suppliers sold the company a defective product that injured a customer. Another person expresses her concern about suggesting specific climbs to patrons. Since she has no way to be sure that a customer's climbing ability is what he claims it to be, she is concerned that she might put the Lair's reputation at risk—along with the well-being of that customer—if she recommends a tough climb to a person who falsely claims to be an expert.

Questions:
1. Explain how an MPR professional could help the management of The Falcon's Lair identify potential crises.
2. List five to ten situations that might cause an MPR crisis at The Falcon's Lair. Discuss the likelihood of their occurring and the impact they would have on the business should they come to pass.
3. Discuss a strategy for the crisis scenario that you deem most likely to happen.

Rules for Implementing the Crisis Management Plan

As a marketer, you must strive to avoid dealing with crises in the passive and defensive modes. However, while you should make every effort to handle your crisis MPR with a preemptive approach, the following guidelines can help when you have no choice but to be reactive:

- *Move swiftly.* If possible, break the story yourself. Speed allows you to control the message and avoid speculation and exaggeration by the media or consumers. Remember, stories travel at the speed of light these days, and you do not want to have opposing points of view dominating the dialogue on an issue that concerns your company. In 2007, Apple's swift response to the commotion that erupted following a $200 price cut of the formerly $599 iPhone is an example of how getting right on a problem can avert long-term damage to a firm's image and sales. Within twenty-four hours of announcing the price break, Apple CEO Steve Jobs posted a letter to the company's Web site offering a $100 credit to anyone who had paid the top price for the phone. Fifteen minutes after the letter appeared, the Web site had in excess of 2,000 "digs" (people who bookmarked the site http://www.digg.com); within days industry pundits were predicting that any backlash would be short-lived.[11] Sales of the iPhone in subsequent years have proven the predictions to be correct.

- *Keep all stakeholders informed.* People with an interest in your organization should not be surprised. Think about how you would feel if you found out you were about to be laid off from your job by reading it in the newspaper rather than by hearing it from your boss. Consider all of the stakeholders involved in the situation and make sure that they hear about a crisis at a time and in a way that is appropriate to their relationship to the firm and the issue at hand. Good stakeholder communication also keeps everyone "on the same page" and minimizes the chance of conflicting stories reaching the media.

- *Be truthful.* Although you may be tempted to veil things in a crisis, that veil will look like a cover-up as time marches on. Even trivializing an event or action by using softer language can make the firm appear as though it does not understand the seriousness of the situation. Professional football player Michael Vick demonstrated a prime example of using inappropriate language in a crisis when he responded to allegations of dog strangling by characterizing his actions as "immature."[12]

- *Be an information resource.* If connectors know they can come to you for reliable information, the chances of them telling your side of the story and assisting in shining a favorable light on the firm in resulting coverage will increase.

- *Be decisive.* Say, "This is what happened, here is what we are doing to deal with it, and here are the future ramifications." The 1982 Tylenol case is an archetype of decisiveness. The company took action in the media on the national and local levels to communicate that they were putting public safety and well-being first by conducting a total recall. This action was risky as it effectively brought sales to zero for a time, but it paid off in the end—Tylenol retains top market share to this day.[13]

- *Apologize and move on.* It's okay to say that you're sorry. In fact, if you have something to be sorry for, it's a good idea to apologize. However, be sure not to dwell on the apology. At best, overapologizing keeps the issue in the public eye for longer than necessary; at worst, it can make the company appear weak. Apple's iPhone example above illustrates the right way to handle an apology as well. Jobs admitted a mistake, gave a plausible reason, and started pointing to the future.

- *Keep the media up to date.* When they can't get information directly from the source, journalists and bloggers will look elsewhere. They might turn to industry analysts, former employees, or even your competitors. If you are trying to manage a message and keep your firm in a positive light, these are probably the last people you want commenting on the situation. Make sure that at least a few visible outlets are reporting your side of the story. You may even consider giving a journalist inside access to show that you are being candid with all stakeholders.

- *Use video.* According to Andy Sernovitz, contributing editor of Smart Blog on Social Media, "Video is the only medium where your original message stays intact.... Text gets re-written, but your CEO talking on screen gets imbedded instead of edited."[14]

Exhibit 13.2 No firm looks forward to a crisis, but planning can avert an MPR disaster and even put the firm in a positive light for its adept handling of a bad situation.

akva/Shutterstock.

CHAPTER OBJECTIVE 5
Post-crisis Opportunities and Evaluation

The Tylenol case is a testament to the fact that good planning and decision-making that puts the customer and public first during a crisis can, in the long run, serve the firm, its image, and its bottom line. When a company handles a crisis well, it has an opportunity to use its adept recovery for additional publicity that reinforces its positioning with customers and other stakeholders. People can be suspicious of business and cynically expect firms to put their own interests before the consumers'. When the reverse happens, it can have a positive impact on the way the public sees the firm and its brands. The marketer's responsibility is to help ensure that the business makes the customer its priority, and to demonstrate to customers how this is so.

A situation that involved the fast-food chain Jack-in-the-Box demonstrates a classic example of communicating the use of a good business solution to help a company recover from a devastating crisis and regain its position as market leader. In 1993 *E. coli* poisoning killed three toddlers who had eaten at a Jack-in-the-Box, nearly closing down the country's fifth-largest hamburger chain. But, rather than let the business go under, Jack-in-the-Box took a proactive and public approach to remedying customers' concerns. Within days of the outbreak, the firm hired a microbiologist as the vice president of quality assurance and product safety. It revamped the chain's entire food-cooking process to include the testing of products arriving from suppliers, store inspections, and employee training.[15]

While it took some time for this new "customer safety first" philosophy to take hold, the combination of operational changes and the communication of the company's new position through public relations and other elements of the marketing mix enabled the company to move from a $25 million loss in 2001 to a record $4.8 billion profit in 2008.[16]

After a crisis has passed, marketers must take the time to look back upon the cause of the crisis, the actions taken, and the results of those actions. Each crisis is a learning experience from which you can gain valuable insight on preventing, planning for, and dealing with future crises.

Concept Case 13.2: **It Happened!**

Despite consulting with a trained staff member and purchasing equipment that was working properly, a Falcon's Lair customer failed to follow directions on a safety component and wound up falling more than twenty feet. Although the customer sustained substantial injuries, he is expected to make a full recovery. Learning of the incident almost immediately from a store-sponsored social network, the Lair's staff begins working with the equipment manufacturer, local authorities, and the customer himself to determine the cause of the fall. The Lair's staff is also diligent about communicating with local media as well as with online hiking and climbing communities and their customers. The local newspaper even runs a story depicting the fallen climber emerging from the hospital, bandaged and on crutches, in which he admits to being careless and credits The Falcon's Lair staff for teaching him about and supplying him with additional safety equipment that ultimately saved his life.

Questions:
1. Discuss what can be done from an MPR standpoint in the future to further minimize the likelihood of such an incident recurring.
2. Explain how you might use the handling of this crisis to help strengthen the image of The Falcon's Lair with its customers and the public.

 Reflection Questions

1. Compare and contrast the different approaches that firms typically use during an MPR crisis. (Chapter Objective 1)

2. How has new media contributed to the acceleration of the spread of news of crises? Give some examples. (Chapter Objective 2)

3. In what ways can new media be a tool for firms to contain the damage caused by a crisis situation? (Chapter Objective 2)

4. Describe the creation and utility of a vulnerability audit. (Chapter Objective 3)

5. Why is testing a crisis plan so vital to a firm's response to a crisis? (Chapter Objective 3)

6. What are the key elements of crisis plan implementation? (Chapter Objective 3)

7. Discuss the impact that using video on modern crisis communications has on a firm. (Chapter Objective 4)

8. Describe how a firm can use the handling of a crisis to improve its image or positioning. (Chapter Objective 5)

Chapter Key Terms

Scenario statement The portion of an MPR crisis plan that maps out the "who, what, when, where, why, and how" of specific potential crises (p. 215)

Vulnerability audit An exercise for identifying and documenting potential MPR crises for planning purposes (p. 214)

Application Assignments

1. Select one of the following real MPR crises and describe the events that caused the need for crisis MPR. In addition, discuss how the organization handled the crisis, pointing to what the firm did well, and explaining what it could have done better. Possible cases for exploration:

   • Tylenol poisoning (1982)
   • Ford-Firestone (2001)
   • *Exxon Valdez* (1989)
   • Union Carbide, Bhopal, India (1984)
   • Tom Cruise's odd public behavior (2005–2006)
   • Harvard University president Lawrence Summer's remarks about women scientists (2005)
   • Merck-Vioxx (2005)

2. Search the Internet and other media to find a current example of an MPR crisis. Explain the nature of the crisis and discuss how the firm used post-crisis MPR to restore the company's reputation in the eyes of customers and other stakeholders.

Practice Portfolio

This Practice Portfolio can be based on a fictitious company or on a real company that your instructor assigns to you. (If you used a company in previous Practice Portfolio exercises, continue to use that company.) Add your completed assignment to your portfolio to present to prospective employers.

Conduct a vulnerability audit for your practice company using the information that you have available to you. List the media that you would contact and the media and blogs with coverage you intend to follow for the duration of a crisis. Explain your protocol for keeping your employees, stockholders, and vendors informed about the crisis, as well as any non-MPR vehicles that you might consider using to communicate with all stakeholders, including customers. List the top five crises that are likely to strike your firm in the next five years and rank them by likelihood of occurrence and impact on the company.

14

Planning and Measuring

CHAPTER OBJECTIVES
After studying this chapter, you should be able to:

1. Explain how MPR planning overlaps with other planning efforts within a firm.

2. Describe the importance of defining the MPR problem and understanding the firm's positioning and resources when conducting a situation analysis.

3. Explain how one firm can have multiple target markets.

4. Discuss how MPR's interactions with other elements of the marketing communications mix affect planning.

5. Formulate goals and objectives for an MPR plan.

6. Explain the primary MPR strategy and formulate a statement of tactics.

7. Describe the purpose and methodologies used in measuring media mentions and word-of-mouth.

8. Construct a formal MPR plan.

CLASSIC AND CUTTING EDGE *Caffeine "Buzz" Agents*

In the fall of 2005, national coffee and donut franchise Dunkin' Donuts hired a word-of-mouth marketing and media company, BzzAgent, to complement traditional advertising programs supporting the launch of a new espresso beverage, Latte Lite®. The 2005 launch called for in-store point-of-purchase advertising, radio advertising in select markets, and word-of-mouth to support Latte Lite. The goal for the effort as a whole was to create brand awareness and drive sales of this new product.

BzzAgent designed a twelve-week word-of-mouth (WOM) program made up of 3,000 trained volunteers (BzzAgents), who would experience the Latte Lite, form their own opinions about the beverage, engage in natural conversations about the product, and report those episodes back to BzzAgent via the company's reporting interface. The company planned to run the program in several regional markets across the country.

To measure the efficacy of the WOM campaign, BzzAgent and Dunkin' Donuts created a control scenario in which they would compare sales in the test markets with those in control markets. The control markets had similar advertising campaigns but did not include the WOM component. For example, if the control market just used radio advertising, then the test market used both radio advertising and a WOM campaign. Test markets included Boston, New York City, Cleveland, and Detroit. Control markets included Hartford, Philadelphia, Atlanta, and Chicago. Geographic selection accounted for market size, franchise penetration (number of stores), and existing brand awareness. The company selected BzzAgents to fit Dunkin' Donuts' demographic and psychographic profile for a Latte Lite.

Once volunteers enrolled in a BzzAgent WOM campaign, they:

- Received a mailing (BzzKit®) that contained a product experience element (in this case, six cards, each redeemable for a Latte Lite), an informational guide about the product, and a code of conduct. (This tactic allowed the BzzAgents to experience a risk-free trial of the product and to also convey their authentic experiences to their social networks.)
- Were given access to the reporting interface at http://www.bzzagent.com to report their social interactions back to the company.
- Were surveyed at three points during the twelve-week campaign.
- Were kept up to date with news and information via e-mail updates.

BzzAgent.™

BzzAgent approximated the number of WOM episodes and people reached by compiling reports that the campaign participants filed and by conducting surveys to account for additional, unreported WOM incidents. The survey was important because agents rarely report all of their WOM episodes. Reasons for this lack of complete reporting include:

- Lack of time, procrastination, or forgetfulness on the part of the agent.
- A mediocre reaction from the conversational partner or a reaction that doesn't seem important enough to report.
- Experiencing a WOM episode that is very similar to another incident that the participant has previously reported.

Over 63 percent of BzzAgents submitted at least one report documenting their WOM episodes about Latte Lite. In total, they filed 5,004 reports. On average, agents reported having 2.5 conversational partners per episode. In addition, survey results indicate that each agent neglected to report an average of 3.8 WOM episodes. At the end of the campaign, BzzAgent estimated that WOM reached at least 108,272 individuals.

Exhibit 14.1 BzzAgent Graph

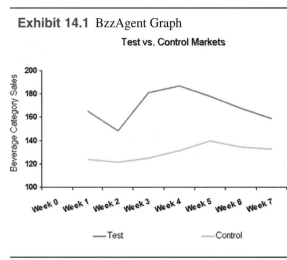

Test vs. Control Markets

Beverage Category Sales

—— Test   ——Control

Source: BzzAgent.™

When the company compared data from the test markets to the control markets, they noted a clear correlation of a sudden and sharp increase in sales during the campaign, while control markets did not experience such an increase. Exhibit 14.1 illustrates the overall sales in the beverage category in both the test and control markets. As the chart demonstrates, there was a clear positive increase in sales after the WOM program launched, resulting in 26 percent higher sales by the end of week four than in week two. Control markets experienced an 8 percent increase during the same time period.[1]

According to BZZAgent founder and CEO Dave Balter, "Providing quantifiable results for marketing and advertising programs—including word-of-mouth—is a major focus for marketers.... The Dunkin Donuts campaign results clearly illustrate the positive impact word-of-mouth has on brand awareness and sales." This WOM campaign plainly worked both to raise awareness and add credibility to Latte Lite and the espresso line. This case is an example of how word-of-mouth can be an extremely effective addition to the marketing communications mix of a campaign, especially when a company has clear goals, objectives, strategies, and tactics. It also demonstrates that companies can implement systems to measure and evaluate the effectiveness of word-of-mouth campaigns, even though these systems are not as developed as methods for traditional marketing.

MPR Plans Are Multifunctional

Conventional business wisdom says that businesses should plan. Companies have over-all strategic business plans, financial plans, marketing plans, and plans for just about every business function and subfunction. MPR is no exception in its need for smart planning. The difficulty, however, can be that MPR crosses strategic and tactical lines and business disciplines. For example, MPR needs to be a part of a firm's strategic marketing plan, yet may also be called upon to participate tactically in a product launch or to deal with a crisis. Additionally, many larger organizations have separate marketing and communication functions, so MPR may need to operate within the corporate com-munications context and coordinate its efforts with investor relations, employee rela-tions, and community relations activities. As a result, MPR professionals can expect to create several different plans over the course of the year. The good news is that they can follow a basic formula regardless of the type of plan they are creating. An MPR plan should articulate the current situation of the firm, brand, or product, define the goals for the effort at hand, describe the means for achieving these goals, and define a way for measuring progress. In short, a good MPR plan should describe where the firm is now, where it wants to go, and how it plans to get there.

Situation Analysis
Define the Problem

The first step in producing an MPR plan—regardless of whether it is long- or short-term in scope—is to define the problem. If it is part of a firm's broader marketing plan, the problem may be determining how to increase product sales. For a product launch, on the other hand, the problem could be determining how to increase awareness of the new offering. In a crisis, the problem might be deciding how to preserve the image of a brand or company executive. In all of these cases, however, the MPR professional must define the problem clearly so that he or she can determine an effective course of action. In MPR terms, the quest to solve a given problem is often referred to as a *campaign*.

Positioning and Resources

Well-marketed companies, brands, and products are consciously positioned in the marketplace in such a way that they have a sustainable advantage over competitors on some level. The firm's mission typically helps produce and support this position, so marketers endeavoring to create a successful MPR plan need to understand both the mission and the position. The marketer must also realize that any position has both benefits and challenges. (For example, a position as a low-cost leader can drive demand among price-conscious consumers, but it may also signal that the products or services are cheap or inferior to others in the market.)

Along with positioning, marketers need to consider the resources they have available to them to support their efforts. Resources can be tangible, like money, a large retail presence in the market, or a large existing customer base. They can also be less tangible, like a strong brand image or a wealth of expertise within the firm. Positioning, combined with resources—or lack thereof—affect the implementation of any plan, so marketers must thoroughly understand and evaluate them before setting goals or formulating strategies or tactics. At this point, marketers should consider conducting a **SWOT analysis**.

Target Market

As discussed throughout the text, MPR is different from other segments of the marketing communications mix in that it has a two-stage target market consisting of the ultimate audience (consumers, publics, stakeholders, etc.) and the connectors (the media, bloggers, and influential and well-connected individuals and institutions) who communicate with that audience. If a firm is conducting MPR for the first time, it will have to create a connector list. On the other hand, if the firm is experienced in MPR, it likely has an existing, ever-evolving list.

In either case, the marketer is unlikely to use all available connectors for any one campaign. As a result, he or she has to pare down the list to just the connectors who will reach the right final audience with the intended impact for this particular campaign. The marketer does this by evaluating the ultimate audience, determining the connectors to which that audience is exposed, and then finding the connectors who will deliver the message in the desired way.

For example, a marketer might recognize that both a respected business magazine and a popular blog reach the right consumer segment for an upcoming campaign to launch a new product. While both touch the same people, the marketer also needs to consider the difference in impact between the two media. He or she may see the magazine as having a high level of credibility with the audience, but it may take days, weeks, or even months to cover the topic. The blog, on the other hand, may be able to publish a story within a day, but it lacks the perception of authority held by a long-established traditional media outlet. Both connectors may still remain on the list, but the marketer needs to recognize the differences between connectors and must consider both reach and impact during list creation.

Interaction with Other Functions

The various elements of the marketing communications mix rarely work by themselves. They can work in sequence or in tandem and are often designed to solve the same problem or achieve the same goal. The result of activities within one area of the marketing mix often influences or is used in another. For example, the media frenzy that resulted from Super Bowl commercials (discussed in Chapter 2) was a case of MPR and advertising working together. Having salespeople use reprints of articles written about the firm or its products is an example of MPR and sales working together. Regardless of whether the plan originates from the MPR level or a broader level that encompasses the entire marketing communications mix, the plan should include analysis of the interactions between all marketing functions.

Likewise, MPR can overlap with or be an integral part of corporate communications endeavors. As a result, MPR professionals must understand how the various areas of communications interrelate. For example, in a large public company, investor relations would likely be the first of the communications departments to learn about a potential financial concern at the firm. That department would have the responsibility to work with investors and the financial press to ensure that they disseminate information in a fashion that is favorable to the company with regard to the firm's stockholders. Employee relations would concentrate on informing and educating the firm's management and staff to keep them aware of the situation and to let them know what is expected of them and how the issue will affect them. Marketing Public Relations would handle the issue relative to existing and prospective customers.

The American automotive industry's predicament in 2008 illustrates the importance of these three communications areas working together. Gasoline prices hit all-time highs, putting a drag on demand for automobiles, which in turn jeopardized the jobs of thousands of employees and sent stock prices falling. While the solution to the problem is largely financial and managerial in scope, the various communications teams had to coordinate efforts to ensure that employees remained reasonably calm, stockholders held onto their shares, and some consumers continued to buy. Panic in any one of these areas will exacerbate the other two and contribute to a downward spiral for the company at large.

Goals and Objectives

CHAPTER
OBJECTIVE
5

By this point in the course, you have no doubt gleaned that the prime directives for MPR professionals are to garner media mentions and create word-of-mouth that contribute to the achievement of the firm's broader goals. To be successful, you, the MPR professional, need to take a top-down approach to goal setting. In this case the top consists of the firm's mission and vision, its overall marketing goals, and the problem that you have defined to start the planning process. The problem statement is the place to begin formulating your primary goal, which ultimately leads to the creation of your strategy. As discussed in Chapter 3, the primary goal(s) need to be S.M.A.R.T.: specific, measurable, attainable, relevant, and tangible. In other words, a goal that states that you are aiming to increase brand awareness is not enough. A more appropriate goal would be the following: "We will increase brand-name recognition among American college and university students, as determined by an online survey, to 65 percent by the end of the calendar year."

To accomplish this goal, you will have some supporting objectives to drive the tactical portion of the plan. These objectives will encompass all of your media mention and word-of-mouth aspirations for the campaign and they will be very specific. Following are examples of good supporting objectives:

- Place at least one feature article in one of the following publications (list publications) in the next six months.
- Receive product reviews in at least 100 college newspapers in the next six months.

Key Terms

SWOT analysis An evaluation of a firm's internal strengths and weaknesses, and external opportunities and threats compiled for use in business planning situations

Exhibit 14.2 Setting goals helps marketers formulate MPR plans and provides a method for evaluating performance.

rob:ocquyt/Shutterstock.

- Receive one review on an identified target blog (refer to connector list) each day over the next six months.
- Increase mention of the company, brand, and its products on Twitter, Digg, and Delicious by 15 percent a month between now and the end of the calendar year.

Remember, each of these objectives needs to be S.M.A.R.T. as well, and they can be quite numerous. You must also realize that, although the plan has its elements ordered, you cannot write an effective MPR plan by thinking of each element in a vacuum. To properly set goals, for example, you will need to have an understanding of the target market and the available strategies and tactics that you can employ to reach them. Without this understanding, you have no way of gauging if your objectives are in fact attainable or relevant.

CHAPTER
OBJECTIVE
6

Formulating Strategies and Tactics

When you formulate your strategies and tactics, you spell out what you plan to do in order to reach your goals and objectives. As you have seen, the strategy component of MPR is very straightforward; for planning purposes it will almost always be a statement of how you plan on getting media mentions and spreading word-of-mouth to achieve the primary goal or goals of the campaign. You will spend the most time in planning in the tactical area. The tactics are the details of what will be done, how it will be done, as well as when, why, and by whom. Each tactical item should refer back to an objective; you can think of your list of tactics as the battle plan of the campaign.

A sample **statement of tactics** in this section of the plan may look like the following:

To achieve our objective of receiving product reviews in at least 100 college newspapers in the next six months, we will create a connector list consisting of the editors of the nation's top 1,000 college and university newspapers (ranked by size of the school's undergraduate resident population). We will formulate a press release that describes the uses of the product and its benefits to students, along with a suggested format for reviewing the product. We will send the press release and a product sample to each editor, along with a pitch letter explaining how writing a review can benefit the editor and her audience. [Name] will draft the press release and pitch letter(s) by [date], and [name or department] will approve them by [date]. [Name] will send the packages before [date]. [Names] will make follow up phone calls between [date] and [date]. We will monitor results through our third-party clipping service and additional follow-up.

Since there may be multiple methods for achieving a given objective, you may have multiple statements like this. However, you should have at least one per objective.

You should base every tactical element upon one or more of the tools discussed in the text:

- Blogging
- Case studies
- Creating brand authors
- Creating thought leaders
- Events—self-produced
- Events—third party
- Micro-blogging
- Pitching new media
- Pitching traditional media
- Podcasting
- Press conferences
- Social networks—private

- Social networks—public
- Source filing
- Speaking
- User-generated content
- Video sharing
- White papers
- Wikis
- Writing a book—self-/electronic publishing
- Writing a book—traditional publishing
- Writing bylined articles

In addition, be sure to discuss support elements such as press releases, pitch letters, press kits and their components, and follow-up protocol in each statement of tactics. You can also use this section of the plan to create a timeline and budget for its implementation. The timeline is a simplified version of the overall plan and is a great management tool. Since MPR expenses are usually limited to the time that team members spend planning and implementing campaigns, budgets tend to be simple and can be incorporated into the timeline. Note that a firm may have multiple MPR plans active

Key Terms

Statement of tactics A detailed description of activities coordinated in pursuit of achieving an objective including staff and managerial responsibilities, and required resources at the same time. Typically, a firm will have a yearly plan that outlines the MPR function's continuing efforts to support its long-term strategy, along with individual plans that lay out the details for specific campaigns.

Table 14–1

Objective	Action	Start Date	End Date	Action Leader	Cost*
Receive product reviews in at least 100 college newspapers in the next six months	Create a connector list consisting of the editors of the nation's top 1,000 college and university newspapers (ranked by size of the school's undergraduate resident population).	05/24/10	4-Jun-10	I. Balog	$ -
	Draft a press release that describes the uses of the product and its benefits to students, along with a suggested format for reviewing the product.	05/24/10	4-Jun-10	W.M. Donovan	$ -
	Write medium-specific pitch letters.	06/04/10	11-Jun-10	C. Duelfer	$ -
	Approve press release and pitch letters.	06/11/10	18-Jun-10	R. Getz	$ -
	Send pitch letters, press release, and product sample to connectors.	06/21/10	25-Jun-10	A. Peltola	$ -
	Make follow-up phone calls.	07/12/10	30-Jul-10	A. Wilson	$ -
	Monitor results (with third-party service).	07/12/10	15-Nov-10	I. Balog	$1,000 (estimated portion of yearly subscription to third-party service)

*Excluding salary

Concept Case 14.1: Tactics

Soon after learning the importance of MPR (see Chapter 3), the management of The Falcon's Lair set out some strategic marketing goals for the company. Two of them are:

1. Increase the number of times the media mention The Falcon's Lair to at least once per month in one year's time and to twice a month in five years.

2. Create both a live and a virtual customer community that allows customers to communicate with each other and The Falcon's Lair staff. Twenty percent of The Falcon's Lair customers will participate in this community in five years' time.

The managers recognize that in order to create an MPR plan, they will need to support these strategic goals by tactical objectives, which in turn become actionable tactics.

Questions:
1. Compose at least one tactical objective for each of the goals listed.
2. Write a detailed statement of tactics for one of the objectives you formulated for question 1.

Measuring Success

In order to know if any plan is successful, you must be able to measure your results with respect to your goals. Since firms plan and execute MPR campaigns fairly frequently (all firms should execute at least one per year), good **metrics** also provide you with an indication of how effective a particular MPR tool is for a given purpose and how well a tool was used. You may find it useful to think of MPR metrics in two categories, media mentions and word-of-mouth.

Media Mentions

Media mentions have been the backbone of Marketing Public Relations since its inception, and techniques for measuring them can range from the exceedingly simple to the extraordinarily complex. For a narrow and quickly executed campaign in which you are pitching a reasonably small number of connectors, you may be able to personally monitor each medium and to keep in touch with your connectors. You can then compare how much pickup you received versus the number of pitches you made, gauge the depth of coverage (for example, was it a sentence or two or a feature article?) and decide whether that coverage was favorable or not.

At the other extreme, a firm may be conducting multiple, widespread campaigns that originate in different parts of the country or the world. Campaigns may overlap by product or brand, and most contribute to the firm's overall brand image and, therefore, marketing strategy. In cases with multiple campaigns, a firm's MPR staff will find it difficult if not impossible to keep track of all media mentions and their impact via monitoring a few media and some simple follow-up.

For this type of case, most firms turn to media monitoring services to provide both media monitoring and analysis. Monitoring services typically just identify and catalog the medium and date of coverage and provide some basic detail on the scope of coverage.

Key Terms

Metrics Means for measuring changes to critical data

Analysis runs much deeper than simply monitoring, although the type of analysis depends on the objectives of the firm conducting MPR. For example, BurrellesLuce's media measuring service can report on editorial tone, the delivery of key messages, the prominence of the mention, the type of story, whether the mention included views of a spokesperson, the importance of the reporter, and whether the coverage included a photo or other graphic.[2]

Exhibit 14.3 The Cision report is an example of one way for marketers to monitor an MPR campaign's performance.

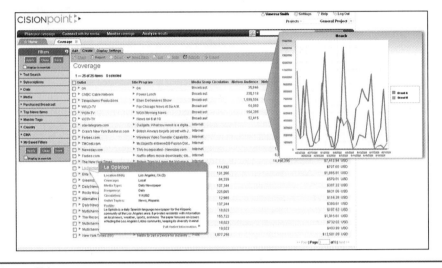

Source: Cision.

Some of the firms that provide PR database services also offer monitoring and/or analytical services. Most of these firms now offer monitoring and analysis of Web, blog, and social media mentions. Among them are:

- *BurrellesLuce*: http://www.burrellesluce.com
- *Business Wire*: http://www.businesswire.com
- *Cision*: http://www.cision.com
- *Marketwire/Media Hub*: http://www.marketwire.com
- *PR Newswire*: http://www.prnewswire.com
- *PR Web*: http://www.prweb.com
- *Vocus*: http://www.vocus.com

Word-of-Mouth

Despite the potential for complexity, monitoring media mentions has the advantage of having established monitoring systems and of always having some physical manifestation. Word-of-mouth (WOM), on the other hand, is a bit harder to track. It takes place in face-to-face conversations, over the phone, in e-mails, and in the interstices of social networks. Any trace of a message being spread by the human voice vanishes as quickly as the person speaks the words. E-mails typically remain viewable only to those who have sent or received them, and even person-to-person dialogue within most social networking environments is off-limits to curious marketers. Although monitoring online WOM is becoming more sophisticated and can be helpful in understanding the spread of WOM, it is still a challenge, especially since research has shown that approximately 90 percent of WOM takes place in offline forums.[3] Exhibit 14.4 illustrates the distribution of the different forms of WOM.

Exhibit 14.4 Word-of-Mouth Distribution

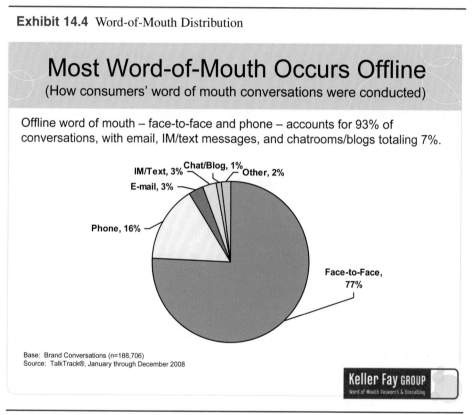

Most Word-of-Mouth Occurs Offline
(How consumers' word of mouth conversations were conducted)

Offline word of mouth – face-to-face and phone – accounts for 93% of conversations, with email, IM/text messages, and chatrooms/blogs totaling 7%.

IM/Text, 3% — Chat/Blog, 1% — Other, 2%
E-mail, 3%
Phone, 16%
Face-to-Face, 77%

Base: Brand Conversations (n=188,706)
Source: TalkTrack®, January through December 2008

Keller Fay GROUP
Word of Mouth Research & Consulting

Source: Keller Fay Group, LLC. Reprinted with permission.

Despite the challenges, marketers need to measure WOM in some form in order to gain some knowledge on the effectiveness of their campaigns. For offline campaigns, marketers can build in monitoring mechanisms to gauge the efficacy of their WOM program. For example, firms have employed their **customer relationship management (CRM)**[4]

Key Terms

Customer relationship management (CRM)
A technology-based system that seeks to create more meaningful one-on-one communications with the customer by applying customer data (demographic, industry, buying history, etc.) to every communications vehicle

systems to track whether new customers found out about the firm, its brands, or products through WOM or were influenced by it in some way. This form of monitoring takes place at the point of purchase or when a potential customer inquires about a product; it can easily work for both large and small firms. Firms can also employ referral or "tell-a-friend" programs, which enlist existing customers to get someone they know to try a certain product by giving them a coupon. The firm can then estimate WOM by monitoring coupon redemptions. Companies can also quantify word-of-mouth by conducting surveys. Surveys can include polling existing customers to determine how they first encountered the product and questioning a statistically significant sample of the target audience to see if they have been exposed to WOM relative to the product.

Many methods are available to measure online word-of-mouth. According to David Meerman Scott, author of *The New Rules of Marketing and PR: How to Use News Releases, Blogs, Podcasts, Viral Marketing and Online Media to Reach Your Buyers Directly,* a powerful yet easy approach is just to answer the following questions:

- Where do you appear in the Google search results? (Ranking is indicative of the number of views, links, bookmarks, etc.)
- How many people are viewing your stuff? (Presumably, more WOM leads to more views of Web pages associated with your product.)
- Are bloggers talking about you? (Bloggers are key online connectors with their own established audience.)
- If so, what are the bloggers saying? (This will give you an indication of whether the spreading word is positive or negative, and allow you to act accordingly.)

Of course, services exist that will track the mention of products on popular social networks, as well as responses and links to blogs mentioning the product. They can even monitor rating and review sites for evidence of WOM. For example, Nielsen Company used HeyNielsen.com (http://www.heynielsen.com) and Nielsen BuzzMetrics to measure and analyze the response to commercials run in Super Bowl XLII in February 2008. HeyNielsen.com was essentially an online focus group that encouraged pop culture enthusiasts to share their views, while BuzzMetrics monitored approximately 70 million blogs, message boards, online communities, video sharing sites, and sports enthusiast forums, the results of which were provided to Nielsen clients.[5] With the lion's share of WOM taking place offline, however, there is debate over whether measurements of online buzz accurately reflect reality. As a result, further study of this issue is under way. For the time being, as Pete Blackshaw, CMO of BuzzMetrics, put it in an interview with *AdWeek,* "Marketers are using the information like radar."[6]

In addition to monitoring campaigns designed with a WOM component, firms should be conscious of monitoring incidental word-of-mouth. Consider the fact that extreme satisfaction or dissatisfaction with a product, along with controversy, advertising, and product exclusivity tend to generate the most word-of-mouth.[7] As a result, information about your products that did not originate intentionally from the firm may be spreading from person to person. This unintended WOM is likely to be either very good, very bad, or a product of your advertising. It may also be the result of a strong brand image with customers. Clearly, recognizing any of these possibilities is worth the effort and can lead to feedback that helps you continue to add value to your organization.

Concept Case 14.2: Measuring the Buzz

As a small company, The Falcon's Lair is planning and implementing all of its MPR initiatives on its own. Likewise, the Lair's management team is hoping to measure the effectiveness of its efforts and to get some feedback for future planning purposes by only using The Falcon's Lair's staff to collect this data.

Questions:

1. Discuss how members of The Falcon's Lair's staff can go about monitoring the number of media mentions received and how they might interpret the value of each mention.
2. Describe the methods you would use to measure and evaluate word-of-mouth resulting from The Falcon's Lair's MPR campaigns.

MPR Plan: The Document

As mentioned above, every firm should have one MPR plan covering all of its activities for the year. In addition, the firm may create multiple plans specific to individual campaigns aimed at meeting specific objectives. In both cases the format of the document should be as follows:

- *Problem Definition*: This is a broad statement of purpose for your planning efforts and will be the basis for your goals and strategies.
- *Positioning and Resource Considerations*: In this section, frame the boundaries of the plan by affirming where your firm, brand, or product stands relative to competitors in the eyes of the consuming public, and identify the resources (time, money, personnel, etc.) available for implementing your plan.
- *Target Market*: This portion should include both a definition of the target consumer by demographic, psychographic, and behavioral factors and a detailed list of the connectors who reach these consumers.
- *Cross-Functional Interactions*: Rarely does MPR act on its own. Broader marketing and communications initiatives often share goals, messaging, and resources with MPR activities, and this section defines MPR's interactivity with other functions.
- *Goals and Objectives*: Use this section to define S.M.A.R.T. goals and objectives.
- *Strategies and Tactics*: This portion includes a description of the overall MPR strategy supported by statements of tactic spelling out the implementation of the plan.
- *Timeline and Budget*: Typically, this section includes a spreadsheet-based management tool laying out the *who, what, where, when, why*, and *how* and the cost of each activity within the MPR plan.
- *Measurement and Analysis*: The final piece should include a framework for monitoring and interpreting the success of the campaign and a mechanism for providing feedback for future plans.

Note that some companies, especially smaller ones, embed the elements of the MPR plan in their overall marketing and/or communications plan. Even in this case, however, the firm must properly plan and execute all of the components listed above to ensure that the firm effectively uses MPR over the long term.

Reflection Questions

1. Discuss how MPR planning can be a part of a firm's overall marketing planning. Do the same for communications planning. (Chapter Objective 1)

2. How do a company's positioning and resources figure into the situation analysis of an MPR plan? (Chapter Objective 2)

3. Why might the connectors on a firm's master connector list not be included on a connector list for an individual campaign? (Chapter Objective 3)

4. Discuss some areas where MPR works in sequence with or in tandem with other areas of the marketing communications mix. (Chapter Objective 4)

5. What are the elements of a well-constructed MPR objective? (Chapter Objective 5)

6. Discuss how to construct a timeline and how it contributes to the implementation of an MPR plan. (Chapter Objective 6)

7. Compare and contrast the methods of measuring media mentions and word-of-mouth. (Chapter Objective 7)

 Chapter Key Terms

Customer relationship management (CRM) A technology-based system that seeks to create more meaningful one-on-one communications with the customer by applying customer data (demographic, industry, buying history, etc.) to every communications vehicle (p. 233)

Metrics Means for measuring changes to critical data (p. 231)

Statement of tactics A detailed description of activities coordinated in pursuit of achieving an objective including staff and managerial responsibilities and required resources (p. 229)

SWOT analysis An evaluation of a firm's internal strengths and weaknesses, and external opportunities and threats compiled for use in business planning situations (p. 226)

Application Assignments

1. Search the Internet for the term "new product of the year." Using the search results, find a product you think is particularly interesting and innovative. Conduct a SWOT analysis for that product and describe its target market. (Remember to identify both the ultimate target and connectors.)

2. Write at least three objectives and corresponding statements of tactic for a campaign aimed at creating media mentions and spreading WOM for the company you chose for Application Assignment 1 (above).

3. Search *one* of the following Web sites and describe the information that it provides to companies wishing to monitor media mentions and word-of-mouth. Describe how this information is useful to a firm's MPR efforts.

   a. http://www.burrellesluce.com

   b. http://www.businesswire.com

   c. http://www.cision.com

   d. http://www.marketwire.com

   e. http://www.prnewswire.com

   f. http://www.prweb.com

   g. http://www.vocus.com

Practice Portfolio

This Practice Portfolio can be based on a fictitious company or on a real company that your instructor assigns to you. (If you used a company in previous Practice Portfolio exercises, continue to use that company.) Add your completed assignment to your portfolio to present to prospective employers.

Use all of the previous Practice Portfolio assignments to help you construct a complete MPR plan for your company using the framework described in the chapter.

APPENDIX 1

Course Capstone Project

1. If not pre-assigned, choose a company and have it approved by the professor.

2. Write a positioning statement for your company that meets all of the criteria described in Chapter 2 (three sentences, maximum).

3. Present a document (500 words, maximum) of organizational considerations, including the following:

   a. Explain how the MPR function fits into the overall strategy of your company. (Hint: Think about MPR's role in each of the five elements of the Business Strategy Diamond.)

   b. Develop a list of goals for establishing and maintaining your brand that can be facilitated by MPR. (Remember that goals are long-term and strategy-focused. You will set specific objectives as you progress through the text.)

   c. Describe how your company will use MPR to engage external authors in developing its brand stories, images, and associations.

   d. Describe your company's brand value and categorize the different elements of value by the four brand value components discussed in Chapter 3. (Remember: Not every company has brand value in each of the four components, and a given company may have multiple brands that offer different value sets.)

4. In a single document (500 words, maximum), outline your MPR framework, briefly addressing each of the following:

   a. List some basic objectives for conducting a public relations consumer-generated marketing campaign for your practice company.

   b. Outline the buying process for your company's products and discuss what you can do as a marketer to influence this process.

   c. Using demographic, psychographic, and behavioral criteria, define as many potential market segments for your company as you can identify.

   d. Considering the five criteria for effective target segmentation selection, narrow the list of market segments you have listed to one to three target markets. Explain why you chose to keep the ones you kept, why you disqualified those you eliminated, and why you combined those you consolidated.

   e. List as many types of media, groups, and individuals as you can think of that would be appropriate connectors for your company. Briefly explain why you have chosen each one.

    f. With your positioning statement in mind, what message could you distribute to your connectors that would be of value to them and that would also effectively translate to your target audience to meet your objectives?

5. Consider potential media connectors for your company, using the following exercises to guide you. (This is a brainstorming exercise; no documentation is required.)

    a. Using your positioning statement as a guide, list the media classifications that will best help you to reach your MPR goals. Briefly explain why you chose each classification. (Hint: Creating a table of all media classifications and listing their pros and cons relative to your company is an effective method for completing this task.)

    b. Using the list you created above as a starting point, select the media outlets that best fit the classifications you have chosen. You may add or delete media types from your list based on this analysis.

    c. Explore four media outlets on your list and identify the journalists who would be most interested in covering your company or products. List their names and their beats. (Hint: A single medium may have more than one journalist who would be interested in your company or products.)

    d. List the types of media opportunities that will contribute most effectively to achieving your goals and briefly explain your selection. In addition, find an example of each opportunity within one of the media on your media list.

6. Consider potential non-media connectors for your company, using the following exercises to guide you. (This is a brainstorming exercise; no documentation is required.)

    a. Write a short statement describing how your product is fun or intriguing and explain why, in general, NMCs need to share your story with their audiences.

    b. Using the target market you defined (see question 4 d.) as your guide, list the types of reference groups you might use to reach your audience. List an example of each.

    c. Explain how experts and opinion leaders influence your target market during the buying process. Give an example of an expert and an opinion leader whom you believe will influence this audience.

    d. Devise a preliminary plan for creating online and offline word-of-mouth using Citizen Marketers and explain how you can get people to spread the message about your product.

7. Use one or more of the sources listed in Chapter 7's *Resources for Finding Connectors* in conjunction with material supplied by individual connectors and auditing bureaus to create a comprehensive media list for your company. Briefly describe why you chose each connector. Submit as an Excel spreadsheet.

8. Using Chapter 8 as your guide, write the following for your company:

    a. Backgrounder

    b. Fact sheet

    c. *One* of the following: a press release for the launch of a new product or service OR a press release to announce a special event

9. Write a pitch letter for the press release that you wrote for item 8.

10. Conceive and describe a concept for promoting your company, using one of the following (500 words or less):

   a. Social network

   b. Wiki

   c. Co-created content

11. Select a community event or charitable cause that aligns with your firm's MPR goals and explain how you would produce such an event. Be sure to:

   a. Select an event format and explain why you have chosen that format.

   b. Decide on a venue and explain why you have chosen it.

   c. Describe in detail who you will invite to the event (remember both target audience and connectors).

   d. Determine which members of your firm will attend the event and explain what they are expected to do while they are there.

   e. Explain what you will prepare as a takeaway for those attending the event. Be sure to differentiate between what you give to members of the target audience and what you give to connectors.

   f. Discuss your strategy for recapping the event.

12. Write a case study for one of the products or services that your company provides.

13. Choose a connector from your list and explain how you would prepare one of your company's executives or experts for an interview with this connector. Include the following:

   a. A written description of the connector and his or her medium in order to give the interviewee an understanding of the style and tone of the interview

   b. A list of ten likely questions and their answers

   c. A summary of facts, statistics, quotes, and anecdotes to be used during the interview

14. Construct an MPR Plan.

   a. Problem Definition: This is a broad statement of purpose for your planning efforts and will be the basis for your goals and strategies.

   b. Positioning and Resource Considerations: In this section, frame the boundaries of the plan by affirming where your firm, brand, or product stands relative to competitors in the eyes of the consuming public, and identify the resources (time, money, personnel, etc.) available for implementing your plan.

   c. Target Market: This portion should include both a definition of the target consumer by demographic, psychographic, and behavioral factors and a detailed list of the connectors who reach these consumers.

   d. Cross-functional Interactions: This section defines MPR's interactivity with other functions. Rarely does MPR act on its own. Broader marketing and communications initiatives often share goals, messaging, and resources with MPR activities.

e. Goals and Objectives: Use this section to define S.M.A.R.T. goals and objectives.

f. Strategies and Tactics: This portion includes a description of the overall MPR strategy supported by statements of tactics, spelling out the implementation of the plan.

g. Timeline and Budget: Typically, this section includes a spreadsheet-based management tool laying out the who, what, where, when, and why and the cost of each activity within the MPR plan.

h. Measurement and Analysis: The final piece should include a framework for monitoring and interpreting the success of the campaign and a mechanism for providing feedback for future plans.

Introduction to Blogs: A Quick Guide to Understanding and Maximizing Communications Efforts in the Blogosphere

Introduction to Weblogs

Perhaps more than any other communications format since the advent of the Internet, weblogs—or "blogs"—have been heralded as a revolution in mass communication. Communications professionals in particular are in a position to use blogs to better listen to and reach their publics in new ways. This paper will explain how blogs fit into the new media landscape and how marketing and communications professionals, once they understand blogs' unique rules of the game, can use them not only as promotion platforms but also as a means to a conversation with their audience and customers. Technically speaking, blogs are just like any other Web site on the Internet. They exist solely online, are capable of accepting advertising, and are designed to be consumed by a specific audience—either the general public or a targeted niche group. The popularity of blogs is primarily due to four factors:

1. Many services will host blogs at no charge. There are several popular blog-hosting services available on the Web, such as Blogger (a Google-owned company), Bloglines (now owned by Ask.com), and LiveJournal (owned by SixApart), which offer free basic hosting with extra features available for a monthly fee. There are other companies such as TypePad that charge for all levels of service.

2. Blogs have given an outlet to anyone who feels his voice has not been represented in the mainstream media. Blogs enable anyone to become a micro-publisher virtually overnight.

3. Blogs are timely, allowing for content updates at any time without an editorial review and without sophisticated knowledge of Web publishing. The immediacy of blogs gives them the leverage to pick up on breaking news stories and instantly create their own stories with new angles and investigations. In fact, the most popular blogs tend to be those that are updated often.

4. There is a strong sense of community among blog writers and visitors. Because most blogs are not regulated by an editorial board or influenced by corporate interests, visitors rely on them for the unvarnished truth. They also value the transparency that

blogs have. Unlike mainstream media, whose philosophy is geared toward keeping the audience on their own site, blogs thrive on posting links to other sites of interest, even other blogs that cover the same topic. The audience of one blog immediately has access to a wide range of opinions and styles.

Types of Blogs

There are four general types of blogs in existence:

1. **Personal blogs** that focus on a passion or hobby. Many people start a blog to express their personal opinions or share their interests and knowledge with others. These types of blogs can still have an enormous impact on a company spreading the current version of "word of mouth."

2. **Topic or industry-specific blogs** are perhaps the most pervasive type, covering everything from current events to marketing/public relations to home entertainment to car maintenance. Bloggers are often acknowledged experts in their specific industry who have a built-in audience.

3. **Publication-sponsored blogs** are growing as traditional media outlets seek to ride the blog wave. Increasingly, newspapers, magazines, and even television and radio stations are adding blogs to their Web sites. These blogs tend to be written by an established journalist with the publication and have been added to lend a sense of immediacy to the content.

4. **Corporate blogs** are another relatively new addition to the blog world. The best ones are written by an executive within the company and are devoted to that company. You won't find here the extensive list of outside links or freedom of opinion that is to be found on other blogs. Corporate blogging is still in its infancy and is just beginning to find its place as part of an overall corporate communications effort.

Blogs and the News

The public has become increasingly distrustful of mainstream news outlets, perceiving them as beholden to either the government or large corporations. Blogs, on the other hand, have the unique power to cut out organizations that traditionally act as gatekeepers. Many bloggers still rely on the mainstream media for source material but then conduct their own research and write subsequent articles independently. For this reason, blog visitors feel they are getting an unvarnished and pure take on a topic, whether that is a political or current events story or an opinion on a video game or movie.

Bloggers are also more adept at breaking stories. For example, the PR/Marketing industry blogs are a great source of news on developments from the major search engine companies. More general news blogs break stories relating to politics or society. They are often the first to take a public figure to task for statements he or she has made.

In a recent survey, people were asked to indicate their reasons for reading blogs. The top three reasons were "news I can't find elsewhere," "a better perspective," and "faster news." This focus on better, faster news has given blogs the power to move from being simply commentators on the news to being opinion leaders. Blogs have become the new op-ed page.

Indeed bloggers' efforts have led to the resignation of at least one high-profile media personality. When Dan Rather, during the 2004 presidential race, reported on the CBS news magazine "60 Minutes" that evidence existed showing problems with President Bush's National Guard record, the blogging community quickly disputed the story. The documents Rather had been given and used as evidence didn't look quite right for the era in which they would have been produced. The blogosphere produced experts on typesets and document creation who quickly and loudly refuted the items Rather had used. Charges were leveled at Rather and segment producers for shoddy reporting and a liberal bias. CBS sanctioned the producers involved and Rather announced what he termed a planned resignation shortly after the controversy started.

In early 2005, CNN head Eason Jordan was pressured into resigning after making what some saw as disparaging remarks about U.S. troops in Iraq. Conservative bloggers attacked Jordan as being unpatriotic and within two weeks he had tendered his resignation.

Working with Blog Writers

Marketing and public relations professionals, marketers, and other media planners are increasingly attracted to this unique blogging community that seems immune to blatant PR spins. If they can pitch a product or story to a blog and get coverage, then they have gained access to an audience seen as lucrative and influential. And due to the popularity of search engines and the cross-linking so commonplace with blogs, the potential for increased impression values is huge. One successful pitch can result in dozens of pick-ups. You can increase your name and brand recognition with a wider span of audiences than you had originally thought possible.

Most blogs include some sort of contact information for the writer. But how should you pitch a writer? What tone should your pitch take? Here are some tips when approaching blog writers with story pitches:

1. Expose all potential conflicts of interest or corporate ties right off the bat. If these relationships are not admitted initially, the blogger will find them. By being up front, you have inoculated yourself to some extent against a potential backlash that could cause negative publicity for your company.

2. Be familiar not only with the blog you are pitching but also with other blogs linked from that site that cover the same topic. Remember that blogs thrive on a sense of community. Bloggers want information to be shared and are not as concerned with exclusives as traditional media outlets.

3. Personalize your pitch. Don't just include their e-mail in a blast mailing of a press release. Bloggers like to feel special and a generic e-mail is likely to fall on deaf ears.

4. Remember that blog writers, in order to stay relevant in the eyes of their readers, need to be honest above all else. They will publish their unvarnished opinion of a product—warts and all. Keep in mind that the risks associated with blogs need to be accepted along with their potential benefits.

5. Like traditional media outlets, the more popular blogs are often the most difficult to break into. Find a mid-tier blog for that first impression and let the story work its way out from there. Because there is a good deal of cross-linking among blogs within a niche, if one picks it up there is a good chance others will report on the story or do their own investigation. By incorporating some form of blog monitoring, you will be able to see how effectively this works and react appropriately.

Monitoring the Blogosphere

As with any media outlet, marketing and communications professionals want to monitor blogs not only to gauge the effectiveness of a specific campaign but also to contain potential communications crises, gather competitive intelligence, or simply monitor their coverage on a real-time basis. They require tools that will allow them to monitor the blogs, evaluate the coverage, and react to the coverage when appropriate.

The larger media monitoring companies now offer blogs as part of their comprehensive monitoring packages. Some go for sheer numbers, stating they search thousands, tens of thousands, or hundreds of thousands of blogs across the entire Internet. Others offer a smaller number of monitored blogs, choosing instead to handpick those that they include in their service. These are mostly blogs by established journalists or other experts in a given field. In some cases companies contracting with a media monitoring firm have the option of requesting that blogs be added to the service as project needs change. The choice you make is dependent on what best meets your monitoring needs: quantity or quality?

Other important factors to consider when selecting a blog monitoring service are ease of use and advanced searching capabilities. It's important that the service you choose gives you the ability to edit, compare, search through, and organize the results you receive. And by choosing a service that delivers your results in an instantly usable format and gives you the tools to keep your results organized, you can save your staff time and money by avoiding the laborious process of manually sorting through the clutter of results.

There are some tools available for free, such as Technorati, Blogdigger, and Google Blog Search, that act as search engines and are useful if you are tracking where your company name has popped up in posts recently. There is an important distinction between these services and traditional media monitoring firms: the search engines do not deliver any research results to your desktop, while some of the established media monitoring firms do provide customized content directly to you, around the clock.

Using Blogs as a Marketing Tool

In addition to using blogs as one facet of a media pitch plan, some advisors recommend setting up a corporately owned blog to build buzz for a company or product. While the allure of this concept is obvious, the downsides can be dangerous.

The goal of a corporate-owned blog should be to reach out to constituents and be more transparent, and if you've got a good or interesting product, hopefully it will build buzz.

First, the positives. Blogs can create a direct outlet between a company and its target consumers. The immediacy is attractive since the company could avoid long advertising production cycles. The company can be seen as cutting-edge and will attempt to be perceived as honest and untouched by PR spin.

The negatives, however, can open up a company to more scrutiny and bad press than it ever expected. Internet users in general and blogosphere citizens specifically are increasingly savvy to blatant pitches. In the past, corporate blogs have not fared well for one or both of two reasons:

1. The companies' message has rung false. If there is any misleading information on a blog, it will be found through the use of today's powerful search engines, and the falsehood will be exposed throughout the blog community.

2. A company has created a blog but not identified it as a corporately owned blog. Frequently referred to as "viral marketing," this effort leads companies to establish blogs and attempt to pass them off as impartial and unaffiliated sites praising the virtues of a new product or service. Bloggers have an almost visceral reaction to these and see them as intruding on sacred ground. Blogs pride themselves on their transparency and independence from corporate ties. When a blog pops up that is obviously biased and lacks these two important traits, it is immediately suspect.

The negative word-of-mouth that can result from either of these missteps could be disastrous. Companies should carefully consider the role a blog could play in their media plan and use it accordingly. Blogs can add a great deal of value to the reputation of a company if used as a means to communicate with—not just to—their base.

Corporate blogs have been most successful when they have been run by—and subsequently identified with—one individual. Often this is the CEO or another high ranking officer in a company. These tend to reflect the best aspects of the most popular blogs: (1) they have a personal touch and do not seem to have the "Approved by the PR Department" stamp on them and (2) they touch on a variety of subjects. A CEO who only writes about his company and how wonderful it is will quickly be ignored. One that reflects interesting articles he or she has come across and other random musings in addition to company information will be more popular among "legitimate" bloggers.

APPENDIX 3

Beyond Blogs: Learn How RSS and Podcasting Can Influence Your Communications Efforts

The ability for anyone to access both the written word and audio broadcasts through online and portable devices is revolutionizing the way marketing and PR can be conducted. Today's marketing and communications professionals can leverage blogs, RSS feeds, podcasts, and more to gain a deeper understanding of their target audiences and provide highly selective messages to an increasingly fragmented population. This appendix will explain the latest content distribution tools, such as RSS, and how they can be used to further the goals of today's communicators and marketers.

What Is RSS?

RSS is the latest method of delivering content from the Internet for personal viewing.

For early technology adopters, RSS is becoming the preferred method of electronic delivery of content from businesses, newspapers, magazines, and blogs. In an age when e-mail inboxes are becoming increasingly full of spam and other unsolicited content, RSS feeds have emerged as the primary tool used by those who want to stay informed.

The most common definition of RSS is Really Simple Syndication. The technology behind RSS is both impressively complex and yet astoundingly simple to use. It uses the XML Web language to create metadata. Think of metadata as the exterior of an airplane: you don't need to see the moving parts within the metal exterior to understand it's an airplane. This metadata then gets delivered to a service called a news aggregator or reader.

The power of a news reader is that it brings information from numerous and assorted Web sites into one place, an excellent alternative to the time-consuming task of visiting Web sites individually to determine if new information has been posted. When a Web site, to which you have subscribed, publishes new content it is delivered in the form of either headlines or the full article or post to the RSS reader, which marks those items as unread in much the same way as most e-mail programs. Your news reader will refresh many times a day, and if a site has not updated its content, you will not have any new items to view. The information is "pushed" out to the RSS readers, ensuring that it is only the RSS feeds that one subscribes to are received. Compared to working through a series of browser-based bookmarks to visit sites of interest, the news reader is a productivity windfall.

Since RSS readers make surfing the Web so much easier and quicker, users can subscribe to the feeds from more sites than they could visit regularly. You couldn't realistically surf through the entire online editions of *The New York Times, The Washington Post*, as well as 100 blogs in a day and still get any work done. For example, with RSS you can surf through all the headlines from *The New York Times* delivered in the last 12 hours in less than five minutes. You then have the choice to pick out the stories most interesting to you and click through to read the full text.

RSS and Blogs

RSS was originally developed by Netscape back in the mid-1990s as an easier way to organize and distribute news. RSS began to gain more popularity in 2002, once bloggers implemented the technology due to the many advantages of publishing and syndicating content. If blogging fulfilled the promise of citizens everywhere being able to publish their views and opinions, then RSS provided the solution to the distribution problem. It was all well and good for someone to start a blog and have good content, but getting it read was a major hurdle. Readership was dependent on search engine results or word-of-mouth. With RSS, visitors (including other bloggers) can subscribe to a feed and easily view a blog's content.

As those bloggers gained widespread recognition and mainstream exposure, so did RSS. Eventually, major news outlets began offering RSS feeds. The bloggers who already had experience with this technology jumped on it as a way to easily read their favorite publications. Bloggers began to copy those links to their blogs, where they could comment on the story. The widespread copying and pasting of links is what makes the blogosphere an interconnected, cohesive web.

Getting Started with RSS Feeds

The first step in using RSS is to set yourself up with a news reader (also sometimes called a news aggregator). Many different readers are available on the Internet either as Web-based applications or downloadable software. Bloglines, for example, is a popular free Web-based service that not only allows for easy RSS reading but also incorporates the ability to push items found via those feeds to a blog of your own. The Web browser Mozilla Firefox comes with a built-in RSS reader, and the latest versions of Microsoft Internet Explorer and Outlook will have built-in RSS readers. With Microsoft embracing RSS in its software, expect to see even wider adoption and acceptance of RSS technology.

The major advantage of the Web-based applications is that they offer access from any Internet-enabled computer. Whether at a home PC or a shared computer at a library or other location, the user will always have access to his or her RSS subscriptions. As portability has become more and more popular, RSS reading functionality has also begun to be integrated into applications for handheld PC devices and cell phones. This means users do not need to carry around a laptop in search of Wi-Fi hotspots in order to check their subscriptions. All they need is a Web-enabled hand held device or mobile phone.

Once you have set up an RSS reader, you must then subscribe to a Web site's XML or RSS feed. Often this is as simple as copying and pasting a link. Most blogs now have these links under the headings such as "Syndicate This Site" or "Subscribe to My Feed" or have the now-common orange "XML" button. Professional media intelligence companies have recently begun listing which sites offer RSS feeds. Having a database with this information allows communications professionals to discern better the breadth of reach of an article from one of those sites. This is a vital part of evaluating any media mention and should be used by anyone reliant on these numbers.

Traditional media outlets have increasingly been catching on to the RSS wave. Early adopters of the format include CNN, *The Washington Post*, *The New York Times*, and the BBC, and it is beginning to reach even more widespread adoption. In most cases the publisher will push a headline and brief summary or extract of the article to the RSS feed, meaning readers will have to click the headline and go to the publication's Web site to read the whole story.

How RSS Can Benefit Your Communications Efforts

So how can RSS help marketing, public relations, and other communications professionals benefit both themselves and their client or company?

The main point to remember about RSS is that it is not a content creation tool but a content distribution tool. Blog posts, news stories, or marketing and public relations materials, such as press releases and white papers, must still be produced by human beings. The RSS feed simply allows that post or story to have a wider audience than it may have had previously. While corporations may look at blogs as a new way to reach an audience, the simple addition of an RSS-enabled press room or marketing materials can have the same impact as a blog.

Monitoring RSS feeds is one of the most efficient ways to gain a big-picture perspective of the industry and world your company operates in, allowing you to scan headlines from dozens of sites in a fraction of the time it would take to actually visit each one. At the same time, news readers such as Bloglines or Newsgator can instantly alert you to breaking news about your company, client, or industry and enable you to respond quickly.

Setting yourself up with a number of RSS subscriptions relevant to your industry or company can be an important tool. It can be a good supplement to a professional monitoring service that encompasses the many types of media that make up the core of your PR programs. The monitoring service also provides you with alerts of mentions of keywords and enables you to receive your coverage on your desktop multiple times a day with the ability to sort and search articles online using many different criteria. You can also use such tools to generate customized press reports and track qualitative criteria such as trend analysis, issue positioning, and tone.

Subscribing to a number of RSS feeds can give you a big-picture perspective just like subscriptions to print publications can. It is certainly not a replacement for a monitoring service, especially one integrating all forms of media: blogs, Internet sites, print outlets, and broadcast stations.

In addition to the monitoring benefits, RSS offers a chance to stay in touch with constituents who have opted to receive your information (which is not always the case with e-mail). A feed should increase Web site traffic as individuals click through to access information, and the Web site's position on major search engines should increase as well. In April 2005, *The New York Times* reported that RSS feed click-through increased traffic to its Web site by over 300 percent. Not only is this a boon for those companies mentioned in news stories and editorials but also for those advertising on the *Times'* Web site. In a sentence, RSS is a big time-saver for executives that are looking to stay on top of trends and news but want it pushed to them when they want the information.

Podcasting

Podcasts are a form of, for lack of a better phrase, do-it-yourself radio. Podcasting started in late 2004 and has skyrocketed in popularity. Co-created by former MTV veejay Adam Curry and blogging pioneer Dave Winer, the concept was for individuals to produce and distribute an audio version of blogs. Someone with something to say was no longer constrained by the relative bare-bones world of text-only blogging.

In the short time since its inception, podcasts have become simpler and simpler to create. Software is widely available at little or no charge to facilitate recording, hosting and distributing podcasts. This means that anyone with a PC and a microphone can create a "show" and then have it mass distributed.

Like blogs, podcasts originated with people outside the mainstream media. Over time, though, large media outlets have begun offering podcasts. Radio programs would seem a natural fit for podcasts and some have adopted the technology but only a few have jumped on the bandwagon to date. Along with them, newspapers and television outlets have also begun offering podcasts as a way to extend their branding efforts and increase viewer/reader/listener loyalty.

RSS has played a large part in the adoption of podcasts. The RSS feed for a podcast can be subscribed to via an ordinary RSS reader, such as Bloglines, or in a special aggregator, called a podcatcher. This podcatcher software not only notifies the user that a new podcast is available but automatically downloads it to the user's PC. The user can then either listen to it on the PC or transfer it to a portable MP3 player. In fact many people differentiate podcasting from simple audio file hosting based on the RSS delivery mechanism. The two have become interlocked and are inseparable.

The one piece of the podcasting puzzle that has yet to be put in place is the monitoring question. The issue remains of how to search for a keyword in an audio presentation. This is an Important component of any brand awareness and brand management monitoring, so the absence of such a service has come to be seen as a large missing piece. Most podcast producers post "show notes," or an outline of the issues, companies, and people mentioned in the show to a blog. That blog can, of course, be searched by either individuals or by a media monitoring agency they've contracted with. The problem with this approach is that it misses the nuance and context of the keyword mention.

Podcasts are increasingly being seen as a viable means of delivering advertising messages. More and more podcast producers are accepting either straight advertisements or sponsorships. The problem for advertising professionals seems to be in finding the right tone for the message. Scripted copy, such as you find on the radio, will ring false to a podcasts media–savvy audience. It would be good for any communications professional considering advertising on a podcast to work with the producer to create a genuine, plain-spoken set of copy.

What's Next?

So now that you know about RSS and podcasting, you may be wondering what's coming next. The most likely answer is video blogging. This has already started to some extent and works in much the same way podcasting does. Someone creates a video file, increasingly easy to do with digital video cameras, and hosts it on his or her blog or Web site. The one roadblock yet to be overcome for this medium is the lack of portable video players. Right now there are a few, but they are still high-priced and the integration with easily usable software has not yet happened.

Many other inventions are on the horizon. The bottom line? It's incumbent upon communications professionals of all stripes to keep their ear to the ground in order to know how best to reach their customer base.

Source: Courtesy of Cision. © 2008. Reprinted with permission. All rights reserved.

APPENDIX 4

Staying Afloat in a Sea of Social Media: An Intelligent Approach to Managing and Monitoring Social Media

The Challenge: Taking Advantage of a Communications Revolution

Marketing and PR professionals today must successfully navigate a sea of social media. But the social media universe is broader, more complex, and quicker to change than mainstream media.

There are more than a hundred million blogs—and millions more users of social media networking sites, podcasts, video sharing sites, RSS feeds, traditional bulletin boards, Twitter groups, wikis, and countless other modes of interaction. In total, they represent an exciting, transformative grassroots revolution in communication. Anyone with knowledge to share or a lot of passion can become a blogger. "Citizen journalists" who provide indispensable information and credible opinion can become opinion-shapers whose impact can be felt in newsrooms in Manhattan, Washington, and London, in boardrooms around the world, and by millions of individual consumers.

For marketing and public relations professionals and other communicators, social media present huge opportunities. To engage effectively, you need the right tools and skill set. Navigating the social media sea starts with a common-sense understanding of how individuals and social groups communicate and relate to each other. When social-media mavens say marketing is now participating in and managing a "conversation," they are talking about managing relationships at their most fundamental level.

The social media phenomenon is less a singular movement than a vast, loosely affiliated universe of discrete communities—some of them large and many of them very small—with each devoted to a particular and sometimes narrow set of interests or topics. Engaging in the conversations with these groups in a meaningful way requires developing relationships with them. Communicating your story credibly and effectively over time requires managing these relationships with care.

The Goal: Identify, Engage, and Monitor the Right Communities

Building and managing relationships with the individuals and groups most important to you requires an understanding of whom you need to engage with and why. By concentrating on the right communities, you can begin a fruitful conversation with both professionals and consumers. While there are millions of blogs (including personal and corporate blogs), social media communities, and video sharing sites, in almost every category there is a relatively small subset of truly influential voices with the credibility or the cachet to set the tone and agenda for the rest. If you identify, monitor, and engage with those top-tier influencers, you will start to get the control over your story and message you could otherwise lose.

Start by asking these questions:

- How can I discover the most influential blogs and social media vehicles that affect my products, services, or corporate reputation?
- How can I monitor them? How much time should I, or my team, spend on social media monitoring and outreach?
- How do I communicate effectively with them?
- Most important, how can I evaluate and measure the impact that social media conversations are having on my business or my client's business?

Answering these questions is the key to successfully navigating the social media waters. Here are four steps public relations professionals can follow:

1. **PRIORITIZE. How do social media rank in importance to your overall media relations strategy?**

   One of the first decisions to reach is basic: are social media fundamental to the success of your company and stakeholders' decision to do business with your company? The answer is *yes*, if:

   - Your brand can be affected (positively or negatively) by social media conversation. A full range of consumer product categories—from clothing to home/interior design items to cars—are now dependent on social media to create buzz that both supplements and takes the place of traditional advertising.
   - Your brand depends on early adopters and passionate "evangelists" to build momentum for your products or services—something business-to-business communicators are accustomed to, especially in high technology and consumer tech.
   - Key blogs or social media sites are authored by or influence market analysts, other "thought leaders" about your industry, or mainstream media that cover your company.
   - Your corporate reputation or your shareholder relations may be vulnerable to attack-blogging by unhappy customers and investors—or your company runs the risk of being depositioned by aggressive competitors who have infiltrated social media.

   Understanding the relative importance of social media in your entire communications and marketing mix will guide you to the right strategies for engaging with social media.

For example, if you represent the latest low-priced, consumer-friendly product, you might focus much time and energy on sites reaching masses of consumers; e.g., music companies interact with MySpace music sites or with YouTube video communities to promote artists and songs. On the other hand, if your client is the chief executive of that consumer products company, you'd devote your energy to engaging with individual bloggers at analyst firms, trade journals, and Web sites of top business publications to position the CEO as an expert for both customer and investor audiences.

Clearly, many companies must recognize social media as a critical communication channel. But, as important as social media may be, they seldom will be the *only* channels. For strategic and tactical planning, and to properly manage your time (or your staff's), you also need an understanding of social media's context within the mix of all other communications channels that you must engage and monitor.

2. TARGET. All blogs are not created equal. How do you separate wheat from chaff?

Once you have determined where social media fit into your overall communications mix, it is imperative to understand which social media are most important to your cause. Focusing most of your efforts on the relatively small number of the most influential social media will most likely provide the best results. This requires identification of top-tier social media outlets and a detailed analysis of their impact on customer behavior.

The complex social media environment makes it more important than ever to leverage best-in-class research, targeting and monitoring tools when identifying and engaging with influential bloggers, and participating in other social media venues. With superior research intelligence and ongoing monitoring of the conversation, you will add value when contacting and interacting with social media.

The goal should be establishment of a strong *relationship management platform*, combining best-in-class media research, monitoring, and evaluation of issues being aired by bloggers and in other social-media venues. CisionPoint, with its integrated media database and monitoring and evaluation modules, is one such platform. It contains critical information, updated continuously, on thousands of blogs and social media outlets, and includes tools to identify the most important blogs and monitor ongoing conversations. This information includes who runs the blog or site and their interests, background, and credibility with your target audiences.

A relationship management platform also lets you know the basis on which they prefer to engage with you. Will they accept press releases from you? Do they encourage comments on their site? Do they edit or delete comments before they are posted?

You also need to understand the demographics and reach of the site. A relationship management platform contains tools and services that allow you to discern how well informed and well connected a site may be, with measurable data on a number of fronts, including:

- Traffic and Links: You need to determine the number of page views and unique visitors to the site. How many other bloggers have linked to the blog in question? The more links, the more powerful an influence the blog may be.

- RSS Subscriptions: Does the blog's home page or About Us page list newsfeed subscriptions? The number of subscribers may influence whether you consider the blog to be critical to your campaigns.
- Post Frequency: How frequently is the blog updated?
- Bookmarks and Social Media Network Tools: Does the blog make it easy for users to bookmark or to join communities?

3. **ENGAGE. Once you know whom you need to deal with, how do you join the conversation?**

The social media are the ultimate uncontrolled communications channel. The lack of the editorial filters seen in the mainstream media and the low barrier to entry are two of social media's most compelling attributes. But this immediacy and accessibility also present challenges. The tolerance of pseudonyms and anonymous comments can lead to misleading posts and flaming—harsh and negative counter-posts and reactions—that can get ugly and personal.

In addition, the social media demand a greater degree of transparency in communications than many mainstream channels. In the past few years, public relations professionals have undergone some painful learning experiences when they have treated social media as a "traditional publicity vehicle" rather than as a forum for open, frank and honest conversation among interested parties. Dissembling or pretending to be a happy consumer versus a paid advocate for a product, company, or cause can cause a serious backlash, whereas honest identification of your interest, knowledge, affiliation, and honest point of view are most often welcomed.

At the same time, the common-sense rules of engagement with mainstream media apply equally to engagement with social media:

- As with traditional journalists, what are their positive and negative biases? What's their history—the longevity and "positioning" of their outlet? What's their bandwidth? When and how often do they post?
- Understand and capitalize on niche outlets. Some blogs that narrowly focus on specific topics or products claim to have only 100 readers, but they may be "the right (i.e., most influential) 100 readers" for your company or product.
- Also know and monitor who in the blogosphere is negatively disposed toward your industry or company (even its strategic partners). They could be the point of origination for damaging coverage or rumors.

Some sites will welcome input from a company spokesperson. In the blogosphere—and elsewhere in social media—everyone has an ax to grind. You have a right to "have a take"—to promote your product, to correct a mistake or misperception—but your communication must be transparent, credible, and honest. Decisions on whether (or how) to respond to sites that are innately hostile to your company, industry, or profession should be made on a case-by-case basis.

When you engage, don't spam. Make your messaging and communication appropriate to the outlet. Get your story straight, and tell it transparently and honestly. Make it useful, credible, and robust enough to withstand challenging comments. When you comment on blog posts, discuss wide-ranging changes, trends, and issues in your industry as candidly as possible; don't simply plug your product. To avoid tit-for-tat arguments, redirect the discussion by linking to credible third-party sources that can provide perspective and a fuller understanding of the issue at hand.

Once you engage properly, you will have started building the relationships you need to meet your communications goals in the social media environment.

4. **MONITOR AND ANALYZE. Track important conversations in key blogs and begin to measure the impact of social media communications.**

It is important to be aware that conversations and relationships evolve over time. Therefore, rigorous monitoring of the conversations in your target blogs and social media outlets is important to understand the strength of your relationships and the traction that your story is getting in the communities where you have engaged. Track the issues being aired that are important to your organization, and summarize the discussion. Leverage positive social media interactions and blog mentions with mainstream media when it makes sense to do so.

At the outset of your monitoring and analysis activity, determine how you will measure success and set benchmarks for results. The conversational nature of social media requires that you make decisions about whether to participate (and how) in near real-time; you will need to develop a means of assessing issues that you are monitoring as they are aired. As in all multiple-spokespeople situations, you also may need to develop guidelines for employees or management who wish to engage social media on those issues.

Reporting is critical. Roll up real-time and daily evaluations into weekly, monthly, quarterly, and annual trend reports to provide context. Then publish and disseminate your findings to as broad an internal audience as possible on a regular basis. Use the feedback for ongoing updates to your own messaging, positioning, and strategies for contributing to the social media conversation.

The Fundamentals Still Apply

The brave new world of social media has revolutionized communication while creating unprecedented challenges for professional communicators. But you can meet the main challenges to effective social media engagement by following fundamental and time-tested principles of public relations practice:

- Identify a finite universe of key outlets.
- Communicate clearly and transparently.
- Know your audience and stay on top of the dialogue in those key outlets.
- Engage in the dialogue in intelligent and constructive ways.
- Endeavor to understand the impact these conversations are having on your brand and corporate reputation.
- Evaluate in real-time and be ready to adjust the dialogue as it evolves and address new issues as they arise.
- Use the feedback to give back to the conversation in intelligent ways.

Communicating in the right ways is imperative if you want to stay afloat and successfully navigate the sea of social media. Productive participation in this environment has until now been more art than science. But the tools required for an effective relationship management platform are improving daily. And—as with traditional PR—common-sense application of the fundamental rules of communication and relationship building will take you a long way.

APPENDIX 5

Identifying Story Ideas

Does this sound like you?

- You can't understand why the business reporter at your local newspaper has quoted your competitor in five separate stories but has not called you once.
- Your company sends out more than two dozen news releases every year about new employees and promotions, but these efforts result in little more than a few lines of type.
- The twelve-page speech your boss wrote when she spoke at the local Rotary Club luncheon would have made an excellent column for the local business magazine, but after you mailed it to the magazine's editor, you never heard a word.

If your attempts at media coverage have fallen flat, quit grumbling and start taking a proactive approach to free publicity by identifying interesting, compelling story ideas the media need. Yes, *need*. Newspapers, magazines, and trade publications must fill hundreds of thousands of column inches. TV and radio stations must broadcast hundreds of hours of news and community interest programs. The number of media outlets is greater than ever, and competition is fierce for advertising dollars, viewers, and subscribers. The secret to savvy media relations is knowing exactly what they want and then giving it to them.

Here are tickler questions designed to help you identify the best story ideas within your company or organization:

What's Different?

Is your company doing anything unique or different than your competitors? Some examples might include a professional speaker who gives a quirky, memorable free gift to every meeting planner who hires her, a Web site company that gives its customers discount coupons good for a Web site update for every referral a customer sends, or an agency that buys creative toys for its employees to use during brainstorming sessions to get their creative juices flowing.

The Local Angle

Are you the local angle to a national or regional event? During the war in Kosovo, many local newspapers and TV stations ran stories about people in their own communities who kept in touch with their relatives in the war zone. In early 2009, when Madonna was attempting to adopt a child from Malawi, many local news outlets ran stories about local couples trying to adopt children internationally.

Piggyback on a News Event

After severe rains in Milwaukee a few years ago, a Minnesota company got several minutes of free advertising on a Milwaukee radio station by talking to the drive-time radio host about a special pump that removes standing water and moisture in the air. The host interviewed a company representative and gave out the company's toll-free number.

Piggyback on Trends

Do you sell a product or service tied to a national trend? A credit counseling agency might offer themselves as a source for stories about the whopping credit card debt owned by many college students. A nonprofit agency that advocates safety for women can promote its community classes by offering the media tips on how businesswomen can avoid losing their laptop computers to thieves in crowded places such as airports.

Piggyback on a Holiday

Are you doing something different on a particular holiday? Are you a management consultant who can suggest ways that companies can keep their employees productive during the holidays? Have you determined that it is more efficient for your business to simply close down during the week between Christmas and New Year's? If you are of Irish descent and give all your employees a half-day off on St. Patrick's Day, that story might interest the media. Remember that the week between Christmas and New Year's is the slowest news week of the year, so it is an excellent time to seek coverage. A Wisconsin company got a six-minute story on the local TV station after it announced at the annual Christmas party that every employee was being treated to a trip to Disney World.

Tell the Media about Trends

Have you spotted a new trend in your industry? Let the media know. For example, many accountants are becoming certified as investment counselors. If it is a trend that a reporter is interested in, don't be surprised if he or she interviews you for the story.

Offer Free Advice

What advice can you offer that will help someone else solve his or her problems? Tell reporters they can call on you for advice when writing stories about your area of expertise. Give them specific examples of how you help people save time and money.

Write How-to Articles

Editors of many newspapers, magazines, and trade publications want articles that tell their readers how to do something, such as get out of debt, discipline their children, make their work environment safer, set up a home office, or acquire a business loan. Think of the number one problem your customers face and then write a how-to article about it. If it is printed, try to recycle the article for a different publication.

Take a Stand on Issues

Is there a local, state, or national industry or political issue for which you lobby or about which you feel strongly? Find the reporters who cover that issue and share your thoughts with them. If, for example, your trade group is supporting local gun control legislation, call and offer to comment on the issue.

Publicize an Upcoming Event

Are you sponsoring classes, an open house, a free demonstration, or a fun event? Don't just send a news release. Think of something visual that ties into the event. Then call your local TV station and ask if they are interested in doing a story a day or two before. Coverage *before* the event helps spark interest and boost attendance.

Think Technology

How are you using technology in interesting or unique ways? Have you found a way to draw lots of traffic to your Web site–with resulting orders? Are you using the latest technology during your speaking engagements? Is your sales force using technology to stay in touch with existing customers and seek new ones?

Your Lifestyle

Does the type of clothing you wear, the home you live in, your hobbies, your relation-ships with your family, the food you eat, and where you travel on vacation say some-thing unusual about you? These stories are ideal for lifestyle sections, food pages, trav-el pages, and special-interest magazines. Even though the articles are not necessarily business-related, the reporter most likely will ask you what you do for a living, and that is a chance to plug your company or organization, particularly if it ties into the reason they are writing. (Example: You speak internationally and have an extensive collection of wine you have bought during your travels. This would be a *great* story for food page editors, and it would publicize the fact that you are a professional speaker.)

Alliances and Partnerships

Has your organization formed an interesting alliance or partnership with another business or nonprofit? Call the business reporter and share the information. Be willing to explain the results you expect to see from such an arrangement, and be sure your partner is also willing to speak with a reporter.

Talk about Your Problems

What are the three biggest business problems you are facing? Find out the name of the reporters who cover your industry. Then share the information with them. Who knows? Someone might read your story and call you with a solution you might not have found otherwise.

Talk about Your Mistakes

What are the biggest mistakes you have made, and how would you advise other people to avoid making the same ones? Don't be embarrassed. Everyone makes mistakes, and if you are willing to discuss yours, there is a good chance the media will be willing to write about you.

Polls and Surveys

Are you taking a poll or survey, either among your customers or among the public? Homewood Suites, a Texas hotel chain, got great publicity from results of a survey that asked guests what they do in hotel rooms. Almost one in five respondents said they jump on the bed. Iams pet food company surveyed its customers about their relationship with their pets. An overwhelming 91 percent of the people polled admitted saying "I love you" to their pets. In addition, 63 percent of respondents sleep with their pets. Results of the poll were released several weeks before Valentine's Day. (Brilliant!) How about taking a poll asking your customers about the most unusual way they use your product or service?

Clever Contests

Have you thought about sponsoring a clever contest? To celebrate its hundredth anniversary, OshKosh B'Gosh® launched a six-month nationwide search for the oldest pair of bib overalls. Thrifty Rent-a-Car® sponsors an annual Honeymoon Disasters Contest. Entries result in amusing feature stories printed in major newspapers and magazines throughout the country. For additional publicity mileage, the company announces results near Valentine's Day, giving the media a perfect story that piggybacks on a holiday.

The Four Seasons

Think about story ideas that tie into the four seasons. Has your company found a way to keep cool or cut utility costs? Suggest it during the dog days of summer. Hospitals, clinics, and medical schools can offer the media a list of experts to pass along helpful tips on how to avoid getting colds and flu during the winter. Lawn care companies can share tips on how to prepare a lawn during the spring.

Celebrating an Anniversary?

The fact that your company is celebrating an anniversary or birthday is not news, but that information would be more enticing to the media if you could tie it in to a clever event. A button manufacturer published a lavish photo history of the button—including its uses—on shoes, clothing, furniture, and accessories. An accounting firm celebrated its centennial by publishing a giveaway book of commissioned original renditions of select artists' thoughts about what it means to be a hundred years old. A national rental car company rented out its fleet of cars for free for one day.

Create Tip Sheets

Can you write a tip sheet that explains how to solve a particular problem or how to do something? It should include helpful free advice such as the following: Eleven Ways to Snag More Business from Your Web Site; the Seven Secrets of Profitable Self-Promotion; or Nine Ways to Save Money on Insurance Premiums. Each tip sheet should have a short introduction of a sentence or two. At the end, include a paragraph that states the name of the author, the author's credentials, and contact information such as phone number, e-mail address, and Web site URL. Think of the number one problem your customers are facing and offer tips on how to solve it.

Changing Your Focus

Is your company changing its focus, switching product lines, expanding services, entering new niche markets, or making any major changes in the way it does business? If so, let the media know. Be willing, however, to talk about the reasons behind the change. If you are trying a new product line because the first one flopped, be willing to say so.

Source: Reprinted with permission of Joan Steward aka *The Publicity Hound* (www.thepublicityhound.com)

GLOSSARY

A

Action-oriented Behaviors Marketing behaviors that include the performance of a specific task, such as trying or buying a product for the first time, continuing to buy a product, casting a vote, or visiting a Web site, 53

Advertising Any paid form of nonpersonal presentation and promotion of ideas, goods, or services by an identified sponsor, 16

Advertising Media Segment of the media business focused on generating revenue through the sales of advertisements, 70

Arena The combination of products a firm offers and the distribution channels it uses to get the products to the consumer, 39

Attitude A person's overall evaluation of a concept; a response involving general feelings of liking or favorability, 53

Audience The intended receivers of a promotional message, 27

Audit Bureau An independent organization that verifies audience reach and demographics for media outlets, 105

B

Backgrounder Fact-oriented MPR document that takes the form of a narrative about a company, product, or person, 121

Balance Theory A communications theory that asserts that receivers feel uncomfortable, or out of balance, when their attitude toward the sender of a message does not match their attitude about the topic of the message, 141

Beat A journalist's area of interest or specialty, 75

Benefits A behavioral segmentation that groups buyers according to the different benefits they seek from a product, 62

Blog A hybrid form of Internet communication that combines a column, diary, and directory. The term, short for "Web log," refers to a frequently updated collection of short articles on various subjects with links to further resources, 72

Blogosphere A collective term encompassing all blogs and their interconnections. It is the perception that blogs exist together as a connected community (or as a collection of connected communities) or as a social network, 164

Boilerplate A short description of a company for editorial use, 128

Booth The exhibit or other area occupied by a firm on the floor of a trade show, 178

Brand Authors The companies, customers, and influencers, along with popular culture, who create the stories, images, and associations between brands and consumers, 31

Bridging An interview technique that allows an interviewee to address an interviewer's question and move onto a topic that aligns with the interviewee's goals for the interview, 204

B-Roll Video footage produced by a firm and supplied to connectors in support of an MPR effort, 145

Buzz Synonymous with *word-of-mouth*, 15

Byline The line of text indicating the author of an article or other published work, 193

C

Case Study A short-format article based upon the expertise of a professional or organization that takes a problem-solution approach to a particular issue, 197

Circulation Impressions The number of times the story was covered multiplied by the circulation of the publications in which it was covered, 101

Citizen Marketer A hyperengaged consumer, not in the employ of any media outlet, freely giving a personal expression of the passion he or she has for a product or an industry, 92

Clipping Evidence of the coverage of a firm or its products by the media or other connectors, 125

Co-created Content Web content resulting from a collaboration of a firm and one or more consumers, 168

Conference Gathering of people from a particular industry or profession or who simply share a common interest who come together to share information on a topic, 179

Connectors Media, groups, or individuals who act as a channel for a marketing message, resulting in media mentions or the creation of word-of-mouth, 26

Consumer-Generated Marketing (CGM) Marketing efforts designed to encourage consumers to create marketing messages and other brand exchanges themselves, 4

Consumer Potential The gap between a consumer's current and ideal state of being, 55

Consumption Stories Stories created by consumers about how they use or consume products, which they then share with their friends and which become the fuel for word-of-mouth, 42

Content All non-advertising elements of media, including but not limited to articles, columns, feature stories, and editorials, 70

Corporate Governance A generic term that describes the ways in which rights and responsibilities are shared between the various corporate participants, especially the management and the shareholders, 34

Customer Loyalty A behavioral segmentation that groups buyers according to how likely they are to switch from the brand they are currently using to a different brand, 63

Customer Relationship Management (CRM) A technology-based system that seeks to create more meaningful one-on-one communications with the customer by applying customer data (demographic, industry, buying history, etc.) to every communications vehicle, 233

D

Demographics Criteria for dividing a market into groups based on such variables as age, gender, income, occupation, race, and nationality, 59

Differentiators The attributes of a company or product that create its competitive advantage in the marketplace, 39

Direct Marketing The use of direct mail, the telephone, direct-response television, e-mail, the Internet, and other tools to communicate directly with carefully targeted individual consumers in an attempt to obtain an immediate response and to cultivate lasting customer relationships, 17

E

Economic Logic The means by which an organization realizes a return on its investment, 38

Embargo A heading on a news release indicating that the news is not to be published or reported before a specific date, 128; giving information about a story to a connector before the firm wants it released to allow the connector to prepare his or her story, 147

Employee Relations A public relations function that deals with managing communication with existing and prospective employees, 32

Event A special activity, showing, display, or exhibit designed to demonstrate products or to connect the product to favorable products or activities, 79

Exchange A transaction in which a person or organization trades a definite quantity of one substance for a definite quantity of another, 16

Exclusive Giving information about a story to a single connector in order to enhance the firm's coverage in that connector's medium, 147

Expert A person with education and/or experience in a particular field, who is, typically, not a journalist, 90

F

Facilitator A creator or facilitator of a community (usually online) designed either to be a de facto support group for customers of certain products or simply to bring fans of a given product together, 94

Fact Sheet A list of facts designed to entice connectors to cover a firm or its products, while supplying them with information to support their coverage, 121

Fanatic A consumer who acts like a product evangelist by continuously monitoring and analyzing a brand, product, organization, or person and prescribing subsequent courses of action, 93

FAQs An MPR document of questions that a typical audience for a given connector might have related to a firm and its products, along with answers to those questions, 121

Filter A consumer who collects and shares traditional media stories, blogger's rants and raves, podcasts, or fan creations about a specific company or brand and then packages this information into a constant stream of links, story summaries, and observations, 92

Firecracker A consumer who creates a song, animation, video, or novelty that generates a lot of short-term interest in a product. This interest dies out quickly as the consumer goes on with her other work, 94

Frequency The number of times a person, household, or member of a target market is exposed to a media vehicle or an advertiser's media schedule within a given period of time; usually expressed as an average frequency (the average number of exposures during the time period) or as a frequency distribution (the number of people exposed once, twice, three times, etc.), 111

H

Hook A creative ploy to garner attention or interest in a subject, 166

Human Resources The division of a company that is focused on activities relating to employees. These activities normally include recruiting and hiring of new employees, orientation and training of current employees, employee benefits, and retention, 32

I

Influencers Media, groups, or individuals who act as a channel for a marketing message, resulting in media mentions or the creation of word-of-mouth. Synonymous with *connectors*, 43

Information-Oriented Behaviors Behaviors designed to make an audience aware of some aspect of a given product, usually with the goal of supporting an action-based outcome at some point in the future, 53

Integrated Marketing Communications The concept under which a company carefully integrates and coordinates its many communications channels to deliver a clear, consistent, and compelling message about the organization and its products, 16

Interaction Concept A business philosophy that assumes that a firm's two-way interaction with customers is essential to long-term profitability, 37

Intermediaries Organizations or individuals that pass a message about a product from a firm to consumers; this should not be confused with the term "marketing intermediary," which refers to product distribution channels, 4

Inverted Pyramid The concept of presenting information from the general to the specific, 131

Investor Relations A public relations function that manages the communication between a publicly held corporation, its shareholders, and the media and analysts who report on the corporation's financial situation, 34

M

Market Segment A group of consumers who respond in a similar way to a given set of marketing efforts, 58

Marketing Concept The business philosophy of centering an organization's goal on satisfying the needs of the customer, 36

Marketing Mix The variety of tools available to marketers in their quest to manage this process, 6

Marketing Public Relations (MPR) Any program or effort designed to improve, maintain, or protect the sales or image of a product by encouraging intermediaries, such as traditional mass media, the electronic media, or individuals, to voluntarily pass a message about the firm or product to their audience of businesses or consumers, 3

Media In public relations, media are considered to be any communication methods widely distributed to the consumer or business community. *Media* is the plural form of *medium*. Types of media include television, radio, newspapers, magazines, Web sites, and blogs, 4

Media Alert A non-persuasive form of a press release intended simply to inform connectors of a particular fact, 128

Media Convergence The trend of media organizations shifting toward a multiple-format approach to producing and distributing content. This trend is driven by innovations in technology and changing consumer preferences, 80

Media Kit A package of promotional materials relating to a specific advertising media vehicle, including the rate card, audience statistics, case studies showing success stories, and related materials, 105

Media Mentions The spoken, written, or visual reference to a product presented through mass media or other incidence where one source has the attention of many people or organizations, 16

Metrics Means for measuring changes to critical data, 231

Micro-Blog A status update application that logs entries to a common Web site, or a multi-user blog with restrictions on entry length, 165

Mission A firm's core purpose and focus, 36

Moderator The master of ceremonies or facilitator of a press conference, 184

N

New Media Electronically delivered media, 71

News Aggregator Internet-based platform that compiles news stories based on either the tagging of the story by its user community or at the discretion of an individual person or organization, 198

News Media People or entities that gather information of potential interest to a segment of the public, use their editorial skills to turn the raw materials into a distinct work, and make their products available to the general public through purchase, subscription, or free distribution, 70

News Release Synonymous with press release

Newsworthy A subject that is interesting to a medium's audience, is objective, and will not make the media appear as though it has an ulterior motive for covering it, 140

Noise Anything tangible or intangible that interferes with the transmission of a message from a sender to a receiver or with the comprehension of the message by the receiver, 25

Non-Media Connector A person who monitors, analyzes, and shares information about a product or industry. This person may be paid for her efforts, but she is not employed by a media organization, 86

O

Occasion A behavioral segmentation that groups buyers according to when they get the idea to buy, actually make their purchase, or use the purchased item, 62

Offline Word-of-Mouth Information about products spread from consumer to consumer via face-to-face, telephone, or other non-electronic methods, 96

Op-ed An opinion piece, often published in newspapers, and more recently in online publications. The term *op-ed* describes the common placement of these articles in newspapers on the page opposite an editorial, 78

Opinion Leader An individual whose attitudes, opinions, and behaviors greatly influence a group or society, 90

P

Personal Selling Personal presentation by a firm's sales force for the purpose of making sales and building customer relationships, 17

Pick-up Evidence (press clipping, video, etc.) of a media mention, 198

Pitch An attempt to persuade a journalist or other connector to cover a story, 75, 139

Pitch Letter A letter, an e-mail, or another written document used to present a pitch, 143

Positioning The way that consumers perceive a product relative to its competitors, 22

Positioning Statement A statement describing the way that the marketers intend consumers to perceive the product relative to its competitors, 24

Press Conference The convening of representatives of the media by a person or organization to explain, announce, or expand on a particular subject, 183

Press Kit Information compiled by organizations for the purpose of informing media outlets and other connectors about their firm, brands, products, employees, and activities, 120

Press Release Information of timely value distributed by an organization to promote its views, products, or services; also called *news release*, 119

Press Room A room at a trade show where exhibiting firms can leave press materials for the use of members of the media attending the show, 178

Product Any good, service, idea, or personality to which PR can be applied, 4

Product Concept A business philosophy that assumes that consumers will favor products with a higher degree of quality, performance, and available features, 36

Production Concept A business philosophy that assumes that consumers will favor the most widely available and attractively priced products, 36

Psychographics   Criteria for dividing a market into groups based on such variables as social class, lifestyle, or personality characteristics, 60

Public   Any group that has an interest in or effect upon the activities of a firm and that may also be affected by those activities, 4

Public Relations   The function of building good relations with the company's various publics by obtaining favorable publicity, building up a good corporate image, and handling or heading off unfavorable rumors, stories, and events, 17

Publicly Traded Companies   Companies that have issued securities through an offering and that are now traded on the open market, 34

R

Reach   The number of different persons or households exposed to a particular advertising media vehicle or a media schedule during a specified period of time. Also called *cumulative audience, cumulative reach, net audience, net reach, net unduplicated audience,* or *unduplicated audience,* reach is often presented as a percentage of the total number of persons in a specified audience or target market, 111

S

Sales Cycle   Time between initial contact with a prospective customer and the completion of a sale, 192

Sales Promotion   Short-term incentives to encourage the purchase or sale of a product or service, 17

Scenario Statement   The portion of an MPR crisis plan that maps out the "who, what, when, where, why, and how" of specific potential crises, 215

Self-Produced Event   An event conceived and put on by an individual firm to serve its audience with the intent of promoting its products, 174

Selling Concept   A business philosophy in which companies focus on large-scale promotional and selling efforts in order to gain market share, 36

Seminar   A self-produced event in which a firm arranges to have an expert in its industry conduct an informational session for its audience, 179

Social Media   1. Online technologies and practices that people use to share opinions, insights, experiences, and perspectives, including text, images, audio, and video, 71; 2. Electronic media where participants can produce, publish, control, critique, rank, and interact with online content, 157

Social Network   A Web-based community designed to promote interaction, discussion, and sharing of content among its users, 157

Societal Marketing Concept   A business philosophy that goes beyond concentrating on the consumer and considers the long-term interests of society at large, 36

Source Filing   Initiating communication with a connector to inform him or her of the availability of a subject matter expert as a resource for future stories, 199

Sphere of Influence   A term typically applied to nations, marketers use this term to refer to the audience that a connector reaches, 86

Staging   The speed and sequence of implementing a strategic plan, 39

Stakeholders   Customers, prospective customers, employees, stockholders, or, in some cases, even the general public, 6

Statement of Tactics   A detailed description of activities coordinated in pursuit of achieving an objective including staff and managerial responsibilities and required resources, 229

Stock   An instrument that signifies an ownership position (called *equity*) in a corporation, and represents a claim on its proportional share in the corporation's assets and profits, 34

Subject File   A file kept by a journalist or other connector containing information about subjects he is interested in covering, 121

SWOT Analysis   An evaluation of a firm's internal strengths and weaknesses, and external opportunities and threats compiled for use in business planning situations, 226

T

Target Market   A set of buyers sharing common needs or characteristics that a company decides to serve, 58

Third-Party Event   An event created and managed by an organization that opens it up to other firms for participation, 174

Thought Leaders People or firms whom an industry or a consumer group recognize for contributing a new way of thinking and/or original perspectives to their field, 192

Trade Journal A print publication similar in form to either a magazine or newspaper that focuses its content on a specific industry or profession, 73

Trade Show Periodic gathering at which manufacturers, suppliers, and distributors in a particular industry or related industries display their products and provide information for potential retail, wholesale, or industrial buyers, 176

Transparency Essential condition for a free and open exchange whereby the rules and reasons behind regulatory measures are fair and clear to all participants, 34

Tweet An entry onto the micro-blog Twitter, 165

U

Usage Rate A behavioral segmentation that groups buyers according to how frequently they buy or use a product, 63

V

Vehicles The mechanisms for a firm to enter or conduct business within a given arena and to achieve its goals, 39

Vendors Companies that supply parts or services to another company; also called *supplier*, 35

Video News Release (VNR) A publicity device created by a firm, which is designed to look and sound like a television news story. Marketers prepare a sixty- to ninety-second video, which can then be used by television stations as is or after further editing, 134

Viral Marketing A marketing phenomenon that facilitates and encourages people to pass along a marketing message, 20, 87

Vision An organization's aspirations in the mid-term or long-term future. It is intended to serve as a clear guide for choosing current and future courses of action, 36

Vodcast A video podcast, 70

Vulnerability Audit An exercise for identifying and documenting potential MPR crises for planning purposes, 214

W

Wall The space on a social network page where friends, fans, or contacts can write a message to the owner of that space, 159

White Paper An educational report made available to the public that expounds on a particular industry issue, 197

Wiki A repository for content of any sort that can be edited, added to, or updated by the community of those interested in the subject, 161

Work Events Events where attendees actively participate in an activity such as building a house for someone needing shelter, filling sandbags for flood-prone communities, etc., 182

Word-of-Mouth Information spread from person to person through the spoken or written word where the communication is personal, intentional, and concerns a product, 16

NOTES

CHAPTER 1

1. Ann Marie Kerwin, "Harry Potter Must Die: What Everyone Is Talking About," *Advertising Age,* June 27, 2006.
2. Gary Armstrong and Philip Kotler, *Marketing, An Introduction,* 9th ed., pp. 67–68. (Upper Saddle River, NJ: Pearson Prentice Hall, 2009).
3. The Museum of Public Relations, "1923 Soap and Art," http://www.prmuseum.com/bernays/bernays_1923.html (accessed November 6, 2008).
4. Armstrong and Kotler, *Marketing,* pp. 19–20.
5. 3M, "YouTube PostIt Notes Channel," YouTube, http://www.youtube.com/postitnotes (accessed November 6, 2008).
6. "Boston mayor targeting Turner Broadcasting after PR stunt spread terror fears," *USA Today,* February 1, 2007, http://www.usatoday.com/news/nation/2007-01-31-boston_x.htm (accessed November 20, 2008).
7. As quoted in John Karolefski, "PR Stirs it Up," Brandchannel.com, July 14, 2003, http://www.brandchannel.com/features_effect.asp?pf_id=166#more (accessed November 7, 2008).
8. Public Relations Society of America, "Preamble: Public Relations Society of America Member Code of Ethics 2000," http://www.prsa.org/aboutUs/ethics/preamble_en.html (accessed March 2008). Reprinted with permission from the Public Relations Society of America (www.prsa.org).

CHAPTER 2

1. "April Showers Bring the New Season of Hannah Montana!", *TV.com,* January 11, 2007, http://www.tv.com/hannah-montana-blog/april-showers-bring-the-new-season-of-hannah-montana!/topic/76900-628985/show_blog_entry.html?topic_id=628985 (accessed April 18, 2008).
2. David Robinson, "Public Relations Comes of Age," *Business Horizons* 49, no. 3 (2006): 249.
3. William Stanley Jevon, *Money and the Mechanisms of Exchange* (New York: D. Appleton and Company, 1867).
4. Gary Armstrong and Philip Kotler, *Marketing, An Introduction,* 9th ed., p. 351 (Upper Saddle River, NJ: Pearson Prentice Hall, 2009).
5. Ben Rooney, "Super Bowl Ads: $2.7 Million and Worth It," CNNMoney.com, January 25, 2008, http://money.cnn.com/2008/01/25/news/superbowl_ads/index.htm (accessed April 4, 2008).
6. "Giants' Staggering Win over Patriots Watched by Record 97.5 million," ESPN.com, February 5, 2008, http://sports.espn.go.com/nfl/playoffs07/news/story?id=3229763 (accessed April 4, 2008).
7. Stephanie Saul, "Helped by Generics, Inflation of Drug Costs Slows," *The New York Times*, September 21, 2007, http://www.nytimes.com/2007/09/21/business/21generic.html (accessed February 4, 2009).
8. Frank Walsh, "You Won't Sell Diddly until You Establish Trust," *Sunday Times (London),* July 1, 2007.
9. Schwartz Communications, "Case Studies: Sistina Software," http://www.schwartz-pr.com/case_studies_pages.php?ind=12&id=52 (accessed June 24, 2008).
10. American Marketing Association, "Dictionary," http://www.marketingpower.com/_layouts/Dictionary.aspx (accessed June 26, 2008).
11. Donna DeClemente, "OfficeMax's Elf Yourself Reaches 193 Million Visitors," Donna's Promo Talk, January 15, 2008, http://www.donnaspromotalk.com/donnas_promo_talk/2008/01/before-we-get-t.html (accessed June 16, 2008).
12. Armstrong, and Kotler, *Marketing,* 167.
13. David Michaelson and Don Stacks, "Exploring the Comparative Communications Effectiveness of Advertising and Media Placement," 2006 Summit on Measurement. (Gainesville, FL: Institute for Public Relations, 2006), 8.
14. Allison Enright, "Front, Center—From His Position, Ries Looks at Marketing Then, Now," *Marketing News,* March 1, 2006, 11–13.

CHAPTER 3

1. Moira Herbst, "Welcome to Caffeine Country," *BusinessWeek*, January 26, 2007, http://www.businessweek.com/bwdaily/dnflash/content/jan2007/db20070126_163045.htm?chan=top+news_top+news+index_businessweek+exclusives (accessed February 5, 2009).
2. Gerhard Gschwandtner, "The Powerful Sales Strategy behind Red Bull," Sellingpower.com, September 2004, http://www.sellingpower.com/article/display.asp?aid=SP2229597 (accessed May 23, 2008).
3. Melanie Ho, "For Red Bull, It's Here, There and Everywhere; Energy Drink Maker Corners the Marketing." *Washington Post,* August 23, 2006.
4. "Red Bull Sets Up 'Ideas' Network." *Marketing,* August 29, 2007, 3.
5. Liz Rusbridger, "Red Bull Pulls Nativity Ad," Reuters, December 4, 2007, http://www.reuters.com/articlePrint?articleId=USN0447928720071204 (accessed February 5, 2009.
6. Business Dictionary, "Human Resources," http://www.businessdictionary.com/definition/human-resources.html (accessed June 23, 2008).
7. Kevin Sullivan, "Why PR Matters—and What It Can Do for You," *Harvard Managment Update* (May 2007): 2–3.
8. Oliver Blanchard, "Happy Employees = Happy Customers," October 13, 2005, The Brand Builder Blog, http://thebrandbuilder.blogspot.com/2005/10/happy-employees-happy-customers.html (accessed June 19, 2008).
9. Coeli Carr, "Seeking to Attract Top Prospects, Employers Brush Up on Brands," *The New York Times*, September 10, 2006.
10. Ibid.
11. Investorwords.com, "Stock," http://www.investorwords.com/4725/stock.html (accessed June 23, 2008).
12. Investorwords.com, "Publicly Traded," http://www.investorwords.com/3940/publicly_traded.html (accessed June 23, 2008).
13. Investorwords.com, "Corporate Governance," http://www.investorwords.com/5483/corporate_governance.html (accessed June 23, 2008).
14. Investorwords.com, "Transparency," http://www.businessdictionary.com/definition/transparency.html (accessed June 23, 2008).
15. Benita Aw Yeong, and Tettyana Jasli, "Savvy in Investor, Media Relations? Financial PR, IR Firms Want You," *The Business Times Singapore*, March 20, 2007.
16. Investorwords.com, "Vendor," http://www.investorwords.com/5234/vendor.html (accessed June 23, 2008).
17. Investorwords.com, "Mission Statement," http://www.businessdictionary.com/definition/mission-statement.html (accessed June 23, 2008).

18. Investorwords.com, "Vision Statement," http://www. businessdictionary.com/definition/vision-statement.html (accessed June 23, 2008).

19. Sandra Miles and Glynn Mangold, "Positioning Southwest Airlines Through Employee Branding," *Business Horizons* 48, no. 6 (2005): 540–542.

20. Gary Armstrong and Philip Kotler, *Marketing, An Introduction,* 9th ed., p. 11. (Upper Saddle River, NJ: Pearson-Prentice Hall, 2009).

21. Ibid. p. 12

22. Girish Ramani and V. Kumar, "Interaction Orientation and Firm Performance," *Journal of Marketing* 72, no. 1 (January 2008): 27, 41.

23. "A Bookstore by Any Other Name," interview with Jeff Bezos by Commonwealthclub.org, July 27, 1998, http://www. commonwealthclub.org/archive/98/98-07bezos-qa.html (accessed July 23, 2008).

24. Ramani and Kumar, "Interaction Orientation," 27–29.

25. Dave Court et al., "Bringing Customers into the Boardroom," *Harvard Business Review* (November 2004): Vol. 82, 70.

26. Mason Carpenter and William Gerard Sanders, *Strategic Managment* (Upper Saddle River, NJ: Pearson Prentice Hall, 2009), 15.

27. Gary L. Neilson, Karla L. Martin, and Elizabeth Powers, "The Secrets to Successful Strategy Execution," *Harvard Business Review,* Vol. 86 (June 2008): 61–70.

28. Jake Laban and Jack Green, "Communicating Your Strategy," *Graziadio Business Report* 6, no. 1 (2003). Web publication: http://gbr.pepperdine.edu/031/ communication.html

29. Douglas B. Holt, *Brands and Branding* (Boston, MA: Harvard Business School Publishing, 2003).

30. Word of Mouth Marketing Association, "Suzanne Fanning, Fiskars Craft," http://www.womma.org/video/suzanne-fanning-fiskars-craft/ (accessed May 21, 2008).

31. Julianna Goldman, "Obama Campaign Seeks to Translate 'Oprah Effect' to Politics," Bloomberg.com, December 7, 2007, http://www.bloomberg.com/apps/news?pid= 20601103&sid=aMcIXVheFBJo&refer=us (accessed May 21, 2008).

32. Barry B. Kaplan, "Forever Diamonds," Gemnation.com, http:// www.gemnation.com/base?processor=getPage&pageName= forever_diamonds_1 (accessed May 22, 2008).

33. Ibid.

34. Robin Edgerton, "Engagement, Inc.: The Marketing of Diamonds," *Stayfree! Magazine,* Summer 1999, http://www. stayfreemagazine.org/archives/16/diamonds.html (accessed May 21, 2008).

35. Paul J. Meyer, *Attitude Is Everything! If You Want to Succeed Above and Beyond!* (Merced, CA: Leading Edge Publishing Company, 2003).

CHAPTER 4

1. Janet Adamy, "Starbucks Closes Stores to Retrain Baristas," *The Wall Street Journal*, February 26, 2008.

2. As quoted in Natalie Zmuda, "Speedo Makes a Splash with LZR Racer Suit," *Advertising Age*, June 25, 2008, From adage.com http://adage.com/article?article_id=128002

3. Gary Armstrong and Philip Kotler, *Marketing, An Introduction,* 9th ed. (Upper Saddle River, NJ: Pearson Prentice Hall, 2009), 177

4. American Marketing Association, "Dictionary," http://www. marketingpower.com/_layouts/Dictionary.aspx (accessed March 3, 2008

5. As quoted in Beth Snyder Bulik, "How Xerox Plans to Position Itself as the Cool Copier Company," *Advertising Age*, April 16, 2007, 33.

6. C. Harrison, "Recall May Benefit Dell: Company Can Improve Its Image If Process Is Easy for Customers," *The Dallas Morning News*, August 16, 2006.

7. Armstrong and Kotler, *Marketing*.

8. "South Carolina YouTube Video Helps Make Chicago 'Warmer'," Reuters, March 10, 2008, http://www.reuters.com/ article/pressRelease/idUS196775+10-Mar-2008+ PRN20080310 (accessed June 25, 2008).

9. Armstrong and Kotler, *Marketing*, 145–148.

10. "South Carolina YouTube Video Helps Make Chicago 'Warmer'," Reuters.

11. Armstrong and Kotler, *Marketing*.

12. Robert Hof, "Who Needs Blockbusters?", *BusinessWeek*, July 17, 2006. http://www.businessweek.com/magazine/ content/06_29/b3993104.htm.

13. John Cassidy, "Going Long: In the New 'Long Tail' Market-place, Has the Blockbuster Met Its Match?", *The New Yorker*, July 10, 2006, 98.

14. Ibid.

15. Armstrong and Kotler, *Marketing,* 169.

16. Ibid., 171.

17. Ibid., 171.

18. Ibid., 171.

19. Zip-codes.com, "ZIP Code Radius Finder and Calculator," http://www.zip-codes.com/zip-code-radius-finder.asp (accessed March 5, 2008).

20. Paul M. Rand, "Identifying and Reaching Influencers," American Marketing Association, 2004, http://www.marketingpower.com/content20476S0.php (accessed March 7, 2008).

21. Stan Stalnaker, "Here Comes the P2P Economy," *Harvard Business Review,* Vol. 86 (2) (February 2008): 18.

CHAPTER 5

1. Hoover's, "ABC Inc.,Company History," Hoover's, 2008.

2. Quoted in Project for Excellence in Journalism, "2007 State of the News Media Report—Digital Journalism," *Pew Research Center's Project for Excellence in Journalism,* March 12, 2007, http://www.journalism.org/node/7230 (accessed January 12, 2009).

3. Ibid.

4. Ibid.

5. Ibid.

6. American Marketing Association, "Dictionary," http://www.marketingpower.com/_layouts/Dictionary.aspx (accessed June 26, 2008).

7. Brad King, "Editors and Publishers Get Together on Making Money," The Modern Journalist, April 20, 2008, http://www. themodernjournalist.com/2008/04/20/editors-and-publishers-get-together-on-making-money/ (accessed June 3, 2008).

8. David Ardia, "Congress Passes FOIA Reform Bill, Expands Definition of 'News Media'," Citizen Media Law Project, December 20, 2007, http://www.citmedialaw.org/blog/2007/congress-passes-foia-reform-bill-expands-definition-news-media (accessed January 12, 2009).

9. Brian Solis, *Essential Guide to Social Media,* June 9, 2008. http://www.briansolis.com/2008/06/essential-guide-to-social-media-free.html.

10. "Sports Illustrated Media Kit," *Sports Illustrated,* http:// simediakit.com/property-single.xhtml?property_id=38 (accessed January 12, 2009).

11. Mark Dominiak, "Brand Needs Key to Media Allocation," *TV Week,* April 20, 2008, http://www.tvweek.com/news/2008/04/brand_needs_key_to_media_alloc.php (accessed January 12, 2009).

12. American Marketing Association, "Dictionary."

13. Doublas Ahlers, "News Consumption and the New Electronic Media," *Harvard International Journal of Press/Politics* (2006; 11; 29): 31.

14. *The Magazine Handbook 2007/2008* New York: Magazine Publishers of America, 2007–2008), 5–6.

15. Marketing Charts, "comScore Top 50 Properties (U.S.)," April 2008, http://www.marketingcharts.com/interactive/top-50-us-web-rankings-issued-for-april-google-no-1-for-first-time-4614/comscore-top-50-online-properties-us-april-2008jpg/ (accessed June 4, 2008).

16. Technorati Media, "Welcome to Technorati," http://technorati.com/about/ (accessed June 2008, 2008).

17. Heather Green, "With 15.5 Million Active Blogs, New Technorati Data Shows that Blogging Growth Seems to Be Peaking," *BusinessWeek,* April 25, 2007, http://www.businessweek.com/the_thread/blogspotting/archives/2007/04/blogging_growth.html (accessed July 30, 2008).

18. Abbey Klassen, "Measuring the Web Just Got More Complex; Nielsen Adds Yet Another Metric, Total Minutes to Convoluted Process," *Advertising Age,* July 16, 2007, 3.

19. Richard Laermer, *Full Frontal PR* (Princeton, NJ: Bloomberg, 2003): 24.

20. Ibid. p.101

21. Ibid. p.168

22. Dennis L. Wilcox and Glen T. Cameron, *Public Relations Strategies and Tactics,* 8th ed. (Boston, MA: Allyn and Bacon, 2007): 91–92

23. Society of Professional Journalists, "Code of Ethics," http://www.spj.org/ethicscode.asp (accessed June 6, 2008).

24. Ibid.

25. Quoted in Eamon Javers, "A Columnist Backed by Monsanto," *Business Week,* January 13, 2006.

26. The New York Times Company, "The New York Times Company Policy on Ethics in Journalism," October 2005, http://www.nytco.com/press/ethics.html#A7 (accessed August 1, 2008).

27. Hasan, "What Is an Op-Ed?", *Directory Journal,* June 6, 2007, http://www.dirjournal.com/articles/what-is-an-op-ed/ (accessed August 6, 2008).

28. American Marketing Association, "Dictionary."

29. State Farm, "State Farm® and The 50 Million Pound Challenge Win Highest Honor in Public Relations," June 17, 2008, http://www.statefarm.com/about/media/media_releases/sfanvil.asp (accessed July 1, 2008).

30. Jose Alberto García-Avilés and Miguel Carvajal, "Integrated and Cross-Media Newsroom Convergence," *Convergence: The International Journal of Research into New Media Technologies* 14, no. 2 (2008): 221–222.

31. Frank Washkuch, "State of Transition," *PR Week,* March 30, 2008. http://www.prweekus.com/State-of-transition/article/108309/

32. Richard Perez-Pena, "Washington Post Signals Shift with a New Editor," *The New York Times*, July 8, 2008.

CHAPTER 6

1. Brains on Fire, "How Earshot (an Independent Record Store) Became an Inspiration Destination," http://brainsonfire.com/FIRE/ (accessed August 6, 2008).

2. PQ Media, *Word-of-Mouth Marketing Forecast 2007–2011* (Stamford, CT: PQ Media, 2007): 8.

3. Chartreuse, "3 Questions with Steve Johnson of Clear Digital Media," January 31, 2006, http://chartreuse.wordpress.com/2006/01/31/3-questions-with-steve-johnson-of-clear-digital-media/ (accessed July 24, 2008).

4. Joan Voight, "The New Brand Ambassadors," *Ad Week*, December 31, 2007 http://www.adweek.com/aw/content_display/news/strategy/e3i9ec32f006d17a91cccd2559f612b0f42 (accessed January 2, 2008).

5. The Nielsen Company, "Word-of-Mouth the Most Powerful Selling Tool: Nielsen Global Survey," October 1, 2007, http://www.nielsen.com/media/2007/pr_071001.html (accessed July 25, 2008).

6. Sinclair Stewart, "More Marketers Using Word of Mouth to Whip Up Sales," *Toronto Globe and Mail*, December 23, 2007.

7. American Marketing Association, "Dictionary," http://www.marketingpower.com/_layouts/Dictionary.aspx (accessed June 26, 2008).

8. Angela Dobele, David Toleman, and Michael Beverland, "Controlled Infection! Spreading the Brand Message Through Viral Marketing," *Business Horizons* 48, no. 2 (2005): 146–149.

9. American Marketing Association, "Dictionary."

10. Ibid.

11. Ben McConnell and Jackie Hub, *Citizen Marketer* (Chicago: Kaplan, 2007): 5.

12. American Dental Association, "American Dental Association Home Page," 2008, http://www.ada.org/index.asp (accessed July 28, 2008).

13. David Santillo et al., *Missed Call: The iPhone's Hazardous Chemicals* (Amsterdam: Greenpeace International, 2007).

14. Apple, Inc., "Apple and the Environment," http://www.apple.com/environment/ (accessed July 28, 2008).

15. Jack Neff, "How to Get Your Brand on 'Oprah'," *Advertising Age*, June 2, 2008, 3.

16. "Social Networks Impact the Drugs Physicians Prescribe According to Stanford Business School Research," *Biotech Business Week,* June 4, 2007, 156.

17. Ben McConnell and Jackie Huba, *Citizen Marketer* (Chicago: Kaplan, 2007): 1–30.

18. Mike Kaltschue, "Hacking Netflix Disclosure Statement," March 5, 2005, http://www.hackingnetflix.com/netflix/2005/03/hacking_netflix.html (accessed July 29, 2008).

19. Adotas, "NYU Study Shows the Power of Viral Marketing," February 7, 2008, http://www.adotas.com/2008/02/nyu-study-shows-the-power-of-viral-marketing/ (accessed July 28, 2008).

20. "Targeting Blogs—Are Bloggers Fair Game for PROs?", *PR Week,* March 28, 2008, 22.

21. Quoted in Tanya Lewis, "A Whole New World," *PR Week*, August 13, 2007, 17.

22. Ed Keller and Jon Berry, "Word-of-mouth: The Real Action Is Offline," *Advertising Age*, December 4, 2006, 20.

23. Ibid.

CHAPTER 7

1. The Pew Research Center for the People & the Press, *News Consumption and Believability Study* (Washington DC: The Pew Research Center for the People & the Press, 2006, 1–4).

2. Megan McIlroy, "Serving Other Media Up with TV Ups Appetite for Products," *Advertising Age*, June 2, 2008. http://adage.com/mediaworks/article?article_id=127454

3. "New Media Measurement, Best Stories for Radio, More," *PR Week,* January 15, 2007, 29.

4. Inc.com, "Creating a Target Media List," http://www.inc.com/articles/2000/03/18673.html (accessed August 25, 2008).

5. American Marketing Association, "Dictionary," http://www.marketingpower.com/_layouts/Dictionary.aspx (accessed August 24, 2008).

6. Ibid.

7. Ibid.

8. Christ Lynn Wilson, interview by Gaetan Giannini, *PR Professional* (August 2008).

9. American Marketing Association, "Dictionary."

CHAPTER 8

1. American Marketing Association, "Dictionary," http://www.marketingpower.com/_layouts/Dictionary.aspx (accessed August 24, 2008).

2. Mark Wright, "Help Reporters Find You . . . Before They Need You," 2005, http://www.markwright.com/backgrounder. htm (accessed August 29, 2008).

3. National Association of Social Workers, "How To Write and Use an Effective Backgrounder in Public Relations," socialworkers.org, http://www.socialworkers.org/pressroom/ mediaToolkit/toolkit/WriteBackgrounder.pdf (accessed August 29, 2008).

4. Mindy McAdams, "Journalism 101: Pictures Sell News," 2007, http://mindymcadams.com/tojou/2007/journalism-101-pictures-sell-news/ (accessed September 24, 2008).

5. American Marketing Association, "Dictionary," http://www.marketingpower.com/_layouts/Dictionary.aspx (accessed August 24, 2008).

6. Public Relations Institute of Ireland, "Glossary of PR terms," 2008, http://www.prii.ie/show_content.aspx? idcategory=19&idsubcategory=0#lnke (accessed September 6, 2008).

7. Marketing-Playbook, "Boilerplate," http://www.marketing-playbook.com/glossary/index.php/term/definition:+What+does+this+B2B+Marketing+term%252C+terminology+mean%3F,Boilerplate.xhtml (accessed September 6, 2008 http://www.marketing-playbook.com/glossary/index. php/term/%26%23160%3B,Boilerplate.xhtml

8. Jay Conrad Levinson, Rick Frishman, and Jill Lublin, *Guerilla Publicity* (Avon, MA: Adams Media, 2002).

9. Ibid.

10. Sid Smith, "How to Write a Press Release," Business Word-smiths, Inc., March 5, 2007, http://www.businesswordsmiths. com/marketing-tips/publicity/how-to-write-a-press-release/ (accessed September 2, 2008).

11. Elisabeth Sullivan, "The Elements of a Press Release," *Marketing News*, April 15, 2008, 8.

12. Lora Kolondny, "The Art of the Press Release," *Inc. Magazine*, March 2005. http://www.inc.com/magazine/ 20050301/marketing.html

13. "Tips, Guidelines and Templates for Writing an Effective Press Release," PRWeb Direct, 2005, http://www.prwebdirect. com/pressreleasetips.php#template (accessed September 2, 2008).

14. Kolondny, "The Art of the Press Release." http://www.inc. com/magazine/20050301/marketing.html

15. American Marketing Association, "Dictionary."

16. American Marketing Association, "Dictionary."

17. William Triplett, "Views on Fake News," *Daily Variety*, November 15, 2006, 6.

18. Tonya Garcia, "VNR debate intensifies as FCC fines Comcast," *PR Week*, October 1, 2007, 4.

19. Erica Iacono, "Broadcast PR Companies Unite Amid Ongoing Scrutiny of VNRs," *PR Week*, October 16, 2006, 1.

20. VideoNewsRelease.net, "VNRs," http://www.videonewsrelease. net/VNRs.htm (accessed September 5, 2008).

CHAPTER 9

1. Sandra Beckwith, *Streetwise Complete Publicity Plans* (Avon, MA: Adams Media, 2003, 37).

2. Jay Conrad Levinson, Rick Frishman, and Jill Lublin, *Guerilla Publicity* (Avon, MA: Adams Media, 2002, 54).

3. Richard Shell and Mario Moussa, *The Art of Woo: Using Strategic Persuasion to Sell Your Ideas* (New York: NY Portfolio/Penguin, 2007, 13–17).

4. William Rogers *Persuasion* (Lanham, MD: Rowman and Littlefield, 2007, 157).

5. Christina Bielaszka-DuVernay, "Take a Strategic Approach to Persuasion," *Harvard Management Update* (July 2008): 2, Vol 13, No 7.

6. Rogers, *Persuasion,* 196–197.

7. Bielaszka-DuVernay, "Take a Strategic Approach to Persuasion," 3.

8. Michael Renderman, "Tip Sheet: The Art of the Pitch, the Science of the Sale," *PR News*, December 4, 2006. Lexus/Nexis.

9. Jason Karpf, "How to . . . Sell the Media," *PR News*, November 5, 2007. Lexus/Nexis.

10. Richard Laermer, *Full Frontal PR* (Princeton, NJ: Bloomburg Press, 2003), 106.

11. Harvard Business School Publishing, "Managing the Media," *Harvard Management Communications Letter*, January 2000.

12. Cision Inc., "What Never to Do When Targeting the Media," 2007, http://us.cision.com/campaigns/targeting_white_paper_fv/ wp_request.asp (accessed February 10, 2009)

13. Ibid., 101.

14. Ibid., 101.

15. Todd Defren, "The PR Professional's Credo—7 Promises," May 12, 2008, http://www.pr-squared.com/2008/05/the_pr_ professionals_credo_7_p.html (accessed September 15, 2008).

16. Karpf, "How to . . . Sell the Media." Lexus/Nexis.

17. Cision Inc., "What Never to Do When Targeting the Media."

18. Robina Gangemi, "Publicity: Write a Better Pitch Letter," *Inc. Magazine*, September 1995. http://www.inc.com/maga-zine/19950901/2403.html

19. Joun Greer, "Why Journalists Need PR People," April 1, 2008, http://blogs.bnet.com/pr/?p=193 (accessed September 15, 2008).

20. David Ward, "Now & Zen Shows Good Timing," *PR Week*, December 3, 2007. Lexus/Nexis.

21. David Ward, "Now & Zen Shows Good Timing," *PR Week*, December 3, 2007. Lexus/Nexis.

22. Allen Stern, "My Take On Embargoes—Break Them and No More for You!", Center Networks, December 12, 2007, http://www.centernetworks.com/my-take-on-embargoes (accessed September 18, 2008).

23. Cece Salomon-Lee, "Embargoes—Valid in the Brave New World of PR?", December 19, 2007, http://prmeetsmarketing. wordpress.com/2007/12/19/embargoes-%E2%80%93-valid-in-the-brave-new-world-of-pr/ (accessed September 20, 2008).

24. Laermer, *Full Frontal PR,* 56.

25. Christine Shock, "Using Editorial Calendars to Pitch on Time, on Target," Side Road, http://www.sideroad.com/ Public_Relations/editorial_calendar.html.html (accessed September 18, 2008).

26. Laermer, *Full Frontal PR*, 116–126.

CHAPTER 10

1. Gary Vaynerchuk, "About Gary Vaynerchuk," http://garyvaynerchuk.com/about/ (accessed October 16, 2008).
2. Tracy L. Tuten, *Advertising 2.0* (Wesport, CT: Praeger, 2008, 20).
3. Ibid.
4. GamerDNA Inc., "Advertising on GamerDNA and the the GamerDNA Alliance Network," http://www.gamerdna.com/alliance/advertisers.php?partner=gamerdna.com (accessed October 6, 2008).
5. Cone, Inc., "Cone Finds That Americans Expect Companies to Have a Presence in Social Media," September 25, 2008, http://www.coneinc.com/content1182 (accessed October 7, 2008).
6. Michael Bush, "What Is Marketers' Biggest Challenge When It Comes to Social Networks?", *Advertising Age*, March 17, 2008. http://adage.com/digital/article?article_id=125712
7. Laura Petrecca and Jon Swartz, "Marketers to Capitalize on Facebook Enhanced Coverage LinkingFacebook," *USA Today*, November 7, 2007.
8. Marina Strauss, "Molson Ends Facebook Contest," *The Globe and Mail*, November 26, 2007.
9. Michael Arrington, "Ning Worth Half a Billion Dollars," Tech Crunch, April 18, 2008, http://www.techcrunch.com/2008/04/18/ning-worth-half-a-billion-dollars/ (accessed October 8, 2008).
10. Bush, "Marketers' Biggest Challenge."
11. Matt Dickman, "Inside//Out: Facebook," Technomarketer, July 18, 2007, http://technomarketer.typepad.com/technomarketer/2007/07/insideout-faceb.html (accessed October 8, 2008).
12. Wikipatterns.com, "Grass Roots Is Best," http://www.wikipatterns.com/display/wikipatterns/Grassroots+is+best (accessed October 8 2008).
13. Beth Kanter, "The Muppet Wiki! One of the Ten Best Wiki Communities," May 27, 2007, http://beth.typepad.com/beths_blog/2007/05/ten_best_wiki_c.html#comments (accessed October 8, 2008).
14. Ben McConnell, "Small Businesses and Blogging," Church of the Customer, August 2004, http://www.churchofthecustomer.com/blog/2004/08/small_businesse.html (accessed October 9, 2008).
15. Ben McConnell, "Small Businesses and Blogging," Church of the Customer, August 2004, http://www.churchofthecustomer.com/blog/2004/08/small_businesse.html (accessed October 9, 2008).
16. Ben McConnell, "Small Businesses and Blogging," Church of the Customer, August 2004, http://www.churchofthecustomer.com/blog/2004/08/small_businesse.html (accessed October 9, 2008).
17. "Blogosphere," Wikipedia, http://en.wikipedia.org/wiki/Blogosphere (accessed October 16, 2008).
18. Todd Zeigler, "Zappos.com: A Twitter Case Study," The Bivings Report, May 6, 2008, http://www.bivingsreport.com/2008/zapposcom-a-twitter-case-study/ (accessed October 10, 2008).
19. Mike Shields, "ComScore: Web Video Audience Flat, Usage Soars," *AdWeek,* June 18, 2008.
20. eBizMBA.com, "30 Largest Social Bookmarking Sites," October 2008, http://www.ebizmba.com/articles/social30 (accessed October 10, 2008).
21. Liane Bate, "How to Use Social Bookmarking Sites to Your Advantage," American Chronicle, April 28, 2007, http://www.americanchronicle.com/articles/25561 (accessed October 10, 2008).
22. Chrysanthos Dellarocas, "Strategic Manipulation of Internet Opinion Forums: Implications for Consumers and Firms," *Management Science* (2006): 1577–1593, Vol. 52, Num. 10.
23. CBC Arts, "Barenaked Ladies Urging Fans to Participate in Music, Video-making," September 14, 2006, http://www.cbc.ca/technology/story/2006/09/14/barenakedladies-internet.html (accessed October 12, 2008).
24. CBC Arts, "Barenaked Ladies Urging Fans to Participate in Music, Video-making," September 14, 2006, http://www.cbc.ca/technology/story/2006/09/14/barenakedladies-internet.html (accessed October 12, 2008).

CHAPTER 11

1. Lisa Hurley, "Hitting the Street," *Special Events*, November 1, 2006.
2. TBA Global, *Sample New Products,* http://www.tbaglobal.com/case_studies/view/26 (accessed January 28, 2009).
3. American Marketing Association, "Dictionary," http://www.marketingpower.com/_layouts/Dictionary.aspx (accessed June 26, 2008).
4. The Auto Channel, *Mercedes-Benz Takes Its Brand on the Road: C Spot Drive Tour Starts 16-City Road Trip,* June 4, 2003, http://www.theautochannel.com/news/2003/06/04/162556.html (accessed November 4, 2008).
5. Karl Greenberg, *Automakers Cling to Events in Tight Economy,* October 29, 2008, http://www.mediapost.com/publications/?fa=Articles.showArticleHomePage&art_aid=93569 (accessed October 29, 2008).
6. Larry Chiagouris and Ipshita Ray, "Saving the World with Cause Related Marketing," *Marketing Managment* (July/August 2007): 49.
7. American Marketing Association, "Dictionary."
8. Western Organization of Resource Councils, http://www.worc.org/pdfs/pressconf12.pdf.

CHAPTER 12

1. Kevin Sullivan, "Why PR Matters—and What It Can Do for You," *Harvard Management Update* (May 2007): 1, Vol 12, No 5.
2. David X.Manners Company Inc., "Thought-Leadership Content and Communication," http://www.dxmanners.com/DXM_ThoughtLeadership.pdf (accessed November 26, 2008).
3. Rachel Hunt, interview by Gaetan Giannini PUBLICATION (November 5, 2008).
4. Ken Lizotte, "Become a 'Thought Leader' and Separate," In *Handbook of Business Strategy 2005*, ed. Patricia Coate (Bradford: Emerald Group Publishing Limited, 2004).
5. Tim Rausch, "Self-publishing is not as daunting a task as in past," *Augusta Chronicle*, November 2, 2008.
6. "White Paper," http://www.investorwords.com/5856/white_paper.html (accessed November 26, 2008).
7. Daniel B. Honigman, "Make a Statement-White Papers Add Authority, Leadership to Your Marketing Mix," *Marketing News* (May 1, 2008): 8.
8. Paul Boutin, "So You Want to Be a Blogging Star?", *The New York Times*, March 20, 2008.
9. Richard Laermer, *Full Frontal PR* (Princeton, NJ: Bloomberg, 2003).
10. Peter Shankman, "Peter Shankman," http://shankman.com/about/ (accessed November 17, 2008).
11. Julia Stewart, interview by Kai Ryssdal, *Marketplace,* September 25, 2008, http://marketplace.publicradio.org/display/web/2008/09/25/corner_office_stewart_transcript/ (accessed February 14, 2009).

12. Valeria Maltoni, "Ask Away: Storytelling in Marketing, Mark Goren—Part One," May 14, 2007, Conversation Agent, http://www.conversationagent.com/2007/05/ask_away_storyt.html (accessed Novemember 19, 2008).

13. Laermer, *Full Frontal PR*.

CHAPTER 13

1. T. I. Stanley, "Gem Sellers Launch Blitz Against 'Blood Diamond'; DeBeers, Others Build PR to Counter Movie's Harsh Take on Industry," *Advertising Age,* December 12, 2006, 00. http://adage.com/article?article_id=113710

2. Robert G. Eccles, Scott C. Newquist, and Roland Schatz, "Reputaion and Its Risk," *Harvard Business Review* (February 2007): 4.

3. Leslie Wayne and Alex Kuczynski, "Tarnished Image Places Welch in Unlikely Company," *The New York Times*, September 16, 2002.

4. Josephine B. Valle, "Containing a Spill: Best Approaches in Issues and Crisis Management," *Business World*, December 13, 2006, S2/4.

5. Caleb Silver, Chris Kokenes, Mythili Rao, and Katy Byron, "Taco Bell Rats Are Stars for a Day," CNNMoney.com, February 23, 2007, http://money.cnn.com/2007/02/23/news/companies/taco_bell/ (accessed December 4, 2008).

6. Media Caffeine, "Motrin Learns: Hell Hath No Fury Like Baby-Wearing Moms," November 16, 2008, http://mediacaffeine.com/solutions/social-media-marketing-solutions/motrin-learns-hell-hath-no-fury-like-baby-wearing-moms/ (accessed December 5, 2008).

7. Emily Steel, "Car Makers Take Case to the Web," *The Wall Street Journal,* December 5, 2008, http://online.wsj.com/article/SB122843938180981627.html (accessed February 2, 2009).

8. Ailish Smith, "Constant Need for Plan B," *Business and Finance*, August 1, 2008.

9. Deborah L. Vence, "Crisis Management," *Marketing News*, July 15, 2008, 10.

10. Gerard Braud, "Writing Your Crisis Communications Plan," Gerard Braud Communications, http://www.braudcommunications.com/modules/smartsection/pdf/WritingYourPlan.pdf (accessed March 10, 2009).

11. Andrew McMains, "Will Apple's Misstep Give Loyalists Pause?", *Adweek*, September 10, 2007. Lexus Nexis.

12. Eric Webber, "If I Had Been Handling These Crisis Strategies . . .," *Advertising Age*, September 10, 2007: 16.

13. "Lessons Still Resonate 25 years Later," *PR Week,* October 29, 2007, 8.

14. Andy Sernovitz, "Andy's Answers: How Do I Get Ahead of the Bad News?" Smart Blog on Social Media, December 2, 2008, http://smartblogs.com/socialmedia/2008/12/02/andy-answers-how-do-i-get-ahead-of-the-bad-news/ (accessed December 5, 2008).

15. Jon Entine, "How 'Jack' Turned Crisis into Opportunity," Jonentine.com, November/December 1999, http://www.jonentine.com/ethical_corporation/jack_crisis.htm (accessed December 7, 2008).

16. Apple Inc., 2007 Annual Report. Hoover's, "Apple, Inc. Company History," Hoover's, 2008.

CHAPTER 14

1. Valerie Alderson, *Measuring the Value of a Managed WOM Program in Test and Control Markets* (Boston: BzzAgent Inc., 2006), 6.

2. BurrellsLuce, "Quality Rating System," November 7, 2006, http://www.burrellesluce.com/Media_Measurement/Quality_Rating_System.pdf (accessed December 11, 2008).

3. W. J. Carl, Jennifer Oles, and Matt McGlinn, "Measuring the Ripple: Creating the G2X Relay Rate and an Industry Standard Methodology to Measure the Spread of Word of Mouth Conversations and Marketing Relevant Outcomes," *Measuring Word of Mouth,* vol. 3 (Boston: Word of Mouth Marketing Association, 2007), 2.

4. American Marketing Association, "Dictionary," http://www.marketingpower.com/_layouts/Dictionary.aspx (accessed October 24, 2008).

5. McClellan, "Nielsen to Track Super Bowl Ads," *Media Week,* January 28, 2008, http://www.mediaweek.com/mw/esearch/article_display.jsp?vnu_content_id=1003702774 (accessed January 29, 2008).

6. As quoted in Brian Morrissey, "Conversation Quotient," *AdWeek,* March 24, 2008, http://www.adweek.com/aw/content_display/news/agency/e3ibbacf24cbb5b53e808755444 5d8161984 (accessed December 12, 2008).

7. Chrysanthos Dellarocas and Ritu Narayan, "A Statistical Measure of Population's Propensity to Engage in Post-Purchase Online Word-of-Mouth," *Statistical Science* 21, no. 2 (2006): 285.

NAME INDEX

COMPANY AND ORGANIZATION INDEX

SUBJECT INDEX